D1710903

CULTURAL OTHERNESS
AND BEYOND

PHILOSOPHY

OF

HISTORY AND CULTURE

VOLUME 19

CULTURAL OTHERNESS AND BEYOND

EDITED BY

CHHANDA GUPTA

AND

D.P. CHATTOPADHYAYA

BRILL
LEIDEN · BOSTON · KÖLN
1998

This book is printed on acid-free paper.

Library of Congress Cataloging-in-Publication Data

Cultural otherness and beyond / edited by Chhanda Gupta and D.P. Chattopadhyaya.
    p.   cm. — (Philosophy of history and culture, ISSN 0922–6001 ; v. 19)
    Includes bibliographical references and index.
    ISBN 9004100261 (cloth : alk. paper)
    1. Intercultural communication.   2. Ethnocentrism.   I. Gupta, Chhanda.   II. Chattopadhyaya, D. P. (Debi Prasad), 1933–   .
III. Series.
GN345.6.C85   1998
306—DC21
                                  97–48656
                                      CIP

Die Deutsche Bibliothek – CIP-Einheitsaufnahme

Cultural otherness and beyond / ed. by Chhanda Gupta and D.P. Chattopadhyaya – Leiden ; Boston ; Köln : Brill, 1998
(Philosophy of history and culture ; Vol. 19)
ISBN 90–04–10026–1

ISSN 0922–6001
ISBN 90 04 10026 1

PRINTED IN THE NETHERLANDS

CONTENTS

PREFACE

Otherness, heterogeneity, are ideas celebrated in today's cultural ethos. Each of us, as well as any social whole to which we belong, feel a passionate urge to re-examine our socio-historical identity and speak from our own centre of experience. However, to gain voice from one's *own* centre of experience, should *others* be driven to silence? Will not the silence and cultural seclusion deepen lines of division that have fractured society in every aspect of its being—social, economic, political, religious, racial, ethnic and gender? How can we remain rooted socio-historically and still not sink in abysmal loneliness and conflict?

These questions surfaced when we were planning to bring out a volume addressing issues connected with the relationship of the "self" and the "other", and with the possibility of *trans-cultural* and *intra-cultural* understanding. A need was felt for a meeting of minds for an interpretive and interactive dialogue to evolve linkages, if possible, between diverse perceptions of social, cultural and moral realities, especially those that are our most urgent concerns today.

Some of our Euro-American friends have been wondering how we, academics, can contribute our bits to bring about the intended meeting of minds. Earlier, Indian writers as well as Western scholars had given independent presentations of views on various themes, working in isolation, though very often on the same occasion, in encyclopedic volumes, books and journals.

This volume is not intended to assemble similar isolated pieces. It deals with various themes but the focus primarily is on cultural otherness and related issues. A better understanding of the culturally other is an effective means of understanding oneself. It helps one in reviewing one's own situation, in identifying themes which are integral parts of one's own culture, and also in allowing one to speak from one's own centre in contradistinction to that of the other. The orientation native to oneself may also help in removing misconceptions which the cultural other often has while looking at one from an alien point of view.

This does not debar the *other* however from looking at one from a fresh angle and clearer perspective. On the contrary it may remove the gap created by misconceptions and promote better understanding. It may lead to sharing, to some kind of cultural symbiosis, which, in a world that has shrunk, would be mutually fulfilling. In India, numerous periodic incursions followed by mingling of cultures have made this sharing a lived reality since antiquity. From our composite and assimilative centre then, the idea of convergence at a global level, in some matters at least, need not appear entirely problematic, despite the fissures that are seen increasingly on the surface of our society as well as on that of the European's or the American's.

Most of the themes dealt with in this book have emerged in the course of the editors' discussions with their Euro-American colleagues over the decades. Our visits to and stays in Western centres of learning convince us of the need of continuous dialogue making optimal use of *public* reason. It is quite understandable that political and economic policy makers, being placed as they are under practical necessity, have been carrying on this exercise with varying degrees of success. But in the sphere of thought and theory, which in practice is apparently less pressing but actually more lasting in effect, this dialogue is yet to assume its due intensity and dignity. Comparative philosophy or comparative literature is yet to be recognized as a mainstream academic discipline. Most of the "international" conferences on humanistic disciplines turn out to be only one-sidedly international—hardly more than national. The intended audience of the American philosopher is American; the presence of the Indian philosopher or the Chinese philosopher in the gathering, is pointless. For the former has nothing interesting to say for the latter; he is not aware of what is going on in Indian or Chinese philosophy. In contrast many of the modern Indian and Chinese philosophers are more or less aware of the living issues of European and American philosophy.

To rectify this one-sidedness of the world academic scene we think we must have more projects of this kind. If we recall the neglect of Africa's intellectual scene we have every reason to feel even more disturbed. The image of Africa to the Euro-American countries is intimately, if not invariably, linked to the issues of poverty, hunger and civil war. If the North-South dialogue has not yielded positive results, the state of South-South dialogue has not proved encouraging either. The difference between self and other persists. The gulf remains. The gap yawns.

We would like to thank many people and institutions who supported this project and contributed to the volume. In this connection we are particularly grateful to the members of the Centre of Advanced Study in Philosophy, Jadavpur University, the Indian Council of Philosophical Research (ICPR), New Delhi, and the Project of History of Indian Science Philosophy and Culture (PHISPC), Delhi.

Our first and foremost gratitude is to the contributors to this volume. But for their cooperation this volume could not be brought out in time. Individuals in the academic community from outside, ICPR and PHISPC who deserve special thanks are J.N. Mohanty, Hilary Putnam, P.K. Mukhopadhyay, Deen K. Chatterjee, Minakshi Roy Choudhuri and Aparna Chakraborty.

We also wish to thank Elisabeth Erdman-Visser and Julian Deahl of Brill. They have been extremely patient and helpful in putting this volume together.

We would also like to put on record our thanks to Asit Kumar Datta and Debaprasad Bhattacharya for their dedicated secretarial assistance.

INTRODUCTION

I

The word *culture* is used both conceptually, *i.e.*, generally, and historically, *i.e.*, particularly. Conceptually speaking, culture is due to human activities, ideas and ideals and their more or less durable expressions. Belief, knowledge, art and crafts, customs and morals are all constituents of culture. Human abilities and dispositions are also to be included within culture. Although some social thinkers of the naturalist persuasion have tried to discuss culture in a positivist or value-neutral manner, we think that they have not been quite successful in this enterprise. It is difficult to deny that artistic and moral considerations deeply orient human ideas and actions. Many of us tend to forget that value consciousness among humans is *more or less* universal and even "savages" and "tribals" have their arts, morals, sense of beauty and sense of justice. The more one can leave behind the pejorative sense often precritically attributed to such words as *savage* and *tribe*, the easier it becomes for one to understand the peoples who do not belong to one's own culture. Many of us are so enclosed within our own narrow cultural "tribalism" that we often fail to appreciate the normative traits or excellence of *other* cultures.

It is not surprising that many people of the industrially developed countries think that the peoples of the underdeveloped or developing countries are culturally inferior to them. They also believe that their cultures are superior to those of their "cultural others". The hidden assumption is that the cultures of countries like USA, Canada, UK, France, Germany, Italy and Japan, essentially based on modern science and technology, are to be rated higher than those of others. Except Japan, all these countries are Euro-American and the main basis of including Japan in this group (G-7) is her industrial development, not chrysanthemum, *i.e.*, aesthetic disposition, or sword, *i.e.*, valour.

It is interesting to recall that this way of rating and ranking different cultures is prereflectively recognized not only by the peoples of the developed countries but also, in many cases, following their capitalist paradigm, by those of developing countries. Such a mode of evaluation of culture may be and often is attributed to political and cultural hegemony of the developed countries. Control over patents, copyrights and media, particularly the electronic ones, it has been plausibly argued, enables the developed countries to make others believe that they, because of their "achievements" in the fields of science, technology and industry, are models for others to emulate. What about the exploitation of the poor in the colonies and also in the homeland since the Industrial Revolution? What about the industries which survive on wars or threats of war, hot or cold, global or local, nuclear or conventional? *Must we* praise all types of industry and industrialization?

Why should industrial, scientific and technological achievements be accorded very high value or weightage in rating a culture? The techno-economic mode of understanding, explaining and even evaluating a culture, as we know, is of relatively recent origin. But why should not the mode of production and distribution be taken in a purely descriptive way? For example, why should a food-*producing* tribe be regarded superior to a food-*gathering* tribe? To take another example, why an industrial society should be taken as more developed than a feudal society? That production and accumulation of wealth have a positive aspect is obvious and undeniable. All things being equal, the wealthy society is found to be better equipped than the not-so-wealthy society to take care of the problems of poverty and ill-health of its people. At the same time some thinkers like Thoreau, Tolstoy and Gandhi, on the one hand, and Marx, Lenin and Mao-Zedong, on the other, have pointed out in different ways how higher production of wealth engineered by "modern" technology give rise to various negative characteristics like pauperization, polarization, conflict and alienation in industrial society. What is more, it has been pointed out, that the higher production and accumulation without social intervention cannot satisfactorily remove the negative characteristics of development and ensure distributive justice. But apex intervention, once allowed, is likely to increase its frequency and expand its scope. And that invariably encroaches upon individual liberty and tends to promote the cult of state. Given the accent on industrial production, national prosperity and personal/familial enrichment, it is not easy to strike and maintain the right type of balance between individual liberty and the sphere of state. Whose liberty is to be curbed and to benefit whom? Who will do it and on what authority?

The very concept of development is now under critical scrutiny. Must we take *development* only in its economic aspect? How can we neglect the moral, aesthetic, ecological and other aspects which are often found to be relatively neglected in the economically developed societies? Moreover fragmentation and impersonalization of human relationship impart a hardly veiled negative character to the industrial society. Often this criticism of the industrial culture is sought to be met by a notion of post-industrial society and its culture. It is argued that the lack of individualism, *i.e.*, the lack of distinct identity of individual human beings, often attributed to the mass society due to the industrial mode of production and marketing, is soon going to be a matter of the past. But the critic of post-industrial culture points out that social fragmentation and human atomization, largely due to industrialization, are going to be almost unpreventable unless the very model of large-scale and heavy industry is abandoned; and this unmistakably proves the weakness of the moral basis of industrialization which can hardly be read as vindication of normative individualism.

Industry is empowered by technology. And technology is based upon some sort of scientific perception, clear or obscure. There is a widespread view that technology, *i.e.*, *how* to tackle a problem or satisfy a need, precedes science. The controversy over the issue "the primacy of science versus the primacy of technology" however seems to be incorrect. It is only those who are culturally blind can forget that without technology science can neither come into being nor be tested. They also are uncritical who fail to see that without science, a *gestalt* preview of our needs/problems, techniques or technology, cannot be appropriately decided. Man is aware not only of *what* he needs but also of *how* to have it. Science and technology form a virtuous and enlarging circle.

Every culture has its own way of testing its technology for wealth production and problem solution, whatever that problem may be, poverty, disease or natural calamities like drought, flood and earthquake. Both technology and science, rightly understood, are rooted in the life-world. The main reason why most of us, who can read and write, take science and technology at an abstract or theoretical level is that our consciousness is primarily literacy-based. When we closely study the orality-based cultures, we realize the intimate relation between the life-world, on the one hand, and science and technology, on the other. As many of us live in big cities, encircled by big industrial units, constantly watch them on TV screen and read about them in books, journals and newspapers, we unconsciously entertain the view that industry is necessarily large-scale in its character.

But reflection shows that this is not the case everywhere. Industry may be small-scale or even household in nature. Without being romantic or utopian one may be the defender of the thesis of "The Small is Beautiful". After all the scale of a particular industry is need- and resource-based. Within one and the same culture we come across industrial units of different sizes, small, medium and large, and different types of technology defined in terms of its varying sophistication, automatic or semi-automatic character, capital-intensiveness or labour-intensiveness. The hidden presuppositions of technology assessment/ choice are basically human, involving human needs and values.

When attempts are made to define technology without relating it to human needs and resources, *i.e.*, without realizing that technology itself is an important component of human culture, an untenable and pernicious dichotomy appears between technological culture and moral culture. The moral dimension of human existence, man's enterprise to enlarge himself and to realize what is there in him as promise or potentiality encompasses within its frame both the technical and the praxical, both the natural and the cultural. The division often drawn between agriculture and industry, for example, though conceptually understandable, is practically unsustainable. This truth becomes transparent when we recall the research inputs of the agricultural scientists, the machineries used for sowing and harvesting, the chemicals used for fertilization and crop protection, and the like. The point is driven home when we come across such expressions as "food-processing industries".

More positively speaking, the intimate relation between nature and culture, man and machine, becomes increasingly clear when we, in our reflective moments, become aware that we, humans, are simultaneously productive as well as consumable resource. We are producer of goods and their needs, consumer of what we need and produce, and also, what is often forgotten, we, as resource, as manual and intellectual labourer, are used, abused, utilized, rewarded and exploited. In brief, nature-culture and man-machine relations are neither unilateral nor monotonic. They are dialectical, many-sided and cybernetic. If these formulations of culture-specific human beings are true, and we think they are, then two points become undeniable. First, there are some general truths which pervade all cultural configurations, contemporary as well as historical. Cultural otherness, at least in a qualified sense, is not only diachronic but also synchronic. Therefore it comes out of the studies of the anthropologist and also of the

historian. Secondly, the general or structural features of widely separated cultures, separated by space and time, have their distinct personality or identity traits.

These two points provide the main justification of undertaking the
project of Cultural Otherness. The question may be raised, at this
stage, about the rationale of including the "Beyond" within the scope
of this project. As pointed out earlier, both cultural similarity and
distinctness are parts of one and the same social reality, the reality
that is complementarily studied in history, archaeology, philology,
anthropology and other kindred disciplines.

Unfortunately, the point often neglected in these studies is the
ontology of human nature. Human nature, rightly understood, is
neither a transcendental and static essence nor is it a once-for-all-
given and exhaustible resource. It has in it elements of transcendence or inexhaustibility, an intimation and invitation of the *beyond*.
But to understand this one need not be a speculative metaphysician.
Our life-worlds, plans, dreams and practices unmistakably throw up
and bring forth our endless and boundless potentiality and freedom
of creativity of what it entails, conjoined transformation of "the inner" and "the outer".

The controversy between the pattern theory of culture, traceable
to Kroeber, Ruth Benedict and Kluckhohn, and the structural-func-
tional theory of culture, associated with the names of Malinowski,
Radcliffe-Brown and Evans-Pritchard, seems to rest largely on the
unduly dramatized distinction drawn between the self and the other.
According to the former, culture consists of patterns, articulate and
inarticulate, and forms of actions, acquired and transmitted by symbols and expressed in artifacts and mentifacts, concepts and values.
Patterns of culture are both products and determinants of action. In
other words, conditioned by culture, humans author culture. But it
may be mentioned here that all spheres of life are not equally sus-
ceptible to patterning. For example, in the forms of political institution, technology, management and business organization the patterns
are easily discernible. Perceptual or functional definiteness and continuity, existential distinctness and durability of the patterns make
their identification and representation easily possible. But the same
cannot be said of the patterns found in customs of dress, diet, salu-
tation, birth, death and marriage rituals, and works of fine arts. This
is not to deny the *uniformity* observed in the dresses, for example, of
the armed forces, persons belonging to different religious orders, and

the behaviour of some groups of people conforming to stipulated norms. Patterns, like family resemblance, are defined simultaneously by affinity and difference, and their extension. Some patterns are systemic or holistic and durable, some others sub-systemic or local and transient.

Following this analysis it is possible to show that individuals, the architects of history, express themselves in different ways in and through distinct cultural forms. All formations cognitive and emotive, say Cassirer and Susanne Langer, are symbolic. When the individuals are called upon to deal with the law-governed natural events and processes, or the "hardened" societal facts, their ideas and behaviour weave out clearer patterns than, for instance, when they deal with *other* individuals in fluid situations and are quite free in their decision-making and decision-changing. Ultimately, it is the ineliminable human freedom, exercised or not, which is symbolically expressed in and through relatively durable societal facts and changing moods of actors and actresses, styles of art and types of fashion.

In spite of their causal subjugation or probabilistic configuration, natural objects may be transformed into and viewed as cultural objects. This transformation may be brought about not only by the artist but also by the scientist and the technologist who, gifted with imagination, are engaged in seeking, discovering and showing multiple forms of symmetry and harmony. Cultural patterns are often, not always, found to have their correlates in the personality traits of the individuals belonging to the concerned culture. Cultural rootedness and ontological freedom are the basic aspects of all human beings. While the latter is symbolic of the inexhaustible character of human creativity, the former is indicative of the facts and factors which account for and determine the processes and forms of acculturation. The two are deeply interlinked.

Human freedom is not an idle or vacuous competence; essentially expressive in character, it is articulated in different forms of cultural objects. Cultural objects, without ceasing to be a part of causal configuration and *natural* in a sense, "natural" to the relatively uninitiated or unintelligent, are unfailingly symbolic, idealized representative or construct in import. The drift of culture, its ups and downs, are at times primarily internal, *i.e.*, orthogenetic, and at times primarily external, *i.e.*, heterogenetic. Generally speaking, cultural drift is found to be of mixed character. This implies, among other things, that the self of every culture, its personality or identity, is more or less open to and influenced by other cultures, their personalities or identities. Individuals and groups of one culture are obliged to interact with those of other cultures. This interaction may be cooperative or competitive, peaceful or belligerent, interrupted or continuous, depending upon time, environment and motivating factors. In our age of information explosion, intensive communication and mass travel, time "shrinks", and both motivating factors and environment are manipulable from without by others. Drift and patterns of culture therefore often appear to be non-linear or fuzzy.

We have already referred to the exaggerated difference between the pattern theory of culture and the structural theory of culture. Perhaps it will be in order, first, to present the considerations why this exaggeration, blind to the points of similarity between the structuralist views and the patternist views, is indefensible and, then, to make use of the comprehensive and composite patternist-structuralist theory to understand the basic issues of cultural otherness from an Indian point of view.

II

Social structure is said to be a network of relations between different groups, classes and roles, which forms a functional unity. Moral, legal, political, economic, religious, educational and linguistic phenomena hang together and are to be understood in their mutually supportive relation, not in isolation or abstraction. Development of social structure, like that of a biological organism, has to be grasped historically in the context of its growth, growth from simple organization and functions to increasingly complex organization and functions. Initially the structuralists like Radcliffe-Brown focussed their attention on stable, *i.e.*, a-historical, conflict-free, nonliterate, *i.e.*, orality-based, and isolated tribes. It may be recalled here that the subjects of Radcliffe-Brown's early studies were Australian tribes and Andaman Islanders (of India). Later on when his followers started studying complex, modern, large, urban and literacy-based social systems it was realized that the assumptions of stability, orality and isolability cannot be universalized. Absolute isolation, like the physicist's frictionless (perpetual motion) machine, is an abstraction or idealization not to be found in the real world. The anthropologist or for that reason any social scientist has to admit that individuals of all "real" societies have their other(s) and with whom they are obliged to enter into some sort of relations, and therefore, cannot be studied as "primitive isolates". Social structure or, to use Radcliffe-Brown's favourite expression, social physiology cannot be understood without a concept of culture. Structure, like culture, is undoubtedly an idealization, but at the same time, it has to be admitted that both are rooted in a network of empirically ascertainable social relations, roles and values, which "link together certain human beings". Patterns are the ways how some definite human beings and groups act and interact between themselves and orient their behaviour to other *beyond* their culture or country according to certain received norms. What bind individuals together are mutual interests and needs, perceived threats and recognized values. Both patterns and social structure are expressive, although in some more or less abstract ways, of these factors.

In order to bring out clearly the similarity or parallelism between what is called structure and what is called pattern it may be pointed out that neither is purely observational or concrete and that both admit of grades or levels. That is, structure has its superstructure and often nests substructures within it, more stable or less stable, and patterns may be basic or non-basic, macro or micro, more durable or less durable. Another way of clarifying the relation between the two approaches is to highlight the point that the structuralist has his own way of explaining cultural patterns and the patternist, in turn, also knows how to explain social structure in terms of his own theory.

The issue may be illustrated thus. The patternist thinks that a kinship system is a sort of *independent* semantic system, a type of cultural pattern based on a limited number of socially recognized categories of relations defined in terms of generation difference, lineal and collateral difference, sex of relative, difference between relation by marriage and by blood, *etc.* To the structuralist, a kinship system is not like an independent semantic system, and kin terms and social institutions are closely related and interdependent parts of social structure. While the former views structure under cultural pattern, the latter sees culture under or as a component of structural system. The difference is a matter of primacy or priority. The social structures or the cultural patterns of villages, towns, cities, countries, civilizations, and also of economic classes, occupational groups, castes, and religious sects may be analyzed in terms of *how*, *i.e.*, by what process, they become what they are.

Generally speaking, neither the structuralist nor the patternist pays much attention to interpersonal and intergenerational contacts and interactions leading to formation and transformation of different patterns and cultures. It was left to some later anthropologists like Robert Redfield and Raymond Firth to emphasize the fact that without institutionalized social relations the transmission of cultural tradition is not possible. Social organization needs to be distinguished from social structure. The former is concrete and denotes the social structure of a particular tradition. In different traditions the arrangements of roles and statuses of such groups as castes, religious leaders, teachers and students are found to be significantly different. At least in some cases these differences undergo change from age to age, from generation to generation. It has been rightly pointed out by Redfield that every civilization has both a social structure and a cultural structure. The specific systems of social relations like marriage, business, political and judicial institutions are dynamic, exhibit some or other process of cultural transmission.

In India, for example, the forms of marriage and the roles of spouses of today are significantly different from what these were in the yesteryears. The modes and scales of trade and industry have undergone notable, if not fundamental, change. The political administration of free India, to take another example, is substantially different from what it was in the era of imperial rule. The significance of the transition from Raj (imperial rule) to Swaraj (self-rule) is wide-ranging and far reaching, both structurally and functionally. The roles of different professional groups and cultural specialists, of political culture, of business culture, of artistic culture, *etc.* are changing fast, introducing new elements and subtracting old elements from the identity of Indian civilization.

This historical way of understanding and analyzing the social process of a particular civilization with many social groups and communities in it substantially takes away the supposed dualism between the cultural approach and the structural approach. It is true that the composite approach referred to before has its distinct normative underpinning and individualist orientation. But this can hardly be regarded as unjustifiable or criticizable. For, after all, without being reductionist we find that no corporate group or societal fact is a purely theoretical construct. Underlying it are concrete human beings of flesh and blood. In order to avoid individualistic reductionism the only advisable point to be remembered is that these concrete human beings are not isolated atoms and unaffiliated to, or uninfluenced by, societal facts, relatively stable and durable networks of interpersonal, *i.e.*, social, relations.

It may be recalled here that the normative underpinning and individualist orientation of culture and social structure are not at all new. These have been highlighted by anthropologists like E.B. Tylor and creative writers like Mathew Arnold in the last century and poets and cultural critics like T.S. Eliot and Tagore of this century. Without healthy normative elements in culture, it has been rightly pointed out, we are doomed to some form of anarchy or anomie, normlessness. Social structure can neither be formed nor transformed without normative motivation and conduct. We try to leave behind our unlived or dead tradition and recreate what is living and abiding in it; we are engaged in restructuring our social structure; and we are trying to change our civilization in the light of new needs and in search of new values. This search is partly due to our own free and internal impulses and partly due to contacts with alien social forces and cultures. This process of acculturation encourages abandonment of some unlived and outdated norms and acquisition of new norms. It is a historical way of renewing our own cultural heritage and renewing it in the light of critical understanding of our new problems, needs and values.

Our emphasis on such concepts as history, development and change are intended to minimize or, if possible, eliminate a blemish common to patternism and structuralism. Neither the patternist nor the structuralist nor even the defender of the composite theory of structuralism-patternism is adequately aware of the significance of individualism-linked history in understanding social phenomena. It is true that the structuralist, the patternist and their followers occasionally refer to the role of history in the career of culture and social structure. But this does not prove adequate to bring out the full humanistic significance of culture and social structure. Unduly afraid of the possible criticism of their commitment to reductionist individualism, they somehow or other consistently underplay the role of human values and creativity.

III

Even the neo-structuralists like Levi-Strauss seem to have failed to be fair to historical development of distinct social structures and patterns. In their anxious search for cultural universals, common structural features of all cultures, they tend to lose sight of their distinct identity. The well-known controversy between Sartre and Levi-Strauss has brought out the point very clearly. Sartre is of the view that social structures, though clearly formulable in terms of binary relations, are essentially historical products or concrete "totalities" based on human praxis. These totalities, because of the workings of *dialectical* reason underlying human consciousness, get detotalised and are again retotalised maintaining a continuity in the course of history. Sartre critically observes that Levi-Strauss's accent on analytical reason and binary relation, borrowed from structural linguistics, prevents him from seeing the dialectical historical lineage of social structures.

This criticism is rejected by Levi-Strauss who claims that social structures, as conceived by him, are doubly historical, both in their process of formation and in their test through ethnographic application. Neither cultural universals nor structural universals are to be taken as ahistorical simply because of their abstract and formal representations. Taking his criticism to Sartre's own arena, Levi-Strauss claims to have shown that the former's criticism of Straussian structuralism rests on four misconstrued pairs of contrasting concepts, viz., (i) self and other, (ii) civilized and primitive, (iii) dialectical reason and analytical reason and (iv) history and anthropology.

Sartre's ontological individualism and historism are viewed by Levi-Strauss as a modern extension of the Cartesian dualism between (self) consciousness and matter (material other). Sartre is criticized for his alleged attempt to present social history in the model of self's (internal) history without duly recognizing the effects of the material other on it. What Descartes did to liberate physics from self's (subjective) fancies, *i.e.*, to vindicate scientific objectivity against bodily, *i.e.*, causal affections, Sartre tries to re-do it from the other end, keeping self-based history free from other's influences. Singularity of one society, like self's individuality, can hardly be assimilated under, or even rightly viewed in the analogy of, another society. The Sartrean image of social history, alleges Levi-Strauss, makes cultural generalization impossible and subverts the very project of discovering cultural universals. If self in the name of freedom remains enclosed, how other(s) can ever be truly disclosed to it?

The neo-structuralist seems to have failed to understand Sartre. While the Cartesian time, a mode of thought (consciousness), is itself separative or juxtapositional and passively derives its unity from material content, the Sartrean time, essentially active and unitive, confers durational self-identity upon things, simultaneously separates the self from its being-in-the-world and reunites it through praxis with the latter as its other. Situated amidst needs, the self gets more and more involved in group-praxis and transcends its own narrow confines. The poverty-stricken human beings in particular, driven by scarcity, tend to enlarge the scope of their group-praxis and intensify it increasingly. The display of affluence and the consumption patterns of the rich societies in the capitalist world multiply the needs of the exploited peoples of the erstwhile colonies and make them more and more conscious of their scarcity. Richness, exploitation and scarcity perform two seemingly contradictory tasks,—uniting the separate societies and separating the united ones. Strictly speaking, no unity—individual or group—can be absolutely unitive. Freedom-linked tension or conflict informs every unity, feeding its praxis in search of satisfaction of its perceived needs. While the neo-structuralist is basically interested in *explaining* and formulating this almost universal phenomenon, Sartre's main aim seems to lie in articulating and enlarging the scope of freedom by the projects rooted in freedom itself.

The attempts to draw the line of distinction between the civilized and the primitive in terms of the scope and limits of freedom are well known both in the Indian tradition and the Western tradition. All *purusarthas* (human ends),—*dharma* (ethico-religious), *artha* (politico-economic), *kama* (somatic-hedonic) and *moksa* (liberation/liberty/freedom) are often viewed in the Indian tradition as a spectrum of values culminating in the last named value or end, *i.e.*, freedom. Some Indian thinkers speak only of the first three values or ends (*trivarga*) and leave it implied that the realization of these leads one automatically to the realization of freedom as one's *summum bonum*. The so-called European view that freedom is teleological unfoldment or gradual disclosure of God in the World is not peculiarly European. Similar views are available in various other cultures. The freedom-disclosive theme has also been formulated in causal-evolutionary, not necessarily providential, terms.

During the last two hundred years in Europe, as we find, Hegel's providential account of freedom and Marx's secular and techno-economic account of the same have proved very influential. What is common to these two accounts is their reliance on dialectical method and reason. Dialectical method is marked by twin tensions of separation/differentiation and unification/integration at all levels. Dialectical reason is said to be the "living logic of action". Another common feature of the Hegelian view and the Marxist view is historicism, *i.e.*, the process of history in all cultural configurations is claimed to exhibit certain definite and necessary rhythms. The followers of Hegel and Marx have been trying to relate the primitive society and the civilized society in terms of this rhythmic and progressive laws of history. Critics like Karl Popper and Isaiah Berlin have forcefully argued that these so-called laws are only patterns, largely due to theory-construction, and existential, not universal, in scope.

It is not difficult to represent different cultural configurations of the world either synchronically, *i.e.*, in their structural diversity, or diachronically, *i.e.*, in their temporal sequence. When these two types of representations, structural and temporal, are brought together, some problems arise. Are these social structures, pastoral, feudal and capitalist, for example, purely descriptive or do they *inter se* have a normative and ratable character? Are the primitive societies, simply because they appear before the modern ones in time sequence, to be regarded as inferior or simple, innocent and superior? The civilized/primitive distinction, like the value/fact distinction, is systematically ambiguous. This distinction, under certain description, is valid but not invariably. A civilized society, viewed under certain aspects, may be said to be brutal and barbarous. Because of its supposed simplicity and hospitability, primitive society may be deemed to be excellent. A Rousseauite, for example, finds a "natural society" more admirable than a "cultural society". A Nazi Germany or a polluting country, in spite of its high industrialization, "civilization" and technological achievement, is likely to be widely condemned. The grounds of condemnation and appreciation are, on analysis, often found to be culture-specific or language-specific.

Every person's ways of classifying the objects of nature and culture, of what is primitive and what is modern, are in a very important sense linguistically grounded. It is not surprising that Levi-Strauss, following the cues of Peirce and Cassirer, is in favour of viewing anthropology as a branch of semiology, science of signs. What a sign will or can signify, depends much upon the linguistic/cultural affiliation of the sign, symbol or code. Totem, taboo, kin, calender, month, year, era, longitude, latitude, *etc.*, for example, are all signs or codes. What they signify or encode are culture-relative. Whether a particular group of signs is to be treated as *myth*-logic or *science*-logic depends upon who, when and in what context are using the concerned signs, expressions. Levi-Strauss does not find any *natural* inferiority/superiority relation between a steel axe and a stone axe, between the primitive and the civilized. Obviously this approach to *different* cultures is in marked distinction from the positivistic orientation of such anthropologists as Tylor, Frazer and Levi-Bruhl who speak of the pre-logical and pre-scientific mentality of the primitive peoples.

But does this Straussian way of looking at *different* cultures, suspending *judgment* on them, mean a strong form of cultural relativism? NO is Levi-Strauss's own answer. He thinks his version of structuralism is a *natural* recognition of cultural diversity (of human societies). What unite them, undoing the supposed relativistic misgivings, are certain "nature-transforming, unchanged and unchanging powers" lodged in the very structure of the human mind. The cultural and linguistic relativity and contextuality do not and cannot affect or influence the *natural* unity of the humankind, and the *natural* unity of human mind. And in that unity are rooted cultural universals and linguistic/symbolic/coded universals. The fact that these codes can be decoded in, or applied to, such widely different cultural objects like hand tools and machine tools, kinship systems and languages, shows that, in spite of their individuation in (geographical) space and (historical) time, human cultures have a natural but concealed unity of their own.

Obviously this analytical account of cultural unity and amidst diversity is *not* acceptable to the dialectically disposed pro-historical writers like Sartre. The structuralist supposition of unchanged and unchanging powers of the human mind seems to be a pure construct of analytical reason. All human powers, all social structures, are believed to be dialectically constituted and reconstituted by praxis, need-induced group activities. The structuralist, much in the fashion of the scientific positivist from whom he differs in very many ways, uses the latter's paradigm of analytical reason. Reason in its analytical stage is used for definition, classification, subsumption, differentiation, *etc.* But at the next or a higher stage human reason works as an integrative, or totalising, capacity. Man's mind cannot understand nature in its "raw" form. For the purpose the objects of nature need to be "cooked" in terms of prior definition, classification, encoding, *etc.* Thereafter the cooked nature, rather than the precooked one, is totalized or meaningfully integrated, by the human mind and is made a part of living culture. It is impossible today (at present) for the unaided analytical reason to understand culture or even nature as it was cognitively available to the people of yesterday (past). In other words, in the name of structuralization the defender of analytical reason unwittingly destroys or "kills" the *actual* findings of nature, *i.e.*, science, and those of culture, *i.e.*, anthropology, of yesterday.

It is undoubtedly true that in the modern world, or in what *we* call the modern world, different countries and cultures do come in contact with one another, *i.e.*, interact. But this fact, rather this claim, can not be universalized. Every culture has its own identity. Only the neighbouring cultures and the historically proximate ones can be said to be interactive. Without straining the meaning of such expressions as "international relation" and "global interaction" it is difficult to show causal or quasi-causal connection between, say, Europe and USA, on the one hand, and Asian countries, on the other. To make their relation intelligible we are required to fall back upon some cultural, apparently non-causal, factors like political imperialism or market forces. It is to be noted here that both imperialism and market economy have hegemonistic elements built in them. Historically speaking, it is not at all surprising that Britain, for example, has the most intimate relation, besides its European neighbours, with the former colonies in Asia, Africa and North America. The same can be said of France and Holland. Of all the far-flung countries in the world they are closest to their own former colonies. For example, the dominant British presence in South Asia, the dominant French presence in Indo-China and the similar Dutch presence in Indonesia show that the selective character of interaction between distant countries is basically historical, linguistic and cultural, a super-structural result of past politico-economic relations. In spite of the antagonistic past of their historical relations, culturally speaking, they continue to remain close. To illustrate the point: the average educated Indian knows more of British history and culture than those of its next-door Central Asian neighbours. Among other things, this cultural integration, intimate relation of one country with another, is not mainly based on geographical proximity. Rather it depends upon co-sharability of certain myths, events, processes and their memories. Totalization or globalization is bound to be selective and interest-relative. To understand the nature and workings of the globalizing ties between different cultures we need the resources both of analytical reason, for "cooking" or interpreting the "raw", what is uninterpreted, and those of dialectical reason for integrating, comparing, and generalizing the results yielded by analytical reason.

All the above considerations make it clear that the supposed antithetical relation between self and other, civilized and primitive, dialectical reason and analytical reason, and history and anthropology is untenable. For every "self" has its "other". Every "other" presupposes some or other "self". Every "civilized" society has its "primitive" aspects; and every "primitive" society has its "civilized" aspects. "Analytical" reason is marked by its "dialectical" moments; and "dialectical" reason performs some "analytical" functions. Rightly understood, these "paired" concepts are really and functionally complementary and show one main point: anthropology is enfolded history and history is unfolded anthropology.

IV

If our line of approach to anthropology, study of culture, and history, reconstruction of human past from a particular point of view, are correct, then structuralization, although to be recognized to a certain extent, must be viewed under the aspect of the primacy of history. Even structure itself is found to have its own history.

Language, which is said to be structure of structures and readily lends itself to structural analysis and generalization, is also found to be changing. Not only the meanings of words but also the ways of conjoining, uttering and using them undergo change. Whether historical changes of cultural objects, including language, are rupturous, radical or incommensurable, is a matter of interesting controversy between the structuralists like Levi-Strauss and deconstructionists like Derrida. The deconstructionist defends acentricity and attacks the theses of knowledge without subject, art without artist, and the like. He discounts the claim of the structuralist that music and myth, for example, are shadowy, *i.e.*, promised, or possibility of actualization but not concrete or historical actualization. If cultural objects are left shadowy in this essentialist manner, then signs and symbols could be claimed to be genuinely meaningful even after the objects they are supposed to signify or symbolize do not turn out to be existential or actual. Respect for structurality, or supposed reality of shadows, Derrida feels, leads to negation or "neutralization of time and history".

How structures come into existence? How do they disappear? If their appearance and/or disappearance are found to be rupturous and without origin or end, then, by implication, reality of time and history are never established. And in that case origin, growth, decline and destruction of all sorts of structures remain enigmatic in the structuralist scheme of cultural studies. Even more enigmatic prove the fundamental concepts of chance and discontinuity, play and contingency. If cultural objects can be deemed to be real, present only by proxy, *i.e.*, without being available to sense perception, then human life is deprived of the significance of what is called play, its playful elements. Without the elements of play or contingency in it, social life becomes monotonous and the process of history mechanically anticipatable. Polytonous and unpredictable characters of society and history are due to play or human freedom. By his emphasis on this point the deconstructionist reminds one of Sartre's ontological individualism. Play is always play of absence *and* presence, a sort of very complex dialectical interplay between the individual praxis and the group praxis. If the origin of structurable cultural objects is *not* available or, plainly speaking, absent, then what remains of a structure can hardly be affirmed. In the structuralist scheme of things affirmation is possible without traceable origin or end, and negation is admissible even in the absence of perceptual justification. In the absence of the *difference* between presence and absence how to determine what is shadowy and what is concrete? This question deeply puzzles the deconstructionist because he always emphasizes the play element, the element of contingency, in our life, individual and social. In this play, he finds, the living space of freedom, freedom of humanism.

Obviously, deconstructionism is a reaction against structuralism, marked by radical relativism, incommensurabilism and uncertainty of the human life. The deconstructionist is opposed to any fixed and permanent difference between received juxtapositional words and expressions. Also he seems to be opposed to the very idea of accepting any word, any context, any culture, as specially privileged. If any name cannot mean "properly" what is intended to be named by it, the very expression "proper name" loses its proclaimed semantic preeminence. In that case many time-honoured philosophical views like realism, correspondence theory of truth, true representation are sure to miss their target. What is more, even the very prevalent ideas about "theory", "context", claimed difference between "analytic" and "dialectic", "nature" and "culture", "literature" and "philosophy", and "anthropology" and "history" become fuzzy. Identity and clarity then prove elusive. Many of these ideas, though in the current Euro-

American tradition, are attributed to thinkers like Heidegger, Foucault, Derrida and Rorty, may be easily traced in different ways to Hegel, Marx, Nietzsche and Freud. Following the anti-methodological approach of deconstructionism, one can look for the genealogy of these views still backward in time to thinkers like Parmenides, Heraclitus, Plato and Protagoras. For, after all, every context, it is claimed, can be differently contextualised, decontextualised, and also recontextualised. In other words, physics or physical time cannot compel the writer to *decide* his own ways of writing. The creative writer is free to write differently, in endlessly different ways.

Since the rejection of *method* because of its alleged tyranny by the structuralists like Foucault and deconstructionists like Derrida is not peculiar to philosophers and social scientists and is also found among philosophers and historians of science like Toulmin, Feyerabend, Kuhn, and Lakatos, no traditionally recognized discipline can be taken to be definitively cognitive. When *method* itself comes under fire, science, scientific method and scientific or physical reductionism cannot claim to have a special cognitive status. Every discipline is an ongoing discourse and nothing is conclusive. Do all these considerations and questions mean cultural anarchy and breakdown of the relation between self and other both within and between cultures? This very question, the deconstructionist tries to point out, makes sense only within a theory. Since theory and the method of forming it are questionable and other theories based on other methods on the same discourse are available, the claim of one particular theory cannot be taken to be specially "privileged" or "true". The way out of the problem regarding the relation between self and other, knowledge and reality, the deconstructionist suggests, lies through lived life, group praxis and similar other enterprises.

In order to stave off the threat of radical relativism realists like Putnam recalls Plato's arguments against Protagoras. If truth is doubted or rejected on the ground of its alleged relativity to some person or some context, then the very act of rejection itself may also be shown to be equally vulnerable or self-refuting. Rejection of truth, like affirmation, may also be said to be contaminated by relativity (to person/context). Another criticism of relativism, particularly moral relativism, is brought forward by thinkers like Thomas Nagel claiming that transcendence from personal and contextual peculiarities is possible. This pro-Kantian view rests on the possibility of self's attainment of a transcendental, Archimedean or universal point of view. This suggests that we can go, or at least try to go, out of our own mind, successfully ignoring the effects of nature and culture on our body-mind complex. Moreover, among the implied claims of this view are the validity of "correspondence" and usefulness of "representation". To try to speak of something extra-linguistic in and by language raises and reopens many problems and questions. If language and reality are juxtapositionally or externally related, what relates them? What, then, happens to representation *of* reality *in* language? Who can answer these questions plausibly and how? Is language a mediumistic instrument?

But it is not difficult to show the infirmities of this strong pro-transcendental view. It has been rightly argued by many writers that it is extremely difficult to show the exact correspondence between what is expressed or stated in a particular language and *what is* (extra-linguistic?) *there*. The ideal of picturesque correspondence has long gone out of fashion after the breakdown of Wittgenstein's *Tractatarian* theory of elementary proposition. It is not without reason that internal realists like Putnam and anthropological rationalists have discounted the theory of privileged access of human mind to God's-eye standpoint. It is impossible for any human mind to stand above or beyond this or that historical context or web of beliefs. Somewhat in a similar vein Davidson points out that there is no chance for any person to take up a vantage point for surveying and comparing different contexts or conceptual schemes by temporarily suspending one's own. The idea of total exile of mind from every context,—linguistic, conceptual or cultural, is as unworkable as its privileged transcendental situation.

Most of the philosophical attempts seem to stand in between two extreme positions, ethnocentrism and universalism. The ethnocentrist thinks that it is impossible for any person to be entirely free from the influences of the culture he is accustomed to live in. The free citizen of the world is an idealized concept. The power of acculturation appears so overwhelming to every one that he is not prepared to believe in his own ability to understand fully his counterparts living in other cultures. He gives the impression that cultural others are constructs of abstract imagination.

Actually, however, this highly idealized extreme position is not ordinarily entertained by any writer. The general-level truth seems to be that in practice each one of us, historian or anthropologist, ethnocentrist or universalist, always lives with, speaks to, or thinks of some other person(s). He, on reflection, realizes that to live all alone is a metaphor, an excerpt from a *social* reality, being-with-others. Similarly, the concept of speaking makes no sense if there is none to whom one can speak and who can somehow understand the speaker. Extending this argument it can be shown that even what we call loud thinking turns out to be impossible. Without a given form of life signs fail to signify and the "possible" ways of using them are just not available. In his argument against the private language Wittgenstein painstakingly shows how private language, like private living or private thinking, is an impossibility. Positively speaking, there cannot be thinking, speaking and living without some sort of language, some form of life. For the purpose we need some language, some publicly sharable institution or way of communication. It is obviously true that one and the same institution of language may be used differently. In fact even the very *difference of use* makes sense only within a commonly sharable institution.

Can the universalist, radicalizing the point of common sharability, make out a plausible case for transcultural universalism? Can he refute the argument for ethnocentrism, cultural singularity? A culture may be singular or peculiar in very many ways, in terms of power (military, industrial, intellectual, spiritual, *etc.*), excellence (artistic, religious, literary, *etc.*), repression (political, sexual, economic, *etc.*). On close analysis, every culture is found to have some distinct traits of its own, which separate, not isolate, it from other cultures. Cultural distinctiveness is not antithetical to universalism. Some of our ideas and ideals, for example, of truth, justice, development, are genuinely universal. This is not to deny the possibility of understanding, defining and following these ideas and ideals differently.

On closer analysis, it can be further shown that commonness or universalistic argument is not uniformly applicable, interculturally or intraculturally. Even within a particular culture the norms and beliefs which are said to be commonly shared are in effect differently perceived and practiced. For example, the same language is differently spoken. The study of linguistic geography, of the shifting relation between different dialects of the same language, makes the point clear. Also it brings out the related point how by speaking a language its speakers change it over the years. The changes in a life of an institution, of a culture, are brought about by how it is lived by the concerned human beings. In the process one institution is influenced by other neighbouring institutions, one culture by other neighbouring cultures.

The ways in which the British speak English are not the same as the Americans speak it. The ways the English-knowing Indians use the language are significantly different from those of the peoples whose mother tongue is English. The point may be pressed further: even in the different parts of Britain this language is spoken or used more or less differently. Can an Indian, whose mother tongue is Bengali or Hindi or Tamil, learn and use English as an Englishman does? This is an intriguing question. The answer to this question may be both "yes" and "no". Obviously in a sense an Indian, like any other foreigner whose mother tongue is not English, can learn it and, given appropriate training and practice, speak and write it with reasonable, but not extraordinary, felicity. It may be recalled here that the English language in which Tagore wrote *Gitanjali*, literally means an offering of songs, and which earned him Nobel Prize in 1913 was critically commented upon on linguistic ground by Yeats, himself a Nobel laureate and who was an admirer and a friend of Tagore in the early phase of his life. Another example. Some years back when Spender during his visit to India was asked at Bhopal "what do you think of English poetry written by Indians?" his cryptic response was "Is there anything like that?" Obviously he refused to recognize the so-called English poetry written by Indians as ideal English, ideal for an Englishman.

It is not surprising that many of us feel amused when a foreigner speaks our language. This is not a phenomenon peculiar to any particular language-speaking group. Proficiency in use of a language is not merely a matter of mastering its grammar, vocabulary and idioms. There are many other things, almost invisibly embedded in the concerned culture, which contribute to linguistic proficiency. Language is indeed a very complex form of life which has many fuzzy subforms nested within it. In it are found many *peculiar* concepts and expressions which do not have their counterparts in most other languages. Linguistic indeterminacy is not merely a philosophical thesis of Quine and some other philosophers. It has its many other nuances.

V

To illustrate the point the English word *history* is ordinarily translated as *Itihasa* in many Sanskrit-rooted Indian languages but the Sanskritic scholars point out that in Indian tradition *Itihasa* comprises *Itivrtta* (chronicle), *Akhyayika* (story/tale/narrative), *Udaharana* (example/in-stance/precedent), *Vamsa* (lineage), *Gatha* (ballad), *etc.* Many European writers, including Hegel and James Mill, are of the view that Indians have no historical sense; and that to them time is unreal. Most of them think that non-dualistic *Vedanta* system, marked by its so-called a-temporal and *maya* interpretation of the world, is the typical way of Indian thinking. Also they are ordinarily unaware of the distinc-tion drawn by several Indian systems between cosmic time, physical time, and historical time. Yet when they speak of ahistority of Indian thought obviously they have a particular concept of history in the back of their mind, apparently forgetting the history of European historiography itself before the mid-eighteenth century. To be more precise on the point, the watershed between the old European historiography and the modern one is often unconsciously drawn mainly in terms of the works of such writers as David Hume (1711–1776) and Edward Gibbon (1737–94). Hume's *History of Great Britain from the Invasion of Julius Caesar to the Revolution of 1688*, 6 Vols. (1754–1762), and Gibbon's *The History of the Decline and Fall of the Roman Empire 1976*, 6 Vols., (1776–78), have been largely influenced by what may be called the scientific way of writing history by spelling out the causes of the historical events and processes. Both French Encyclopedia and British Historiography of the time were deeply influenced by the scientific spirit due to the Newtonian Revo-lution. In brief, the changing perception of history in Europe is a part of its cultural metamorphosis.

Somewhat in the same fashion it may be pointed out that the early historiography of Europe, like the Indian one, was closely asso-ciated with supernaturalism, genealogy, fable, and the like. But when towards the end of the eighteenth century the cultural presence of Europe in general and of Great Britain in particular was effectively established in eastern India, the impact of European historiography was deeply felt in India. The works of William Jones, Hayman Wilson, Prinsep, Elphinston, Colebrooke, Macaulay, Henry Maine, *etc.* unmistakably show the rising influence of the concept of European historiography. Some of them like Jones, Wilson and Colebrooke took the trouble of learning Sanskrit and few other Indian languages to understand India, while most others, like James Mill, openly claimed that one need not learn any Indian language to write on Indian history. This seems to be patently incorrect. This is the point, among other things, which has been argued in "*Itihasa,*

History and Historiography of Civilization". By generalizing this point one can say even this Introduction that we are writing and the language in which we are writing clearly indicate the cultural presence of Europe in India.

A kindred point has been persuasively made out by Richard Shusterman in his essay, "Understanding the Self's Others". His line of presentation is both theoretical and autobiographical. The words chosen by him for formulating his issue are insightful: "we come to understand better by discovering the cultural others in our self". Some of us are born in one country and reared up elsewhere. Many families are bilingual. In the multi-ethnic countries like India, the former USSR, and USA this phenomenon is very common. By mastering a second language one becomes both bilingual and bicultural. Migration of population is nowadays a very common phenomenon. It is interesting to recall that till the late medieval age, when immigration laws, passport and visa systems were not there, the people used to move more freely than we are allowed in the modern age. In a very important sense people's movement implies mobility of their language and culture as well. In India came and permanently settled the Aryans, Bactrians, Scythians, Mongolians, Turks, Arabs and Persians; they have got assimilated in Indian culture. A similar thing happened in the last four hundred years in USA. Therefore it is not surprising that many cultures like the Indian or the American can rightly claim to be composite. It is well known that in the 1930s a large number of European scholars and writers moved to and settled in the USA and Canada. If we forget for the time being the questions of personal difficulties and family tragedies, it is difficult to deny that migration had some positive cultural fall-out. The history of the Vienna Circle and the Frankfurt School during the years 1930–1950 introduced and disseminated many philosophical and social ideas of European origin in USA. The post-war development of American science and technology owes a lot to the academic community from Europe in general, and the Jewish community in particular.

Shusterman's own case, self-understanding, in this context, is very instructive. Born in America with English as mother tongue, educated at Oxford, bearing a Jewish surname, and interested in learning German language and philosophy, he identifies himself "as an American-Israeli binational". Environed by different cultures one's self-identity cannot be absolutely free from an element of ambiguity. This is an experience which has been expressed, among others, by many Jews settled in USA or Canada. Even the black Americans, many of whom have forgotten their ethnic origin, living in America for several generations, and whose mother tongue is English, are not entirely free from an ambiguity in their self-understanding. To take some other examples, most of the Indians who travelled to Mauritius, Fiji and the West Indies do not speak nowadays any Indian language. Still they have not been able to erase completely their ethnic origin or racial-cultural memory. The cases of Creoles in Mauritius and the West Indies, of the Eurasians, Parsis and Armenians in India are even more complex and instructive. Simultaneous affiliation to different cultures and languages are bound to impart some ambiguous traits in the concerned human character. Self and others cannot be easily separated.

The relation between self and other(s), as has been rightly pointed out by Shusterman, is marked by several characteristics, viz., (a) self-understanding, self-discovery, and self-enlargement, (b) comparative and contrasting consciousness, and (c) comparative expression of the self in the light of self's understanding of other persons, other texts, *etc.* in the self. Self-understanding knows no limit. On the conceptual interdependence between self and other(s) much has been written by the philosophers. As already noticed, some anthropologists have tried to show the complementarity between and convergence of them.

Comparative and contrasting approaches to the relation between self and other(s) are beset with various difficulties. The point has been clearly brought out by Shusterman's reference to Eliot. Born in America and settled in England, trained in philosophy and giving best of his time to literary activities, Eliot discovered a new identity of his own. His conversion from Catholicism to the Anglican faith also contributed to the complexity and richness of his self-understanding. These have found expressions in his various writings. His interest in and study of French and Indian cultures made him acutely conscious of the difficulties, in fact impossibility, of *completely* identifying one's own self with other cultures, selves and texts for the sake of understanding.

That true understanding or knowledge involves identification, overcoming the difference between self and other(s), subject and object, has been highlighted not only by Eliot but also Sri Aurobindo and several other Indian thinkers of the Vedantic persuasion. Knowledge by identity, as distinguished from empirical knowing by difference, is extremely difficult to attain and retain. It involves a sort of total self-transformation. This self-transformation or what has been referred to earlier as complete self-transcendence is a very lofty normative invitation. One might say, it is also an ontological invitation which, with difficulty, can be accepted but almost humanly impossible to keep. Therefore it is not surprising that most of us, like Shusterman, are inclined to recognize the presence of others within our own self. This means that in the process of understanding other cultures we do not propose to, rather cannot, completely assimilate or internalize other cultures within ours; nor can we be totally oblivious of our culture, *internal* to ourselves.

No self remains in total seclusion despite the relativist rhetoric concerning "otherness". Shusterman's insight about the presence of others within our own self is widely recognized as noted above. Still one wonders whether this insight can extend to a realm where in response to a normative invitation a self seeks complete autonomy from the "other", other selves, as well as the natural, social and cultural environ which the self faces as the other. Kalyan Sen Gupta writes about this realm, the realm of cultural objects, particularly fine arts, where the creative freedom or autonomy of the artist takes him/her *prima facie* totally beyond the others. Sen Gupta, following Tagore, maintains that art objects are expressions of "the surplus in man". This creative surplus is neither causally related to nature, nor is it even quasi-causally related to the artist's social background. But this is an extreme position which harks back to the false portrayal of the self and the other as binary opposites, which Shusterman has exposed. The artist, like any other individual, cannot be completely unaffiliated. Art critics like Dewey think that works of art are located within the historical and cultural context of both the artists and their appreciators.

To reject outright the view that art has nothing to do with nature raises questions. One cannot be cultural without being natural first. Reason or imagination, whatever may be the main fountain of art, is in a way bound to be located in some human being. The cultural identity of the artist is somehow rooted, thickly or thinly, in the biological identity of the creative artist. This point becomes clear from iconography and art history. The art and architectural forms of every culture, Indian, Chinese, Egyptian and European, have their distinct features. Even within every culture are found different art forms in different regions and periods of history. The "monotony" of the identity of natural objects is broken by the creative artist, it is true. The "surplus" in him enables him to transform natural object into an artistic one. Natural and seasonal sights and sounds, for example, are transformed into different forms of *Raga* by the musician. But this only shows the close link between the "natural" and the "cultural".

If art objects are essentially "expressional" in character as Sen Gupta thinks, can we discover any universal or generic forms in them? If we can, how is that possible? If we cannot, to what is it due? The terms like *style* and *pattern* are indicative of the possibility of generalization. If this possibility is discounted, then one has to defend the claim that the artist's creative freedom is absolute, *i.e.*, unrelatable to anything external to his imagination. But this strong claim seems to be indefensible. Even the creators of so-called radically new styles are, on close analysis, found to be indebted to some tradition, often several traditions. And that is why one feels that different art forms show a trend of convergence. Sen Gupta rightly highlights this concept of convergence. This does not mean that the different art forms or styles found in different countries would exhibit some kind of artistic universals. It is true that some psychologists and anthropologists have tried to extract elements of artistic universals from "collective representations" underlying the art objects of different cultures. But when the art critic is called upon to examine this claim, he finds it very difficult to endorse it. By implication it is suggested that the creative freedom of the artists cannot easily be chained to any "creative representation" or "collective unconscious".

This shows that the conflict between the two extreme positions, universalist and relativist, cannot be easily resolved. The project of discerning convergence, not to speak of essentialist unification, is hazardous. Still most of us avoid the two extremes and operate in the middle region despite the obstacles encountered in comparing different cultures. For alongside the obstacles there are satisfactions as well, as shown and persuasively argued by Frank Hoffman.

VI

It is a common experience of most of us who have tried to study different cultural heritages,—Indian, European and American, that the outcome of this enterprise is almost invariably mixed, partly satisfying and partly disappointing. For example, although we have studied Greek philosophy, our claim to have understood Plato and Aristotle is likely to be rejected on linguistic ground by the classical Greek philosophers. Analogously, the Sanskrit-knowing classical scholars of India often refuse to recognize the knowledge-claim of the modern philosophers who have studied the classical texts only in English, Hindi or any other vernacular translation.

The problem of translation poses a major obstacle to the success of comparative study of philosophy, anthropology and other forms of culture. With the problem of translation is intimately related the issue of semantic variance. On this ground particularly in the areas of fine arts, ethics and law we find it relatively difficult to pass universally acceptable cross-cultural judgment. It is in this problematic context that Hoffman highlights the importance not only of linguistic competence but also of context-sensitivity. Also related to the problem of meaning is the problem of ascertaining the exact identity of the problem. It is true that all philosophical problems are not necessarily linguistic. But that linguistic competence is very important in philosophical and other forms of cultural understanding has been highlighted not only by the followers of later Wittgenstein but also by various other scholars, including the classical scholars. In India *Vyakarana* (linguistic analysis or grammar) has been recognized as a distinct science (*sastra*) right from the Vedic period (*sakalya*) to the modern time and learned treatises have been written on the subject by an illustrious line of authors from Panini (400 BC), Patanjali (150 BC) and Bhartrhari to Bhattoji Diksita (late 16th century), Konda Bhatta (mid-17th century) and Nagesa Bhatta (early 18th century). Even in the recent past some very erudite books have been written following the tradition.

Simply because the problems besetting comparative philosophy are mentioned, one must not think that it provides no reward. Far from that, Hoffman tries to show how Asian philosophy, often presented under the rubric of "orientalism", has been widely misunderstood by many Western scholars. The best way of defining, rather understanding, Asian philosophy would be to use the method of comparison and contrast. To appreciate a particular type of philosophy one need not necessarily praise or deprecate it. Before passing judgment one is expected to try honestly to understand what is going to be judged. Unstudied criticism is as puerile as uninformed admiration. One need not be an Indophile to be a good scholar of Indian culture. Nor an Indian is required to be an Europhile to appreciate the excellence of European culture. To be a good comparative philosopher what are needed most are, in the words of Hoffman, "imaginative sympathy and critical acumen".

The view that there is no self which can possibly internalize within its consciousness *all* that it is conscious of suggests, among other things, that solipsism is untenable. Similarly untenable seems to be the view which claims that the knowing self is reducible to the world or part thereof which it knows. The second view, reductionism, like the first view, solipsism, is a promise which is sometimes made philosophically. But this is never honoured in practice. Rather, one can say, because of its very nature, it cannot be honoured. Both reductionism and solipsism are in the nature of unexecutable programmes. Strictly speaking, there is neither any practicing solipsist nor any practicing reductionist. All of us move in the space between the extremes. Most thinkers who write or speak about their views, scientific, philosophical, anthropological, historical, or literary, may on analysis be shown to be working in between their own selves and for whom they are writing. There is no subject, self, or knower, who is absolutely foundational or self-contained nor is there any object which is foundational or self-contained. The fluxist philosophers of West and East like Heraclitus and Nagarjuna have been drawing our attention to a sort of dynamic continuity on the basis of this kind of unfounded symbiotized unity. Joseph Margolis, referring to the works of such philosophers as Descartes, Husserl, the later Wittgenstein, and Nagarjuna, tries to show the continuative nature of philosophy.

The theoretical thrust of different types of fluxism is anti-presuppositionalist or anti-foundationalist. There is no first philosophy which can be taken as the matrix of all other types of philosophy or theoretical enterprises. It is ordinarily believed that neither self nor other is available without presuppositions. Kant speaks of categorical presuppositions, Vaihinger believes in the hypothetical ones, and Collinwood's "absolute presuppositions" are all historical, epochal and culture-bound. Neither God nor Matter is sovereign, *i.e.*, can be shown to be independent of our ways of apprehending them. Descartes tried to show that the knowing self, thinking consciousness, on its own may not be self-contained but as affiliated to a non-deceiving God is unquestionable. But his argument has apparently failed. Because if we need God to accept the possibility of unquestionable self, one can point out, how can God be thought to be veracious without assuming or presupposing the infallible ability of self to apprehend God? Circularity seems to have vitiated this argument.

If the claim of self-knowledge can be so easily vitiated, how can one be sure of the existence of the physical (other) world as studied in science. Because, after all, world as extended matter as such is not self-shining or self-proving. It is only in self's consciousness or knowing capacity that the true nature of the world is captured. This argument proves either the dependence of the world (as other) on self-consciousness or the cognitive fallibility of the self because of its contingent character and dependence upon the self-contained world. If this thesis of interdependence is accepted, then the primacy claim of *cogito* breaks down; also breaks down with it the primacy claim of the so-called self-existent world. In that case both self and the world (as other), both consciousness and matter, have to be viewed as dependent upon and expressions of God, the only sovereign being. It is precisely this sort of foundationalism which Husserl, for example, following Kant's philosophical anthropology, wanted to combat. He, like Nagarjuna, wanted to vindicate anti-presuppositionalism. Of course their *ways* of attempted vindication are quite different.

Opposed to the thesis of dichotomy between the self and the world, Husserl is persuaded that neither is self-contained. World in its raw or pure physical form, marked by corporeality and temporality, is not available to the knowing mind which variably interprets it in the process of apprehending it. The knowing mind or self is not available even to itself in a finished or fixed form. There is no end to the process of self's self-discovery. The "complexity" of the knowing self is partly due to the presence of life-forms in it. In other words, world without ceasing to be objective, is available, articulately or inarticulately, within self. It is only within self, self-reflective consciousness, that life-forms of the world get coherently related, become objectively meaningful and unified. The unity of world and that of self are inseparable.

Admittedly, this view sounds transcendentally idealist. It is doubly transcendental, both self-wise and world-wise. Self's apprehension of the world and also of itself is endlessly growing. Whatever self apprehends, itself or world, is endlessly intentional, every content of it is said to have its "beyond" in it. Every form of knowledge is a transcendental invitation, promise of the expansion of its meaning-horizon, in it. Every cognitive content is self-exceeding. Neither physical world nor history nor language can set a permanent limit to what self can possibly know. Whenever self knows something new, its existing knowledge undergoes change and in a way is renewed. Viewed thus, one can say, somewhat like Margolis, that Husserl's programme of eidetic reduction or unification cannot be *completely* carried out. It is doubly open-ended, both from the end of the knower and also from that of the known. The symbiotized structure of human knowledge, of subject and object, is being continuously destructuralized. This cognitive process is claimed to be endless.

It is not easy to find a straight way from Descartes or even Husserl to fluxism of Nagarjuna. For, after all both Descartes and Husserl are in favour of "founded and definitive knowledge", a sort of first philosophy. In marked contrast, Wittgenstein discovered that the most natural locus or home of human knowledge is this or that natural language. He discounts the Cartesian search, substantially endorsed by Husserl, for a transcendental form of knowledge which can rise above, not only above the physical temporality and corporeality but also above the natural linguisticality. The nuances of human knowledge and discourse are to be found, says Wittgenstein, in actual *uses* of natural language within different *forms* of life. Words have no unified or unifying metaphysical "home". Their homes or contexts are varied and variable. It is by using the anti-metaphysical and pluralistic tools of natural language that Margolis makes his way to Nagarjuna, understanding and interpreting him.

Undoubtedly Nagarjuna is a fluxist. He believes in no originary or antecedent foundational home of knowledge. Knowledge is neither historical nor futuristic. It is momentary (*ksanabhangura*), a matter of dependent origination (*pratityasamutpada*) and having practical efficacy (*arthakriyakaritva*). These are the basic features of the Nagarjunite fluxism. It is both backward-looking and forward-looking. Every past moment of one's "self"-consciousness collapses. "Self" is bracketed because of its *elusive* nature and which reminds one of the views of self found in Hume, Kant and Wittgenstein. As "self", according to Nagarjuna, is elusive his (*Mahayana*) view is often called *nairatmavada* (non-selfism). The collapsing past of the non-selfist "self" makes its presence, though momentarily, possible. In an important sense "self" is real; otherwise to speak of its *nirvana* makes no sense. The present moment of "self", of "self"-knowledge, dies paving the way for "its" future. However, these moments, though different, are continuous only in terms of practical efficacy. Their causal connection is only a matter of imagination (*kalpana*), not determinate perception. *Kalpana* means making *possible* (by imagination) and possible ways of apprehending past and future are numerous. *Madhyama* literally means the middle. Whatever it is is between no-longer (past) and not-yet (future). *Sunya* is not ontological emptiness. It is reality but without any permanently identifiable/predicable determination of it; we cannot say either *asti* (is) and *nasti* (is not), either *ek* (one) or *anya* (other), about it.

That *Sunya is* reality in a sense and *is not* reality in a sense is clear from the Mahayana dictum: *Samsara* (empirical world of change, of birth and death, of appearance and disappearance) is *Nirvana* (world beyond change, chain of birth and death, *etc.*) and *Nirvana* is *Samsara*. This is also in accord with the principle of fluxism. Nothing is; every thing flows. Translated in the discourse of *self* and *other*, it may be said, *self*, in a sense, is *other* and, in a sense, is *not other*; further, *other*, in a way, is *in self*, and, in a way, is *not in self*. Slightly varying a distinct Vedantin theme, one can say, every *self* is in every *other* self and every *other* is in *self*. For this reason some Vedantins, from Gaudapada to Samkara, have been understandably referred to as crypto-Buddhist (*pracchanna Bauddha*). Vedanta and Buddhism, two main traditions of Indian thought, are not quite antagonistic as ordinarily believed. Their points of convergence and affinity, a modern deconstructionist historian of thought may well say, are numerous and very important.

VII

The dialogue between different cultures, as we have noted before, is an on-going process. It has been going on down the centuries between East and West. Since we are now, for historical reasons, particularly interested in the dialogue between Euro-American countries, on the one hand, and India, on the other, it is quite understandable why writers like Fred Dallmayr focus their critical attention on the hegemonistic and/or global approach of the West to the question of development.

Must the aim of development of all societies be identical or uniform? Should the state authority be exercised in the same way in different societies or even within one society? How should the ideals of justice and freedom for the individual be conceived in the context of uneven political states of affairs? These are some of the basic questions understandably raised and sought to be answered by the social scientists of the developing countries like India. Dallmayr draws our attention to the views of Indian social scientists like Rajni Kothari and Ashis Nandy, both of the Centre for the Study of Developing Societies in Delhi. Apparently encouraged by Gadamer's critique of uniformism and univocal globalization, Dallmayr finds, Kothari's "Search of Humane Alternatives" very refreshing and instructive.

Indian political culture, particularly in the present century, has come under two basic influences, one of Gandhism and another of Marxism. Indigenous tradition has found its most influential articulation in Gandhi and his followers. Gandhi was deeply influenced by the ideals of minimal statism of Thoreau, Emerson and Tolstoy, and above all by the ideal of *Ahimsa* (non-violence) preached by the Buddha and other Indian thinkers. But, right from the early decades of the century, the impact of Marxism was felt in the struggle for independence. Experience of his Russian visit (1927) left a lasting impact on Nehru. It was further deepened by the rise of Nazism in Germany (1933) and the Spanish Civil War (1936). Nehru and Subhash Bose leaned to the Left within the Congress, comprising the Marxists and Socialists.

After independence both in the spheres of politics and economics the relevance of Gandhian thought and that of Marxism has been differently perceived. This difference in perception is clear from the Indian Constitution, marked by federalism with unitary bias, and the initial Five-Year Plans. Haunted by the political and regional diversity of the country and working under the background of partition (1947), the founding fathers of the Constitution wanted to make the Centre very strong. Till date, the Centre-State relations have remained a highly controversial issue. In the sphere of economic planning, mainly because of Nehru and Mahalanobis, both considerably influenced by the Soviet model of planning, India espoused a sort of welfarism. The core sector of the economy came directly under the State control and heavy industries, compared to small-scale and village industries, received higher priority. In effect the Gandhian economic motto, "The Small is Beautiful", was bypassed. The accent on village economy, though notionally recognized, was practically missing. Some Gandhians like Vinoba Bhave and Raja Gopalacari, taking cues from the thought of Gandhi, strongly criticized political centralism and controlled economy. The ideas of alternative approach to economics and politics may be fruitfully traced to the tradition left behind by Gandhi, and the legacy of the mixed economy was partly due to Marx and partly due to Keynes. The experience of the years of depression of 1930s in Europe and America persuaded the Left in the Congress that State intervention in the sphere of economy is absolutely imperative.

The importance of land reforms and that of fast industrial development were more or less recognized by all political parties and the policy-makers. But the question was how to go about these programmes? Should the people themselves and the non-governmental organizations come forward and take the lead? Or, must the state take the initiative both in formulating and executing the action programmes? Over this question the Gandhians and the welfarists understandably differed.

Kothari and others of his persuasion felt that in the name of industrialization and building a nation-state the society was getting increasingly stratified, widening the gulf between the elite and the poor. The state, largely because of its inherited structure of unresponsive bureaucracy, failed to deliver the goods meant for the poor and the exploited. The political policy-makers largely drawn from the upper castes and the propertied sections failed to tackle effectively the growing problems of inequality. The turbulent years of Emergency (1975–77) and the mass movement headed by Jayaprakash Narayan and other Gandhian leaders, backed by intellectuals like Kothari, successfully highlighted the weakness of the political system and of the Government of the time. But the collapse of the Janata Rule and the return of the Congress under the leadership of Indira Gandhi in 1980 once again brought the sad fact to the focus that the needs and say of the masses were yet to reach the level of governmental functioning.

What is worse, the direction of development followed by the Government is unsuitable to the people of a developing country like India. The modern science and technology of West are being allowed to propel the development of the country, resulting in high expenditure and neglect of indigenization of technology. Moreover, the heavy defence expenditure is cutting into the poverty-alleviation programmes. A new civilization is coming up which is westernized, consumption-driven and wasteful.

The main thrust of Kothari's argument is that the right way of developing India and its political-economic system cannot be blindly borrowed from this or that developed and industrialized country. We have to think of different alternatives and choose the one which is most appropriate to the meaningful life of the people of this country. The ideal of decentralization, a corollary of the minimal state, is favoured by both Kothari and Nandy. This does not mean that they are blindly in favour of "privatization" or mindless "liberalization", allowing foreign investment in all sectors of national economy. Critical of colonialism and statism, they are not in favour of importing neo-colonialism.

Nandy is in favour of a social system which has to be built up from the bottom level, on the basis of the needs and values of the poor and the exploited. He, like Kothari, is opposed to western-style modernization which is being defended, wittingly or unwittingly, by the modern elites, professionals, entrepreneurs and intellectuals. Respectful to the age-old tradition of the country, one need not be a traditionalist in the uncritical sense. Critical of the irrational elements of tradition, Nandy refuses to be identified as a traditionalist. But he favours the idea of understanding India and its culture in terms of what he calls "native categories".

Whether one is traditionalist or not, one, together with others, modernist and post-modernist, can hardly escape certain problems or even crises. The difference in the mode of understanding or interpreting problems and crises makes little or no difference to how possibly we can tackle them effectively. Practical compulsion is a hard task master. Even if we agree that different countries/cultures have some different peculiar problems, we cannot deny that the crisis through which the world is passing today affect us all irrespective of our countrywise affiliation.

This crisis has been understood in different ways. Pranab Kumar Sen views the crisis under the heads of economics, politics and ecology. Economic poverty seems to be a very important factor which is aggravating this crisis. Politically speaking, conflict of ideologies is making the situation additionally critical. The ecological crisis can be viewed both independently and also in relation to economic and ideological conflict. Generally speaking, the poverty-stricken people are obliged to live in close touch with nature and depend very much upon it. Yet, paradoxically enough, they are forced, forced by poverty in countries like India, to exploit nature. For example, those who live in the forest or hill areas know very well that deforestation is harmful to their own interests, but because of their inability to pay for commercially marketed fuel, fell the trees and use the wood as fuel and for heating in cold climate.

The economically developed countries often use the less developing or the least developed countries as the captive supplier of their natural resources like oil and iron ore. Because of the latter's poverty the terms of trade between them are also found to be relatively tilted in favour of the developed ones. What is more, underdeveloped in industry, the poor countries rely mostly on trade for their earning in hard currencies. In the process they have to sell out or export most of their non-renewable resources at a relatively cheap price. It is not difficult to see the close relation between the economic, political and ecological aspects of the world crisis. In a different form this crisis is evident also within the bounds of every country.

The essence of the crisis is conflict. Sen points out that conflict is rooted in distrust towards others and in the wrong belief that one can live all by oneself. This misunderstanding of our own situation explains at least partly the absence of the spirit of cooperation between different individuals, groups and countries. The lack of the spirit of cooperation indicates also our failure to appreciate the needs and values of others. At times some of us even willfully reject others' value systems. Thus we land ourselves in a kind of "axiological nihilism".

It has been rightly pointed out by Sen that the spirit of humanism or human unity does not require us to forget our difference based on cultural, political and economic distinctiveness. What is expected of us is the spirit of cosharing our available natural and cultural resources. Practical compromise and adjustment are not only un-avoidable but also positively welcome. To minimize or remove the causes of conflict we must enter into ideological dialogue. The use of public reason makes our communication successful. The more we communicate with each other, the less intense becomes our conflict. Dialogue and communication also instill trust both in ourselves and also in others. Success in communication is reflected in the rising level and different areas of cooperation. Philosophically speaking, that we are not victims of radical relativism or incommensurabilism is evident from our acts of cooperation and cosharing. To show the weakness of relativism Sen makes use of the conceptual resources of Davidson and Strawson.

VIII

The course of history is largely conditioned by trains of ideas which human minds conceive, articulate and propagate. The hand that holds the pen holds the future. Relativism, despite its weakness exposed by Davidson and others, enshrines such a train of ideas which has an immense practical significance. Difference, heterogeneity, otherness, are key relativistic ideas which still have a firm hold on the modern mind. These are ideas celebrated in today's cultural ethos notwithstanding the philosophical warnings against "incommensurabilism" to which radical relativism leads. Each of us as well as any group to which we belong have a strong urge to re-examine our identity and speak from our own centre of experience. The passion to gain voice from one's own centre of experience and to remain rooted in one's own way of being however impels one to drive others into silence. And the silence and seclusion to which the search for singularity eventually leads deepen lines of division that fracture society in every aspect of its being—social, economic, political, religious, racial and gender. Is there a way in which we can *retain otherness*, which relativism rightly stresses, and yet *go beyond otherness* so that the course of history is not fraught with conflict and fragmentation? To move beyond otherness we need a new vision, a vision that eschews the false image of the self and the other as binary opposites. We need to evolve new linkages between the two which may transform the course of history averting anxiety, fear, oppression, discrimination and conflict hitherto aggravated by the false construal of the self-other relationship.

Christina Schües speaks of multiple exploitations, discriminations, and oppressions to which women have been subjected, and contends that feminist philosophy as "practical philosophy" should "conceptualize an alternative project" a "vision" that would not only liberate women from men, but also transform society into a "world of partnership". She envisions a change in the course of human history which will achieve "linking of the two halves of humanity". What has to be given up is the long entrenched misconstrual of the self-other relationship, which, instead of linking the two halves has arrayed men and women in conflict.

Schües finds the genesis of conflict in the history of occidental thinking, in the train of ideas expressed in Hegel's writings for instance. Self-consciousness faced by another self-consciousness has come out of itself or lost itself as it were. Confronted with the "other" the self is haunted by a sense of fear, domination, loss and anxiety. To overcome this, Schües thinks, the autonomous subject establishes "the universal law in the light of his own self-image of rationality" to

which all must conform. This, she thinks is "his story" of rationality
with which "her story" should also merge. If it does not, then women
are simply what men are not. From the 17th century onwards, she
observes, woman is defined by negation and lacks, as nonaggressive,
non-competitive, and private, not public. She is defined by a lack of
autonomy. A drama of antagonism is thus enacted in which the
"other" is a threat to the self. The woman, who is the "other" is
perceived as "nobody", as "nature, matter, irrational *etc.*" She must
therefore be controlled. This androcratic characterization of the "other"
by negation lies at the root of sexual discrimination.

A challenge to occidental tradition has come from two phenomena
according to Schües, the re-emergence of women's movement in the
last thirty years, and the zeal of deconstruction in transforming and
dissolving dualistic thinking underlying dichotomies like male/female,
rational/emotional *etc.*, and their implied hierarchies that tend to
subordinate the second member of each pair under the first.

To avoid such hierarchical *ranking* and live up to the vision of
linking two halves of humanity, a proper understanding of the nature
of the feminine subject is necessary. One must not endorse an oversimplified account of essential characteristics and roles within a specifically female context, a context which Carol Gilligan explores in her
very influential work: *In a Different Voice*. Gilligan is right no doubt in
stressing "otherness" of the feminine subject, but this should not be
seen as a prelude to segregation along essentialist lines, for that might
revive androcratic characterization of the feminine subject by negation. Simon de Beauvoir, Schües approvingly says, was right to raise
her voice against this androcratic characterization. The woman as
"other" must not be reduced to an inessential object, defined by lacks.
But then, though a woman is not born but made, made an object
doomed to inessentiality and immanence, as Simon rightly claims, it
would be wrong to portray the feminine subject as one who is striving to become *like men* in order to attain transcendence, equality and
freedom. For that would destroy her distinctiveness, her positive alternative identity contra Gilligan's correct insistence on the necessity of
speaking "In a Different Voice". Deconstruction of the subject too is
mistaken for the same reason. At the end what remains after deconstruction is "nothing" or "nobody". If feminine subjects are reduced
to "nothings" or "nobodies", who have no distinctive identity, then
they can never find a voice of their own and therefore no direction,
no political programme of liberation. Instead of fluid "nomads" or

"nobodies" Schües envisions a feminine subject who is capable of acting and communicating with others, without isolating herself from and controlling the other. She is one who is not afraid of others and can *link* with others. Her thesis in her own words is "an attempt at linking rather than ranking".

The distinctive identity of the subject however is not completely constituted. Schües is not speaking of a notion of identity, entailed by the metaphysics of presence. The subject is always "a possibility of beginning". She is a being, as noted before, who is capable of acting. Acting means beginning; something begins, and others must help in order to push the beginning forward. So a beginning is always linking up with others. And since being free is synonymous with acting, and acting with beginning which involves linking with others, in being free one must link with others. Liberty is achieved only in relation to others, not by dominating others.

It is by moving beyond the traditional bipolar opposition of self/other that we can have a vision leading to transformation. Neither the selves nor their others however are so radically free that they can transform in the sense of creating. But we are not mere products of a power beyond our control either. We seek to transform by acting and acting is a striving towards making a difference. Making a difference does not amount to creating, nor to mere repetition owing to some controlling power. Bare repetition of traditional values implies status quo. But repetition done reflectively and in a different style can initiate transformation. Transformation for emancipation or liberation, to repeat, is not to be achieved through radically free creation, nor through bare repetition, but by linking with each other.

The false image of an opposition between self and other produces a wrong notion of power as domination. Schües conceives power in a different way following Hannah Arendt. She argues in favour of a notion of "power" which inheres in the condition of linking with other human beings. It is grounded in the acting-together of individuals and groups. It is power as *affiliation* in contrast to power as *control* over others. That is why even if women do demand empowerment, and adopt means like affirmative action for realizing equality they would not and should not want to be accomplices of androcratic power strategies that culminate in aggressive hierarchies and domination, in increasing militarism, economic exploitation of large parts of society and other forms of control and oppression. In stark contrast to this, a non-destructive view of power is vindicated which tries to privilege links with others, caring for others and having a responsibility towards others, in the way a mother has responsibility to help her children and care for them.

It is this power or strength that helps in building a community which has justice as the ideal basis. Unification in a just society may be secured through a sharing of subjectivities though this should not be taken to imply conformity to a fixed common paradigm of understanding. Justice for Schües is based on the responsibility for others, on partnership and linking with others, and on *respect for differences*. In linking with the other through friendship, love and care one does not merely confirm his/her humanity but his/her human *individuality*.

The need for a reconstrual of the self-other relationship which does not erase difference and is still able to secure human unity, stressed so strongly by Shusterman and Schües, is reaffirmed in "Understanding Human Action: Women's Free Acts as a Case-Study". In a specific context the general question is raised once again: How can we remain rooted socio-historically and still not sink in abysmal loneliness and conflict?

Cultural diversity, according to radical relativists, segments society into hermetically sealed worlds, each with an irreducibly native set of norms, beliefs, concepts and customs incomprehensible to the other. Against this thesis, especially in the form given to it by T.S. Kuhn, it is contended that (a) the relativists draw wrong, crypto-absolutist lessons from right relativistic insights; and (b) it is possible to understand, evaluate and learn from others' experiences and actions despite "otherness".

The social investigator or critic or any *other* person should surely try to understand and assess the actions of a feminine subject or "self" from the standpoint of her own centre of experience. However, the assumption of the agent's subjectivity must not be overstressed, for that might result in complete gap in communication. The "other", in this case the critic or the investigator, is shut within the prison of a subjectivity in the same way as the agent is confined within hers. And so the "other" might not be able to reach out beyond the frontier of his/her own culture to understand the actions of the subject belonging to a different culture. The action of a Hindu widow or "sati" who sacrificed herself on the funeral pyre of her husband illustrates such an action. The agent herself perceived this practice as a free act of self-effacement in many cases, for a strong sense of conjugal identity might have generated the feeling that life without her husband was meaningless and insufferable. The practice is now abolished and the values of self-effaciveness and sacrifice which it symbolized are seen as delusions which women have internalized under social pressure. Still there are many women who are engulfed in this mystique and believe that an act, though self-effacive is free. The belief and the acts to which it leads might not be defensible but they do suggest one particular image of being free. And this image can hardly be understood by investigators who have a different cultural background. To an alien investigator therefore who construes freedom as self-assertiveness and self-fulfilment, such a free act of self-effacement would either seem to be incomprehensible or seem to be one which was *forced*.

If the two subjectivities of the agent and the investigator are thus seen to lead to two contradictory characterizations of the same act as "free" and "forced", we seem to face a dilemma. The investigator must either give up all effort to understand and judge the action, acknowledging that the standard of judgment which can be used in this context must be internal to the agent's own culture. The internal standard in that case turns out to be crypto-absolutist which forbids the use of any other external standard. Or, the investigators may continue their efforts and ultimately import their own standards and concepts applying them to a context which is inappropriate and resistant.

The gap however is not so wide as it is imagined to be. The thesis of incommensurability which makes it look so wide is indefensible. Besides, the self-other relationship, when reviewed and reconstrued, is seen to be one of assimilation, absorption and mutual enrichment as Shusterman urges, or of "linking" as Schues contends. The alien investigator need not coerce the feminine subject, the Hindu "sati" into accepting the interpretation, which describes her action as "forced". By "linking" with each other the alien may realize that whatever she did was "free", free in the sense of exercising an option. The agent in her turn may be persuaded *as agent* to absorb freely a new image of freedom which is expressed in self-assertiveness and self-fulfilment. Out of the contrasting images of freedom one particular image may get entrenched on which others converge as a result of cultural interaction, transvaluation and synthesis. Which among these will be entrenched and may reflect a commonly accepted converging viewpoint is a matter that depends largely on experiences of common human concern—of features of humanness which constitute "feelings of recognition and affiliation that link every human being to every other human being" as Aristotle observed (in *Nicomachean Ethics*).

These features of humanness which lie beneath all local traditions and practices can provide the basis of trans-cultural norms, by reference to which we may criticize different local conceptions, not only of women's free acts but of other matters as well. Radical relativists however, refuse to recognize such trans-cultural norms and their relevance for transvaluation of different local conceptions. Traditional ideas, local conceptions of different cultures, they contend, are all immune to criticism on the basis of these norms which are supposed to be justified by reasons of universal validity. Krishna Mallick contests this extreme relativistic contention. She unravels the morally pernicious consequences of the relativist's immunizing strategy in a specific context of gender discrimination, a specific socio-economic, cultural, religious context where accepted practice and local traditional conceptions are utilized for reinforcing the bias against women. She shows how oppression is institutionalized by reference to practice, and how practice is protected from criticism even when it collides with the basic human concern about the worth of life.

The practice Mallick refers to and writes about is the strong preference for male children some countries have, particularly India, on socio-economic, religious and cultural grounds. She reports how this preference has led to the apalling rise in the figure of abortion of female foetuses detected through amniocentesis. Sex determination test through amniocentesis has become an instrument of discrimination against the female foetus for women themselves are culturally conditioned to consider females as burdens to the family, who drain its wealth in the form of dowry, and who do not stay with their parents to take charge of them. Mallick questions whether the sex determination test can relieve Indian society of such burdens, and thereby make a difference to the quality of social life. The answer is no, and she suggests other morally preferable ways of improving the human condition by introducing changes and reforms that would no more allow these oppressed beings to remain as burdens. She points out that far from slowing down overpopulation, as some argue, misuse of amniocentesis for preselection of sex, would aggravate the already existing adverse sex-ratio. Besides, there is no reason to target one gender for trying to solve the problem of overpopulation. Against yet another argument that women themselves are availing of amniocentesis of their own volition and that the test should therefore not be banned, Mallick says that this is not a free choice. The so-called choice results from powerlessness of women who are conditioned to accept that unless they are able to produce male babies they have no social worth.

However, even if the specificity of the social, economic and cultural situation in which the choice is made cannot be ignored, larger questions of common human concern are bound to arise at this juncture. Contrasting images of what choice should be like, pro-life or pro-choice, would emerge. Which among these two contrasting images will get entrenched, and on which of these the other viewpoint may converge, will perhaps be decided by some shared human concern. Such a shared concern is a feature of humanness which is there underlying diverse practices whether or not it is recognized in these practices. So in whatever way the woman acts, she has a responsibility to respect the right to life of the foetus and a responsibility towards her action. Even if late abortion of female foetuses is an accepted practice in India, and even if it is important to understand differences in the accepted practices of different cultures, the practices can and should be appropriately criticized, not immunized. They should be criticized in the light of some trans-cultural norm, in this case respect for life. And this is a feature of humanness, in discerning which one may recall what Aristotle said: in one's travels to distant countries one may observe feelings of recognition and affiliation that link every human being to every other human being.

ITIHASA, HISTORY AND HISTORIOGRAPHY
OF CIVILIZATION

D.P. Chattopadhyaya

Not infrequently we witness a sense of bewilderment among the writers on the human past when they are told that many peoples lack in historical consciousness. To look closely into this issue is culturally very instructive, almost revealing. Ordinarily, modern historians understand by *history* reconstruction of human ideas and activities based on reliable record. This enterprise aims at discovering deeper meanings of the different forms of human life. It is rarely realized that this view of history is neither old nor universal. Before the late eighteenth and early nineteenth centuries, historiography did not figure at the centre of any civilization. For an interpretation or understanding of a form of life as a whole, people used to turn their attention to religion, philosophy, literature and other forms of imagination like myth.

> [H]istorians aim at reconstructing an accurate record of human activities and at achieving a more profound understanding of them ... [It] is quite recent. ... It springs from an outlook that is very new in human experience: the assumption that the study of history is a natural, inevitable kind of human activity. Before the late 18th century, historiography (writing of history) did not stand at the centre of any civilization.[1]

If to reconstruct the meaning of *individual* human activities proves difficult, to undertake this task in the larger field of this or that human civilization as a whole is bound to prove additionally difficult. It is true that the ideas and activities of individuals cannot be understood without referring to their societal background or forms of life. Also it has to be admitted from the other end that the life of a civilization, its rise and fall, cannot be interestingly depicted without making any direct or indirect, specific or generic, reference to the lives of individual human beings who are the architects and carriers of that civilization.

---

[1] Edmund B. Fryde, *Encyclopaedia Britannica, Macropaedia* (Chicago: William Benton, Helen Hemingway Benton, 1974), Vol. 8, p. 945. See also, *Vasistha Dharmasutra*, i, 24, 25, *etc.*

Neither methodological individualism, *i.e.*, historical events are to be understood in terms of concerned individuals, their ideas and actions, nor methodological collectivism, *i.e.*, historical events are best understandable in terms of collectivities like class, culture, race, religion and nation, seems to be plausible as a *reductionist* programme. The composite approach is often found to be more promising and fruitful. The exactly advisable approach depends much upon the nature, scope and level of the issue to be dealt with. When one proposes to reconstruct the history of a civilization, one's approach cannot be comparable to what another historian engaged, for example, in tracing the history of a family, royal or lay, is required to do. The reason is not far to seek. The life of a civilization, embodying the achievements of a people or group of peoples, is much more complex than that of an individual being or family. The heterogeneity of peoples and ideas that is held together in a civilization is marked by diverse customs, styles and values. The diversity of a civilization is manifest in its forms of knowledge, belief, art, moral, law, rites and rituals.

In our understandable eagerness to highlight the heterogeneity and complexity of a civilization, its broad unity, marked by the recognized do's and dont's, should not be forgotten. This unity pervades the whole of a society, from the centre to the periphery. The complexity that defines a civilization, especially its cultural traits, are not uniformly or evenly distributed over the entire society. The complexity that marks the operations of a stock exchange, the administration of a lunatic asylum, and the management of a bachelors' home cannot be identical.

Property and technology impart increasing complexity to a civilization. Another important factor responsible for the growing complexity of a civilization is the introduction of writing. Electronics and telecommunications add new dimensions to the process. Property, technology, writing, *etc.* not only enable different groups of people to assume added roles than the others but also to try to devise institutional means to preserve and increase the same. In the process, the traditional roles of the elite and the laity undergo dissimilar, discriminative and often disorderly change and the changing roles also change the values, norms and goals of different groups of people in different spheres and stages of life. All this contribute to the increasing complexity of a civilization. Historiographical method to deal with the complex phenomena and simple or not-so-complex phenomena cannot be obviously identical.

Historiography, writing of history, and historians are intimately related. Historians, like any other groups of humans beings, belong to a social milieu, and as such their self-image is, to a great extent, influenced by how others in a group identify themselves. Since everybody is born in a family, his self-identity, cannot be completely dissociated from his own familial identity. It is true that every person from the same family does not belong to his/her family in an identical manner. Some people are deeply devoted to their family, the weals and woes of the family members, and religiously follow the family tradition, its ethos, customs, rites and rituals. This is obviously not true of all family members. The persons who are strongly individualist in their disposition have their own distinct ways of viewing themselves and their relations with the family, its past and future. All of us are not equally orthodox or heterodox. These peculiarities of human personality are bound to be there in the nature of genealogists, chroniclers or historians. Besides, what is very important to note, their aims are not identical. Therefore the social milieu as such cannot satisfactorily explain how different members of the same groups would recall their own past, individual, familial or collective.

The Vedic literature provides us long lists of the teachers in the context of describing the ceremonies of different sacrificial rituals. In the *Brahmanas* we come across systematic reference and exposition of the oldest genealogies (*vamsas*). The names of the teachers and their pupils not less then 60 in number are named in the *vamsa Brahmanas* of the Samaveda. Many of these genealogies contain the names of deities like Agni, Vayu, Indra, and of course *Brahmanas*. Many of these names are father-related or patronymic and, interestingly enough, some are mother-related or matronymic. Reference to the family genealogies is mainly intended to lend authenticity to what is said or injuncted in the concerned context.

But it becomes clear by the time of the rise of Buddhism and Jainism that reference to the authority of the *vamsas* has started losing its importance. To neither of these two heterodox religious groups *vamsas* establish their chronological character or binding nature. Even the reference to the names of the gods could not persuade them to accept the authority of the *vamsas* for performing different rituals. The authority of the *vamsa* literature is questioned by the sceptic not only because of the non-chronological character of different *vamsas* mentioned in it but also because of the duplication of the names in different genealogies. The Buddhist and the Jaina critics were additionally suspicious of the authority claim of the *vamsas* on the ground of their proclaimed divine origin.

Beside *vamsa*, the other concepts which one finds in the Vedic literature for tracing the ancestry of different persons and their groups are *gotra* and *pravara*. The term gotra is found both in the *Rgveda* and *Atharvaveda* and also in the *Chandogya Upanisad*. Among its different forms are "family", "clan", or "lineage". The people of the same *gotra* are deemed to be related by blood. In the *Grhyasutras* and elsewhere emphasis is laid on the prohibition of marriage within a *gotra*. Avoidance of marital relation between cognatic and agnatic groups by several degrees, varying from three to six, is *gotra*-based and often claimed to be biologically advisable. But this rule of prohibition of marriage within the *gotra* was not universally insisted upon. Neither *gotra* nor caste appears to be a universal determinant of marriage relation.[2]

Pravara stands for the "summons" addressed to Agni at the time of sacrifice. Since Agni used to be invoked by the names of the ancestors of the priest or Purohita, the word "pravara" means the series of invoked ancestors. Marriage, as stated before, was forbidden not only within the same *gotra* but also within the same *pravara*. The divisions between different groups of people on the basis of *gotra* and *pravara* appear to be separated by long interval. But these principles of classification or grouping were intended to regulate inheritance, succession and title for performance of different rituals. Identification of people in terms of *vamsa, gotra* and *pravara*, though uneven in importance, served some specific social purposes and had a substratum of history underneath.

Compared to *gotra* and *pravara*, historiographically speaking, more significant in the Vedic context are *gathas* (epic song verses) and *narasamsis* (songs in praise of heroes). Songs of victory, praise of valour, gift and benevolence, lengthy and repeated reference to sacrifices, *etc.* essentially literary in character and composition, are deemed to be sacred and recommended to be recited down the generations. *Gathas* refer not only to kings—Janamejaya, Kraivya and Bharata, for example—but also to gods like Indra. These are recited not only in the larger contexts like *Asvamedha* (horse sacrifice) but also in the

---

[2] Gautama Dharmasutra, iv, 16; Baudhayana Dharmasutra, 16, 2-5; and Vasistha Dharmasutra, i, 24, 25, *etc.*

limited domestic contexts. Musicians (*vinaganins*) and lute-players (*vinagathins*) used to compose and sing songs in praise of the sacrifices performed by kings, nobles, household people and their ancestors and, in some cases, for future generations. The authors of the *gathas*, unlike the revealed authorship of the Vedic hymns, seem to be human. The *gatha* and *narasamsi* literature implies the existence of a class of minstrels and its social relevance to the people of the Vedic times. In spite of the courtly exaggerations of the writings of these bards and musicians, they kept people aware of their past and paved the way to the rise of the historical *kavya* and epic poetry.

For the purpose of understanding the mind and activities of the Vedic people the importance of *Itihasa* and *Purana* is to be rated very high,—immediately after *Rgveda*, *Samaveda*, *Yajurveda* and *Atharvaveda* but well above *gathas* and *narasamsis*. *Itihasa*, legends of gods and heroes, and *puranas*, legends of origins, are elevated to the level of the *Vedas*. In all sorts of rituals,—royal, feudal, ordinary household, auspicious and inauspicious, their recitation was very common, almost obligatory. Besides ritual, their other imports were didactic, explanatory and injunctive. The legend of the Flood is found in the *Itihasa*. In the *Puranas* we come across various creation-legends and the legend or origin of the four castes (*varnas*) out of the body of Prajapati. Wars between gods and Asuras are also often referred to. In the absence of specific reference to the places of war and identity of the warring groups definitive historical reconstruction (as we understand it to-day) proves very difficult, almost impossible, and much is left to imagination.

It must be remembered here that the derogatory sense that is now attached to such terms as "imaginary", "mythical", and "legendary" was not there in the minds of the pre-Vedic, Vedic and Puranic peoples of India. The fact that the cast of the ancient mind was different from that of the modern mind is no *argument* to maintain that the former was "pre-logical" and the latter is "logical". Even this so-called rational periodization (ancient/medieval/modern) of history appears to be arbitrary. Synchronically speaking, equally arbitrary seems to be the classification of *different* human minds into such categories as "tribal", "national" and "international". In using the scale of time and place for normative or evaluative purposes in the human context one has to be very circumspect.

It is not surprising that many modern historiographers are critical of such "serious defects" as "mixture of mythology and folklore", "acceptance of the operation of supernatural forces on human affairs", indifference to "topography" and "complete neglect of chronology".[3] But why this surprise? Are "we" justified in criticizing "them" simply because of the different ways of recollecting and representing their past? If we critically reflect on the related issues, then we can *understand*—and *understanding* is the key concept in this very complex context—that our surprise is rooted in our uncritical ethnocentrism and the resulting lack of understanding of *their* points of view, the concepts used by them for self-identification, self-recollection, and self-representation. "We" and "they" can well meet and understand each other; but at no stage of our meeting (of minds) and understanding (of the concerned points of view) our cultural gap can be completely eliminated. Our freedom and individuality, though variable, are ineliminable. Even in our own age of so-called scientific historiography all historians are not unanimous in their appreciation or/and criticism of the history of the people of India. Not only the European historians differ between themselves in their understanding of the past of India but also the Indian historians do so. If the difference between H. Oldenberg, G. Buhler, F.E. Pargiter, M. Elphinstone, James Mill, G.F. Ilynin and A.L. Basham on India is notable, the same between R.G. Bhandarkar, H.C. Raychaudhuri, Radha Kumud Mookerjee, R.C. Majumdar, K.A. Nilakanta Sastri, B.N. Dutt and D.D. Kosambi is no less notable. The presuppositions, values and religious commitments, the composition and complexity of the social milieu, and political inclination of the historians and various other "non-academic" factors silently or explicitly influence their consciousness, views, judgment and finally what they write and/or orally communicate.

The development of the Buddhist historiography in India and neighbouring countries illustrates the point clearly. If most of the people of a culture, including the learned ones, believe, for example, in miracles, doctrines of *karma*, rebirth and incarnation, in the writings or words of their historians, we find their history in a form which fails to be regarded as history in the modern sense. On the ancestry, life, teachings, *nirvana* and the after-effects,—doctrinal, institutional and religious, of the Buddha, his disciples and interpreters, old and new, widely differ. The times and lives of the peoples of the Buddhist era, early and later, as found in the Pali *Tripitaka*, com-

---

[3] U.N. Ghoshal, *Studies In Indian History And Culture* (Calcutta: Orient Longmans, 1957).

mentaries and chronicles, Sanskrit *Mahavastu* and *Lalitavistara*, the tradition due to the *Dipavamsa* and the *Mahavamsa*, *Ambattha-Sutta*,
Mahapadana-Sutta and *Sonadanda-Sutta* of *Digha Nikaya*, and some *Suttas*
of *Majjhima Nikaya* are not coherent or do not agree in details. Even
about the *nirvana* of the Buddha and its significance legends, traditions and authorities are not in agreement. At times one gets the
impression that he was essentially a saintly human being; at times he
appears as a unique superman; also he has been portrayed as a Cosmic
Being, *Dharma Kaya*, an incarnation of Supreme Reality or *avatara*.

Buddhacarita and other works of Asvaghosa (second century AD)
have contributed much to our understanding of the Buddha and
Mahayana Buddhism in different ways,—literary, philosophical, biographical and historical. The life-stories of the Buddha and the accounts of his teachings available in the Pali canon had deeply
influenced the source-books of the Pali commentaries and chronicles,
and later on gave rise to quasi-canonical works in Sanskrit language.

The history of Buddhist art and literature owes much of its substance to the different versions of his Buddha's life and teachings. It
is not at all without point to say, as it has been said, that the Buddha borrowed and assimilated many Vedic insights and interpreted
the same in his own creative way, and that the *Vedanta-Sutras* of
Gaudapada and *Vedanta-Bhasya* of Sankara are doctrinally, not ritually,
indebted heavily to the Buddha. The history of different orthodox or
pro-Vedic systems of philosophy cannot be coherently reconstructed
without reference to the ideas of the Buddha. Both directly and indirectly Buddhism has contributed to the emergence of the Indian
ways of writing history.

It is understandable that the relatively modern writers on history
in their attempts to reconstruct the past of a country or a part thereof
lay emphasis on temporal linearity or chronological time. At the same
time it has to be noted that many of them, especially those who are
philosophically inclined or theory-oriented, are well aware of the limits
of the search for linearity or chronology. Both in perceptual time
and cultural time "gaps" have to be tolerated. At times not only the
historians but also the chroniclers unconsciously or even consciously
skip over some events, segments of time and details thereof. Every
form of representation—legend, story, fable, chronicle, history and
picture—involves elements of selection, elimination and organization.
What precisely has to be done, how and to what extent with respect
to reconstruction and/or deconstruction of history is case-specific,

depends mainly on the aim of the concerned writer or the artist. For example, to write history or to deal with historical time is different from dealing with and writing on cosmological time, cultural time, biographical time, this or that calendrical time. Each of these forms of activity is creative in a way and has its peculiarities. More specifically speaking, different writers on the "history" (history in the modern sense was yet to emerge as *a* discipline) of the peoples of (what we now call) South Asia had their different approaches, individually and collectively. Pre-Vedic, Vedic, Puranic, Buddhist and Jaina ways of recollecting and representing "the past of India" are not identical. Yet the discerning scholars could identify the areas of overlap between different approaches and findings, enabling them to narrate *a* coherent, but not unchanging, historical account of the bygone days, peoples, their ideas and actions.

Some of the five characteristics, *pancalaksana*, of the Puranas like *sarga*, original creation, and *pratisarga*, dissolution and re-creation, may not be of much significance to the historiographers of to-day but *vamsa*, genealogies, and *vamsanucarita*, biographies referred to in the genealogies, continue to be of importance to them for recapturing the past. In this connection the student of Indian historiography is reminded of the works like Bana's *Harsacarita*, the chronicle of King Harsa of Thaneshar (c. 606–648 AD), and, particularly, Kalhana's *Rajatarangini*, the royal and dynastic chronicles of Kashmir written around 1148–50 AD. While Bana focuses his attention on the life of one ruler, Kalhana traces the life-stories of a long line of rulers. But it must be said to the credit of both that in the process of narrating a ruler's life they provide us glimpses of the ways of life of the ruled, forms of administration, diplomacy, *etc*. While writing about the life of Harsa it is interesting to note that he, following the Puranic style, not only refers to the genealogy of the King of Thaneshar but also to his own. To trace simultaneously *self*-ancestry and *other*-ancestry has a deep significance. It brings out the hidden point ordinarily forgotten, viz., *how* other(s) would be depicted in a "historical" narrative depends very much upon the mental make-up, the web of beliefs, of the narrator himself, *who* he is. If the chronicler believes in the operation of supernatural forces upon the human affairs, in the efficacy of dreams, and attributes deep significance to omens and portents, his chronicle is bound to be different from that of another whose cast of mind is "naturalist".

In the western tradition, the ancient historians like Herodotus and

Thucydides (fifth century BC) of the Hellenic world, Livy (first century BC), Tacitus (second century AD) and Polybius (c. 200–118 BC) wrote on history but, during the time, as in India, the distinction between myth, legend, antiquities, literature and history as recognized to-day was not clearly demarcated. Herodotus, referred to by Cicero as the "father of history", was basically a traditionalist. To him history was an "inquiry" and not narration. Like others of his time in the Asia Minor, he was also interested in genealogies. During his visit to Egypt he was told of the descent of their high priests through 345 genera-tions. Both in Babylonia and Egypt genealogies of kings used to be kept in temples. Also there were inscribed the glory of the gods. Some of the Hellenic and Roman historians tried, not always suc-cessfully, to draw a distinction between history and biography. To them history was intended to give true story, while the aim of the biographer was to praise and to edify.[4]

Some ancient scholars like Varro (116–27) tell us that histories, being concerned as they were with chronological accounts of wars and political events, proved narrow in their aim and have to be distinguished from study of the antiquities which relied upon a variety of evidence and was concerned with a broader spectrum of happen-ings. This view echoes Aristotle's dismissive attitude towards history as a branch of literature dealing only with the *particular*, neglecting the things and beings of *general* character.

The rules of rhetoric are found to have considerable influence on the historical writings of the Romans like Cicero and Livy. True to the tradition of the time, they followed the style of oratory. It is interesting to note that the historians of the ancient time were in-variably found to be supportive of their own country, its culture and tradition, which included fictitious and supernatural things.

A similar attitude is evident in the Christian historiography. The Christian writers on history defended their religion against their crit-ics. For example, Eusebius (4th century) tells us how through a long series of acts of Divine providence a Christian Empire was estab-lished by Constantine. St. Augustine and his disciples wrote on the causes of degradation of all the non-Christian societies. Another point to be noted is that many of the ancient and medieval works on history

---

[4] A.J. Toynbee, *Greek Historical Thought from Homer to the Age of Heraclitus* (London: 1924).
[5] Herbert Butterfield, *Christianity and History* (London: 1949).

were concerned with contemporary events and written by the people who themselves participated in those events. This partly explains the subjective character of their writings.

But while we say all these things we should be careful *not* to be critical about their ways. We must try to understand their times and minds. For the writers of history, like other human beings, are products of their own times. This is not to deny that through scrutiny of the evidences used by them and their points of emphasis we can find in their writings a critical element of judgement. In other words, cultural determination of historiography is not inconsistent with the historian's freedom to judge.

It seems that the Western historiography in the medieval age, from the 5th to the 11th century, considerably declined. Most of the writers were learned monks. The learning of the time was quite different from what is meant by it now. The elements of folklore and miracle got mixed up with the lives of the saints or human personalities. Bede's *Ecclesiastical History of the English People (597–731 AD)* are full of supernatural happenings, miracles and visions. The sources used by him were meagre and dubious. Another work which deserves mention in this connection is *Life of Charlemagne* written by Einhard, a courtier of the Carolingian King himself. He is full of praise of the deeds of his King.

To glorify kings, Christian God and saints was the chief aim of the historians of the 12th, 13th and 14th century. This predominant orientation is illustrated by such works as *History of the Kings of Britain* written by Geoffrey of Monmouth, *Chronica* written by Otto, and *Mirror of History* written by Vincent of Beauvais. Otto was a Bishop and descendant of the Holy Roman Emperor Henry IV, and Vincent wrote his book under the patronage of King Louis IX. The royal and the theological associations of the writers are clear from the contents of their histories. Whether one accepts these writings or not, the annals and chronicles of the medieval age help us much to understand the minds and activities of the people of the time, especially those of the leading political and religious personalities.

Criticism of the medieval historiography came mainly from the humanist historians of the 15th century of the early Renaissance period, who started working under the influences of the Byzantine scholars who moved from the East to the West of the crumbling Roman Empire. The works of humanists like Petrarch (fourteenth century), Valla (fifteenth century) and Erasmas (sixteenth century) introduced a new orientation in historical writings. Use of philology and the methods of textual criticism started exerting a sober and disciplining influence on the medieval historiography. With the waning of the spirit of the Middle Age not only the attitude of the general public but also that of the historians as writers started changing in a big way. This is not to suggest that everything medieval was dark or whatever started emerging during the period of Renaissance was right or good. From the historical point of view the main question is to understand the changing mind of the peoples and their attitude to the various objectives, *purusarthas* of life, religious and secular, divine and mundane.

The new astronomical paradigm, the sun-centric hypothesis of the planetary system proposed by Copernicus, a bishop by profession, proved very influential in changing human minds in relation to life and the world. Although the helio-centric hypothesis did not prove immediately acceptable to the Church or even to the then scientific world of learning, it raised a number of fundamental questions with clear bearing on science and society. The helio-centric hypothesis of the Polish theologian challenged (at least in principle) the prevailing Ptolemic paradigm of astronomy. Its fall-out proved widespread and far-reaching. At least some learned persons like Galileo and Bruno started feeling the necessity of rewriting not only the history of science but also that of man.

One of the significant characteristics of the humanist historiography in Europe was to focus the writer's attention on the local pride of a people and their past achievements. A number of histories along the line was written in Spain, Poland and Germany. The opposition between the Catholic historiography and the Protestant historiography is another notable feature of the time. Both in the areas of clerical history and legal history some significant contributions were made during the 16th and the 17th centuries. The voluminous works of such scholars as Le Nain de Tillemont, Pierre Pithou and Andre Duchesne proved a very valuable storehouse for future historians like Edward Gibbon. Gibbon's *The History of the Decline and Fall of the Roman Empire* could not be written without the source materials left behind by the pioneers.

It is well known that, following the works of Copernicus, Kepler and Galileo, significant progress was made in mathematics, astronomy and physics. Some of the prominent scientists of the time like Descartes were definitely hostile to history and dismissed its claim as a branch of genuine knowledge. Leibniz, who was both a historian and a mathematician, in his attempt to make history scientific reduced it to a sort of necessity-bound providential story. Though some historians like Mabillon and jurists like Hugo Grotius tried to give a secular look to their works on history, it took a long time before this discipline could acquire the distinction of being truly "scientific". The French Encyclopaedists taking the wrong lesson from science, were by and large distrustful towards the past human achievements. Though the pro-scientific and anti-religious stance towards the past was tolerated in France, it was strongly rejected in countries like Italy. Several anti-clerical writers on history were punished by the Church and their works were banned. But the "radical" thinkers like Condorcet disregarded the frown of Church and other authorities and devoted themselves to write what may be called histories of civilization based on the thesis of the endless progress of the human mind. Gibbon's monumental *History of the Decline and Fall of the Roman Empire* (1776–88) may be regarded as the most ambitious and successful example of rational and progressive historiography. The scientific revolution of the 17th century, one may say, gave rise to the rational historiography of the 18th century. Still more free and secular historiography of the 19th century was largely due to Darwin's evolutionary theory (1859). When we use such words as "rational", "scientific", "secular" and "progressive" it would be wrong to think that we are favouring a particular ideological approach to history. If we are *committed* to *one* particular ideology, we are bound to be *critical* of the histories written from the *other* ideological standpoints. This intellectual arrogance is often referred to as "scientism" or "abuse of reason". The historian, like everybody else, has the right to have his/her preferred ideology and methodology. Without a definite standpoint *criticism* is impossible. *Genuine* criticism, as distinguished from *sham* criticism, must have its two faces, *internal* and *external*. If we are uncritically committed to one (and only one) particular ideology and doggedly refuse to see the merits of all other ideologies, we are condemned to end up only with *external criticism*. Genuine criticism means both (i) *self's right* to criticize the other and (ii) the *other's right* to criticize the self. Even a so-called "a-historical" and "enclosed" tribal society is informed of the art of internal criticism or self-criticism. In brief, nobody,—nothing—is above criticism. Criticizability is the essence of free and rational creativity of "what is objective" and also of "what is subjective".

It is undeniable that the Indian historiography of today has been largely, almost decisively, influenced by the European historiography as available to and interpreted and followed by the English-knowing intelligentsia. But I think that in order to understand the historians of our time and their writings we have to relate them both to our own past and the changing features of the Western historiography. When I speak of our past I mean not only the past of literati but also, perhaps more so, of the laity. That is by oral tradition, folklore, legends, *etc.*, so-called pre-rational sources deserve much of our attention. It is well known that the Western historians or Indologists have stated repeatedly that, compared to the Hindus, the Muslims had been more history-conscious and disposed to document and keep chronicles of their times, of the events and actions of their polity and society. The said superiority of the Muslim chronicles is often attributed to the fact that they were written mainly by men of affairs, contemporary courtiers and not by theologians. At the same time it must be remembered that a significant part of the history of India written by Muslim historians bears the stamp of Sufism.

The Indian historiography has been often classified under three heads, Hindu, Muslim and British. Like several other ways of classifying or periodising history, this is also unsatisfactory, even misleading at times. For centuries together the Hindu and the Muslim chroniclers had been chronicling the events which fall under the same calendrical periods, assuming that we are following one particular calendar. But it is interesting to note here that several calendars were in use among the peoples of India. Coming close to the British period it may be pointed out that different sets of people,—British, Muslim and Hindu were at work from different points of view on "the same" Indian history. But was the "text" itself on which they were working identical? Hardly. This is not surprising. In spite of its attending difficulty, the classification of Indian historiography under the heads of Hindu, Muslim and British has its relevance and use. Broad—only very broad—similarity is evident in these approaches. Within each approach there is difference. Between the approaches there is overlap. For example, Muslim historiography itself may be viewed under two broad heads, pre-Mughal and Mughal. Ways of living and thinking of the peoples who came from West Asia were more or less different from those who came from Central Asia. Admittedly, their religion, Islam, proved a strong common bond between them.

The chroniclers and the annalists who came to India with the Muslim conquerors and were yet to settle down and identify themselves culturally with the Indian milieu, understandably, had a spectator's approach to the land and people they were writing on. Their "homeland", its people, their past, their religion, customs, manners, *etc.* had been working on their mind. Domiciled in India and close to the ruling families, their mental backdrop, in most cases, was West Asian. Their writings reflect the region, together with its culture, wherefrom they or their immediate ancestors had come.

Secondly, there was a distinct didactic undertone in their writings. Eulogy of the ruler was a common feature of the historiography of the time. In many of these writings of the period from the late 12th century to the 15th century one finds certain characteristics in common, viz., reverential reference to the Prophets, Umayyid and Abbasid Khaliphs, genealogies of the ruling families, principles for pious rulers to follow, chronology of military events, cosmological, geographical and ethnological data. These characteristics lend a sort of unity to their historical writings. The modern critic may ask: "was the stuff they wrote, strictly speaking, *historical*?" Whether our answer would be YES or NO depends largely upon our own standpoint.

In this connection reference may be made to the works of Fakhr-i-Mudabbir Mubarak Shah who came to Lahore with the Ghoris in 1186 and was in the court of Qutb al-din Aibak in 1206. In his work *Shajara-i-ansab-i-Mubarak Shahi*, the author tells us in details the reasons for the eminence and dominance of the Turks on the Muslim world. Referring to the Quran and *Hadith* he counts the virtues which rulers and their learned advisers should acquire and follow. Also he records the Ghori conquest of Hindustan (1192–1206) and the life and deeds of Qutb al-din Aibak. The other works which deserve special mention are *Tabaqat-i-Nasiri* (1259–60) authored by Minhaj al-Siraj Juzjani, *The Ta'rikh-i-Mubarak Shahi* written by Yahya ibn Ahmad Sarhindi (1428–1434), and the *Ta'rikh-i-Muhammadi* by Muhammad Bihamad Khani (1438–1439).

In all these works much attention has been paid to biographical details of the rulers and reference has been made to the ancient and the medieval histories of such different areas of West Asia as Iraq and Persia. History has been treated as a succession of events. Miracles, dreams and visions are liberally used. In most of these works the absence of the spirit of the *Hadith* criticism is notable.

As mentioned earlier, many of the Muslim writers took history as a branch of ethics. To think, as some European writers do, that these features of the writings of the Muslim historians show the "decline in the critical standards of Muslim Historiography" is again misplaced.[6] By bringing history close to religion, ethics and literature the writers of the time were simply following a tradition which was then an accepted practice among the learned people.

We often tend to forget that in future techno-economic or nationalist orientation that is evident in many of our contemporary historical works may be strongly criticized as very one-sided. Even today among the historians there is no unanimity of view regarding the most advisable methodology or guiding principles of history. Even today we find religious underpinnings in the writings of very distinguished historians. One may pertinently raise the question, "why should we think that religious approach to history is outdated, idle or wrong?" Equally pertinent is the question, "must history be scientific in order to be recognized as a respectable branch of knowledge?" One may rightly point out that respectability and acceptability of a discipline is age-bound or/and group-specific.

This does not mean relativism in the bad sense. *Per contra,* this self-critical spirit encourages the enterprise of understanding across the boundaries of historical time and cultural space. For example, it is difficult to deny that the pre-Mughal Muslim historiography of India was deeply influenced by the culture,—political, religious and literary, of such countries as Persia and Iraq. But this is not an altogether new development. Even of the Vedic period the ideas on historiography that we have in relation to the northern India are not certainly of purely local origin. Cultural migration had always an understandable impact on the ways of life of the people and through them on the course of history and historiography. Some people may not be religious in the God-based sense of the term but it is difficult to deny the presence of ethical impulses in normative enterprises of human beings. From the myths and the epics to the treatises on statecraft and administration of every civilization we find endless reference to the importance of religion and ethics. It is often emphasized that in order to be able to follow the maxims of do's and dont's in practice humans are required to attain a degree of inner or spiritual excellence which cannot be always explained in terms of

---

[6] P. Hardy, "Some studies in Pre-Mughal Muslim Historiography" in C.H. Philips, *Historians of India, Pakistan and Ceylon* (London: Oxford University Press, 1961).

discursive reason. An element of mysticism is found in almost all
forms of religious or ethical culture. The doctrines and practices of
the *sufis* have provided rich source materials for writing on Muslim
history in India and various other countries. From the life-stories of
the *sufi* saints in which facts and fictions, miracles and saintliness get
blended it is not easy to extract historical materials. But it is and has
been possible. Even now, at this age of science, many people, both
lay and educated, believe in miracles and attribute supernatural powers
to the *gurus* and charismatic persons who lived in the recent past or
are still living. Simply because I, left to myself, do not believe in
miracles and supernatural powers I, as a historian, cannot refuse to
recognize and lightly dismiss *others'* beliefs.

The biographies of the *sufi* saints in the Indian setting has a unique
historical significance. From the thirteenth century to the fifteenth
century when the Muslim rule in northern India, though established,
was not very strong and many of the conquering people started
accepting this land as an adopted home rather than a conquered
colony, the need to neutralize the forces of the separative factors and
to bring the Indians and Muslims close to each other were being
increasingly felt. What could not be achieved by the traditional forms
of a proselytizing religion and those of a non-proselytizing one, was
being peacefully and constructively attended to by the *sufis*. In the
common mystical quest of the spirit, the Indians and the Muslims, at
least a sizable sections of both, started culturally gravitating to one
another.

While some *sufis* wrote down their views, several others followed
and favoured oral traditions of their teachers. Besides Shaikh Ali
Hajweri who had written the first important *sufi* book, *Kashful Mahjub*,
in India, the other two important *sufi* teachers of the Sultanate period who left lasting influence are Ibn-i-Arabi and Shaikh Shihab-
ud-din Suhrawardi. The Chisti Shaikhs did not believe in writing
down their principles; they used to teach by the ways of their living.
The written literature on the *sufi* principles was produced by the
Suhrawardis. Some of the books, like those authored by Shaikh Hamid
Nagori, because of their abstract and subtle characteristics could be
comprehended only by the learned people. However, the writings,
Maktubat or letters, of persons like Shaikh Sharaf-ud-din Yahya proved
very popular. The *Maktubat* of Mujaddid Alf Sani was devoted to
various subjects like science, technology, metaphysics, politics and
theology. Many of these *sufi* teachers and writers, notwithstanding

their spiritual and devotional pursuits, were in touch with the rulers, high officials and of course common people. Thus their influence proved very pervasive.

The teachings of the great *sufi* saint Shaikh Nizam-ud-din Auliya was faithfully recorded by the poet Amir Hasan Sijzi in his famous book *Fuwaid-ul-Fuad*. From religion and education to the social and economic conditions of the time and the affairs of the state have been dealt with in this work. Nizam-ud-din's reference to Indo-Muslim mystics, difference between the jurists (*Ulama*) and the mystics, and scepticism about miracles are among the notable traits of his teachings. But, following the custom of the time, he makes no reference to the Sultan Ala-uddin Khilji and his senior courtiers or officials. Amir Khwurd, a disciple of Nizam-ud-din Auliya, wrote a history of the Chisti order of the *sufis*. He lived during the reign of Sultan Muhammad bin Tughlak and, ordered by him, was forced to go to the southern Indian with many other mystics. On return to Delhi, after the fall of Tughlak's power in the Deccan, Khwurd started writing *Siyar-ul-Auliya*, giving the history of the Chisti saints from Hazrat Ali to Usman Haruni. Nizam-ud-din's life and teachings have been accorded a special place in the work (c. 1357 AD).

From the research on the lives and teachings of the *sufis* the modern historian gets very valuable information about the political and economic conditions of the Muslims in the medieval India and an insight into the Indian culture of the time.

I have pointed out earlier that European historians found nothing historical in the strict sense in the writings of the Hindus. If they refer to the works like those of Bana and Kalhana, it is because they are recognized as good chroniclers. Chroniclers are at best proto-historians and not historians. A somewhat similar attitude, not surprisingly, is evident from the writings of the European historians on the Muslim chronicles of the period AD 1206–1707. Henry Elliott, Elphinstone, James Mill and Macaulay had nothing very laudable to comment on the Muslim historiography of the Mughal period. By scanning the historical writings of the Portuguese, Dutch, French and Danish historians we find a more or less similar and deprecative assessment. Perhaps the only difference is that most of them are more appreciative of the works of the Muslim chroniclers than those of their Hindu counterparts. Perhaps a plausible way of understanding this difference in assessment is to be found in the hypothesis that the Muslim writers, compared to the Hindus, left more reliable records of their times, places and the rulers. But this hypothesis has to be taken very circumspectly and in a general way.

Henry Elliott tells us that Muslim chroniclers, primarily interested in thrones and imperial powers, had nothing very important to write on popular institutions, general administration, local judicature, commerce and agriculture. Though these observations are not quite correct, perhaps what we can gather as essence of the critical observations of the foreign writers is this: the Muslim historians did not write much about the life of the common people. Elphinston's *History of India* shows its highly critical attitude, if not contempt, towards the Islamic institutions and even the Prophet of Islam. He reminds one of James Mill's highly critical reference to the Hindu ideas, manners and achievements. If the Hindu and the Muslim chroniclers were more interested in chronicling the deeds of their rulers than the events of the period, the institutions of the people, it is mainly because they were the product of their own time, following the traditions prevalent at that time. In spite of the exaggeration that we find in the writings of the Indian chroniclers it would be one-sided to think, as many European historians did and do, that their works have been vitiated by the influences of despotism, bigotry and love of flattery.

The most serious difficulty that one encounters in understanding the history of India from the early thirteenth century to the early eighteenth century is posed by the non-availability of reliable official records and documents. Perhaps most of these evidences have been destroyed or lost. Besides, the remaining kinds of evidence,—numismatic, epigraphic and literary, which are available in the Arabic and Persian languages, cannot be easily grasped by the general public. The European historians are twice removed from the true spirit of the available evidence preserved in foreign languages, foreign to them. Rooted in their conceptual frameworks which in turn, are located in their own languages, their cultural distance from the objects of their study is formidable. Even those who had taken the pains to learn these foreign languages did not, in most cases, have the sympathy in them to understand the intended meanings or spirit of the available evidence. A similar misfortune had befallen also the Hindu historiography. Only by knowing Sanskrit, Pali or Prakrit they could not get into the heart of the ideas and actions of the people of the concerned periods. This linguistic-cum-conceptual road-block also largely prevented the European historians of the last few centuries to grasp the institutional and religious forms of life embedded in cultures alien to the cultures of the writers.

When I say all these I do not intend to give the impression that the European views of the Hindu and the Muslim historiography, because of their critical tone, are to be taken lightly or dismissed summarily. In a way my reservation about their unstudied judgments rests on their own professed aims of writing on the history and historians of India. James Mill, for example, in his well known *History of the British India* frankly tells us that what motivated him most to write this very comprehensive book was to help the British rulers to understand the people of India to be ruled and to apply the Benthamite version of utilitarianism in practice. In the process he had to reject the views of scholars like William Jones, Colebrooke and Prinsep that the Hindus, at least of the early periods, had reached a high degree of civilization, and he arrived at the conclusion that contemporary as well as ancient India was barbarous in science, religion, political economy, law and government.

Many of the Western historians say that Indians, both Muslims and particularly Hindus, were so preoccupied with eulogy, rhetoric and metaphysics that they had little or no interest in documenting particular details. Aristotle writes in his *Rhetoric* that history is useless because it is concerned only with particulars and has nothing to do with general truths. Cicero advises the historian to follow the style of oratory in his writing. Descartes is contemptuous of history because of its alleged disregard of scientific method, indulgence into sophistry and illusion. Even today the controversy over the question whether history is a science or art has not been settled. Within the maze of contrary views it is not easy to decide what should be the aim of a good historian, whether he is Indian, American or European. It seems to me that while the historians' prime concern are particular events and actions of *individual* human beings, they are obliged to use, explicitly or implicitly, *general* facts or truths in order to make their story meaningful and understandable.[7]

Those who have familiarity with such works as Abul Fazal's *Akbar Namah* or *Ain-i-Akbari*, Mulla Abdul Qudir's *Muntakhib-ut-Tawarikh* and Nizamuddin Bakhshi's *Tabaqat-i-Akbari*, can hardly deny their value in terms of factual details. It is true that in all these writings eulogy

---

[7] D.P. Chattopadhyaya, *Individuals and Societies: A Methodological Inquiry* (Calcutta: Scientific Book Agency, 1975).

of the Emperor is there in abundance. At the same time it is interesting to note the *critical* reference of some of these writers to Akbar's
appreciation of other faiths and the encouragement that the Emperor
had given to free thinking.

Of the period from Jehangir to Aurangzeb (1606–1707) we have
an impressive corpus of historical writings. Jehangir's Autobiography,
Tuzak-i-Jehangiri, is itself a very important piece of historical source
material. Partly written by himself and partly by Mutamad Khan
under his own supervision the Memoirs give us details about the
social, cultural and spiritual life of the period. Important works were
written also during the reign of Shajahan. One of these works which
deserves special mention is *Padshah Namah* of Abdul Hamid. Herein
also one gets concrete details of the political, social and cultural life
of the time. Akbar's religious catholicism or eclecticism is not to be
found in Shajahan's period of religious orthodoxy. Aurangzeb himself was not initially opposed to historical writings. Allowed by him,
Muhammad Kazim wrote *Alamgir Namah* and *Maathir-i-Alamgiri*. But
later on he held back permission to make the works public. This
anti-historical stance of the Emperor has been differently interpreted.
It seems that he did not like the events of his time and his own
deeds to be made officially public. Because, he thought, it might
create avoidable political controversy and diplomatic complications.

Understandably, there is no uniformity in the views of the Europeans who wrote on India, her people, institutions and culture. As I
said before, history in its modern sense was not there either in India
or in Europe in the Middle Ages. Rightly or wrongly, the eighteenth
century is generally taken to be the watershed between modern historiography, on the one hand, and chronicles, biographies and other
proto-historical sources, on the other. Again, one has to be careful
about the difference between the development of historiography and
its characteristics in one culture and those in another. The elements
of *Itihasa*, as we have noted earlier, are not identical with those of
history. Nor are the ways of handling or using these source materials
identical. Besides the individual personality of the historian and his
cultural background which enter into his writings, his preferred point
of view and aim also colour his project.

Coming closer to our own time, the so-called British period of
Indian history, we find some historians, primarily the European, are
writing *for* their own countrymen, their needs and taste. For example,
the French historians like Abbe Prevost, Abbe Guyon, Dernis, and

Castonnet des Fosses were writing with different or mixed motives, viz., to inform their countrymen of the peoples in India and their manners, of the French achievements and failures in this part of the world. While some of them were professional historians, the rest were compilers or chroniclers.

The British writers like William Jones, Charles Wilkins, Henry Colebrooke, John Shore, Charles Grant, James Mill, Hayman Wilson, Mountstuart Elphinstone, Munro, Malcolm and Macaulay do not present a homogeneous composition either. Some were basically administrators, some really scholars and what was common to both groups is a scholarly interest in the past of the country and its contemporary affairs. The difference between their approaches, orientations and conclusions, as indicated before, are very notable. While the writers like Mill made no secret of their *British* and *utilitarian* motivations, the scholars like Jones, Wilson and Colebrooke tried to understand the country and its people by learning their language and studying the original sources of Indian culture. Given the limited but understandable objectives of his laborious work, Mill could easily say that historians, in order to be successful in their work, are not required either to know the language of the concerned people or to have personal knowledge of the country in question. Mill became a recognized authority on Indian history without knowing anyone of the classical languages of the country and without ever visiting it despite being a senior executive of the East India Company.

That one's personal familiarity with a country does not necessarily help one to understand it better is illustrated by Macaulay's writings on India. Macaulay's home work for writing on India was apparently not as thorough as that of Mill. But his style was forceful and carrying. His bitter criticism of the Bengalis as coward and liar, feeble and effeminate, is understandably resented by the Bengalis or for that reason by other Indians. But a historian's work must not be assessed solely on the ground of his praise or criticism of a people. This sort of criticism has been levelled against the Indians by the Indians themselves, against the British people by their fellow countrymen.

The main ground on which Macaulay's writings on India have to be assessed is his ability or lack thereof to understand this country and its culture. Was he really interested in understanding the people of India? Was he really qualified for the job he had undertaken? In his self-defence Macaulay observed that, given the systematically anomalous character of the British empire and of the East India Company, it was just not possible either to rule the country rationally or to understand it correctly. It seems that Macaulay consciously accepted the irony of the situation. It is clear from his simultaneous defence of British imperialism, on the one hand, and "progressive" press laws, "just" legal system and "rational" educational system, on the other. Apparently Macaulay did not realize that within the constraints of the politico-economic system of the time it was not possible to give "good" education, "good" laws, "free" press and, at the same time, to preserve the imperial system dictated primarily by the interests of England. Macaulay's accepted standards of historical judgment were clearly anomalous and therefore the conclusions he arrived at about India are untenable.

Macaulay's love of his motherland, England, is perfectly understandable. Also understandable is one's almost unconscious commitment to the values of his time. To Macaulay liberty and progress were the most important values which any civilized country can think of and must try to achieve. But the interesting point to be noted in the writings of Macaulay is his uncritical commitment to the chauvinistic notions of "progress" and "liberty". "The history of England", he thinks, "is emphatically the history of progress". From Milton and the Mills he had his initiation into the English concept of liberty. And he had no doubt whatsoever that "England was 'the greatest and most highly civilized people' not only of the world of his day but of the world of all times".[8] The English notions of liberty and progress of his time and his own passionate love for the motherland set his standard of passing historical judgment on other civilizations like India and their attainments or failures. Referring to Mill's *History of British India* he observes that Mill was right in criticizing the defects and failures of the Indian people and praising them on the counts and scores on which they could rise "in a small degree above the common level of their contemporaries". Macaulay commends: "It is thus that the annals of past times ought to be written". Pieter Geyl clearly points out the difference between two very distinguished historians of the mid-nineteenth centuries, Ranke and Macaulay. While Macaulay was a prisoner of his "national or time-tied delusions", Ranke was trying to explain how, in spite of unavoidable relativism,

---

[8] Pieter Geyl, *Debates With Historians* (Glasgow: Fontana/Collins, 1962), p. 38.

the historian must try to comprehend or understand rather than to judge. He should be as objective as humanly possible. Geyl, in this context, quotes Ranke's words of 1854: "Every period is immediate to God, and its value does not in the least consist in what springs from it, but in its own existence, in its own self".

In effect this view of historiography accords to a certain extent with my own view on the subject. In a way we all, including the historians and the people about whom they write, are located in a particular period and culture and influenced by its tradition and prevalent ideas.[9] If this is true of Macaulay, this is also true in a way of Ranke as well. But Ranke, basically a conservative and, unlike Macaulay, was no believer in the *natural* law of progress. Extremely anxious to be faithful to facts he was always trying to be guided by the source materials. He was totally opposed to introduction of personal, national and political biases and prejudices in history. Since culture in every period of history has its unique or individual characteristics, the historian's "humble" task is to try to show what actually happened. In other words, history should be as factual as possible and least interpretative in its character. Whether Ranke's methodological prescription can be followed in practice is a matter of debate. But it is generally conceded that pro-objectivist approach to historiography is sure to minimize the miseffects of cultural chauvinism and relativism. Even the critic of Ranke who accuses him of fact-fetishism tends to agree that his multi-volume works on the *Latin and Teutonic Nations, Popes, Civil Works and Monarchy in France in the Sixteenth and Seventeenth Centuries, A History of England Principally in the Seventeenth Century*, and even *History of the Reformation in Germany* are remarkably fair and objective.

If the historians like Mill and Macaulay had written *prejudiced* history of the British India, one may pertinently raise the question: was not the history of the Indian society written by pro-nationalist historians *biased*? Before this tricky question is sought to be answered, perhaps it is advisable to take a close look at the writings of those men like Hume, Cotton, Wedderburn, Beveridge, and Yule who started perceiving the rise of the westernized middle class of India and its growing nationalist sentiment. Also of historical interest are the writings of Indians like R.C. Dutt, S.N. Banerjee, Justice Ranade, Firozshah

---

[9] D.P. Chattopadhyaya, *Anthropology and Historiography of Science* (Athens, Ohio: Ohio University Press, 1990).

Mehta and Gokhale who, in spite of their exposure to the Western education, got deeply interested in the tradition of India and started interpreting it. But their interpretations were basically in the light of Western ideas. Their views marked a major shift of Indian historiography from the so-called British period to the pro-Indian period.

An influential section of the nationalist historians, not surprisingly, decided to combat the partisan European historiography on India by an almost equally partisan Indian historiography, defending the Hindus and what their culture stood for. The views and writings of Dayananda Saraswati, Bhudev Mukherji and Bankim Chandra Chatterji could be recalled in this context. The defence of India's past found in the writings of R.G. Bhandarkar, Rajendralal Mitra and R.C. Dutt is admittedly serious and scholarly. The historical *literature*, highlighting the heroic activities of the Rajputs, Marathas, Sikhs and the Muslims, significantly contributed to the growth of nationalist consciousness. In the changed context, the founders of the British Empire like Clive, Warren Hastings and Wellesley came in for sharp criticism. Interestingly enough, the presuppositions of many of these criticisms, on scrutiny, are found to be British or Whig in their inspiration. The gradual shift of focus from politics to culture, from political weakness to cultural richness of India is evident in these nationalist historical writings, marked by the criticism not only of the role of the British Rule but also of its ruling ideas.

Closely related to the pro-cultural approach to history was a renewed emphasis on the theme of Hindu-Muslim unity. Many other old themes started reappearing in new forms. Lala Lajpat Rai, for example, tried to show the positive aspects of the Muslim Rule in India. Attempts were made to deconstruct the Hindu-Muslim relation mainly in terms of collaboration, not domination or hegemonism. The Sepoy Mutiny of 1857, to take another example, was re-interpreted as the First War of Indian Independence.

Apart from the theme of Hindu-Muslim collaboration, yet another notable point which emerged out of the nationalist historiography, is the emphasis on the synthesis of Aryan and Dravidian culture. The very significant contribution made by the peoples of the Deccan, which did not receive its due recognition earlier, started drawing the attention of the historians like Nilakanta Sastri and K.M. Panikkar.

Nationalist historiography is not the only species which flourished before and after the independence of India. Articulately or inarticulately, every historian has a philosophy or method of his/her own. And that philosophy, though ordinarily related to the historian's traditional or cultural background, turns out to be trans-national at times. For example, in the first half of this century most of the Marxist historians, irrespective of their national/cultural affiliation, professed an ideological internationalism. The true Marxist, it is said, belongs to no nation. Because nation is always class-divided, conflict-ridden and never homogeneous in its composition. The distinction often drawn between the pro-nationalist historiography of India and the European/British historiography of the country carries little weight with the Marxist historian. This is evident from the writings of two very well known Marxists, Hiren Mukherji's *India Struggles for Freedom* (1946) and R. Palme Dutt's *India Today* (1947). Because of the writers' ideological predilection it would be wrong to take these works as merely partisan party pamphlets. A distinct and well argued point of view is found in their works. According to the Marxists, there is a general affinity of interests between the British bourgeoisie and the Indian bourgeoisie. Negatively speaking, none of them is willing to accept the rule of the poor in the country. The foreign ruler uses the services of the rich and educated "natives" to maintain his grip over the colony and exploit it effectively. When history is written from this sort of premises, the distinction between the nationalist historiography and the imperialist historiography, between what James Mill writes and what R.C. Dutt writes, ceases to be significant. Is it not an oversimplification of a very complex and changing situation? In fairness to facts it must be admitted that the orthodox phase of Marxism is now a matter of the past, almost forgotten.

On the contrary, some very scholarly works have come from the pens of committed Marxists like D.D. Kosambi, R.S. Sharma and Irfan Habib. Even after professing his firm commitment to Marxism Kosambi writes: "The adoption of Marx's thesis does not mean blind repetition of all his conclusions (and even less, those of the official, party-line Marxists) at all times".[10] The technico-economic historiography of Marx and his followers has one distinct merit, it successfully separates political and dynastic history from the history of the people at large and focuses its attention on the latter. When the historian writes mainly on the community-bound life of the people, highlighting the economic elements of their living, the periodic "storm-clouds of the political sky" are not unduly allowed to obscure the historian's view of the ground-level reality.

---

[10] D.D. Kosambi, *Introduction to the Study of Indian History* (Bombay: Popular Prakashni, 1956 & 1975), p. 10.

In 1940s the leading Marxists of the country like S.A. Dange, P.C. Joshi and B.T. Ranadive were engaged in interpreting differently the tumultuous years of war, communal conflagration and possible independence through partition. Jawaharlal Nehru, lodged in the Ahmadnagar Fort, was writing a sort of history of India during five months, April to September 1944, and, in the process, trying to discover India anew. Nehru's was a complex personality. On his own admission he was "attracted towards the *Advaita* philosophy of the Vedanta" and "Gandhi's ethical approach to life [had] also a strong appeal for [him]". At the same time, "Marx and Lenin", Nehru tells us, "produced a powerful effect on [his] mind and helped [him] to see history and current affairs [and] . . . future" in a meaningful way.[11]

It is well known that Nehru's regard for Marxism and the scientific world-view embedded into it did not prevent him from deeply appreciating the spiritual heritage of Indian culture. But, unlike many other historians, his interest in the past of this country was not only spiritual and scientific but also had a futuristic orientation in it. He wanted to *discover* the covered past of India with a futuristic dream about the country in the back of his mind. Strictly speaking, Nehru was not a professional historian. Nor has he himself ever claimed it. But it must be said to his credit that his grasp of the past of India and the relation he could see between the events, personalities and institutions were remarkable. Deeply distressed by the "arrested growth" of traditional India and convinced of the dynamic impulse of its civilization, he was thinking of the future India, free from alien rule, and making progress peacefully to a democratic and socialist goal. He could easily anticipate the forces of disruption and disorder on the way.

Nehruvian historiography has both classical and romantic elements in it.

> India must break with much of her past and not allow it to dominate the present. . . . But that does not mean a break with, or a forgetting of, the vital and life-giving in that past. We can never forget the ideals that have moved our race, the dreams of the Indian people through the ages, the wisdom of the ancients, the buoyant energy and love of life and nature of our forefathers, their spirit of curiosity and mental adventure, . . . their splendid achievements in literature, art and cul-

---

[11] Jawaharlal Nehru, *The Discovery of India* (New Delhi: Oxford University Press, 1983), pp. 28–31.

ture, their love of truth and beauty and freedom ... their capacity to absorb other peoples and their cultural accomplishments ... we will never forget them. . . . If India forgets them she will no longer remain India.[12]

Without being a professional what Nehru has written is clearly very insightful. His perception of the relation between religion, philosophy and science, is both critical and creative. Religion, in spite of its fanatic deviations, has helped greatly in shaping the development of humanity. Notwithstanding its pitfalls, philosophy has encouraged thought and inquiry. The earth-bound modesty of science has to be taken not only as a cognitive enterprise but also as "a method of acting and associating with our fellow human beings". The long and strong arms of technology should not make us blind to its kind human face.

Nationalist historiography of India has been criticized from various points of view. Apart from the charge of chauvinism that has been levelled against it, some pro-Marxist thinkers have criticized it for its elitist bias and failure to appreciate the contribution of subaltern, of inferior rank, in unleashing the forces of national independence. Captured in the network of colonial institutions and ensnared by its system of education, the elite of India, it has been argued, could not identify itself with the woes, protests and causes of the masses who often fought on their own the alien ruler and/or the national elite.[13] To the subaltern historian almost all protest movements or actions, however disjointed or limited they might be in their scope, are to be taken as visible islands of the submerged continent of discontent, suppressed social psyche. Even transitional frictions are viewed in the image of class-conflict. Many of the basic ideas of subaltern historiography are traceable to Gramsci's "Notes on Italian History" and Straussian structuralism with its sharp accent on binary social relationship.

Immediately after the independence of 1947, it was proved difficult for the Marxists in India to define their attitude to the Indian situation and the Nehru-led Government at the Centre. The moderate section of the Communist Party of India, CPI, under the leadership of P.C. Joshi, in spite of its criticism of Nehru's policies, was

---

[12] *The Discovery of India*, p. 509.
[13] Ranajit Guha (ed.), *Subaltern Studies I: Writings on South Asian History and Society* (New Delhi: Oxford University Press, 1982).

not in favour of taking an insurrectionary line against the Congress Government. But mainly under the influence of the then Soviet authorities on Asia like Dyakov, Zhukov and Zhandnov and after the Cominform Meeting in September 1947, a new line was accepted. Accordingly it was decided by the CPI at its Second Congress in February 1948 that the illusion of the Constitutional Road of Socialism must be rejected and that violent peasant uprisings, as a prelude to the supposedly impending Civil War, should be encouraged. To carry out the new line Joshi was replaced by Ranadive as the General Secretary of the Party. But when the Telengana Peasant Movement failed to trigger off a Civil War-like situation as witnessed by China during the years 1945–49 and the insurrectionary method of the Party could be easily suppressed by the Government, a new centrist line was adopted under the leadership of Ajay Ghosh. The old idea that Nehru was a mere lackey of imperialism was abandoned and it was recognized that he was pursuing a policy of peace, despite its hesitant character.

After the Twentieth Congress of the Communist Party of the Soviet Union in 1956 when the principle of peaceful transition to socialism was affirmed, the old tension between the moderates and the radicals within the CPI resurfaced. When this line was reaffirmed at the 1960 Conference of 81 Parties in Moscow, the difference within the Party became even sharper. The Sino-Soviet ideological difference and the Sino-Indian border dispute significantly influenced the intra-Party conflict of the CPI. The flash point of the difference was reached in 1962 at the time of open border conflict between China and India. Formally the CPI was split into two Groups in 1964: the original Party remained ideologically close to the Soviet Union and the Seceding Group, CPI(M), got openly closer to the Chinese Communist Party and its position. By 1967, when the CPI(M) accepted the Parliamentary method in the Indian context, the Chinese criticized it because of its alleged revisionist character. And a new Communist Party, CPI(Marxist-Leninist), openly came into existence. It advocated the line of armed and guerrilla insurrection which is popularly known as Naxalbari Movement.

Around 1969 when the split between the old guard of the Indian National Congress and others under the leadership of Indira Gandhi was developing, both the Communist Parties found themselves closer to the Congress(I) and started strongly criticizing the Congress(O) for its extreme rightist line on such issues as the Nationalization of Banks and the Abolition of Privy Purses.

During the years of Emergency, 1975–77, the difference between the Communist Parties became clear once again. When the CPI supported the Emergency, the CPI(M) opposed it. During the years of coalition experiment at the Centre, 1977–79, both CPI and CPI(M) supported Janata Dal and BJP enabling the new Government to survive. A section of the Congress, critical of Indira Gandhi, came out of Congress(I) and lent support to the short-lived Government under the leadership of Charan Singh. However after the failure of the Janata experiment Congress(I) returned to power at the Centre in 1980.

This story brings us close to our own time. If we are to believe Hegel's *philosophy* of history, in a way this story marks the "end" of our history. Obviously it is not an end in the literal sense. For the course of events flows on. But we are so close to the events that it is difficult, if not impossible, for us to write history or even *Itihasa* of these events. Events as such devoid of reflective connection between them are not meaningful and historical. But reflection requires some distance between what happens and the historian who wants to write on it. When one brings one's hand very close to one's own eyes, strictly speaking, one cannot see the hand. There is no hard and fast distinction between *contemporary affairs* and history. Yet at times we draw an advised distinction between the two.

The impressions left on us by 1980s may be stated in different ways. One might interpret the years as waning of the age of planning and control. Another feature is the rise of sub-national regionalism, secessionism and the forces of national disintegration. From the international point of view one can relate the happenings of India as the fallout of what was happening elsewhere, in the former Soviet Union, the Far East and the South East Asia. In brief, economic reforms and liberalism had become the accepted goals of most of these countries irrespective of their different ideological commitments and forms of Government.

This trend has become even more pronounced now in 1990s. Economic liberalization, it is being said, is a "right" step toward globalization. The Chinese leadership has been openly saying that political communism and economic capitalism can well go together.[14] In India the main terms of our political discourse on modernity centre

---

[14] Roderick MacFarquhar & John K. Fairbank, (eds.), *The Cambridge History of China, Vol. 15, The People's Republic Part 2* (Cambridge: Cambridge University Press, 1991), pp. 475–539; see also pp. 218–301.

round the desirable pace, not necessarily substance, of economic reforms. Whether this view is a temporary impression or considered historical judgment cannot be said at this moment. As stated before, we are too close to the events to judge them objectively, or, to change the metaphor, one might say, we are inseparably caught up in the flow of the events and unable to rise above it and see it rightly. Yet, as a matter of fact we anticipate, we dream and have our own preferences and priorities in life. In a way, historiography has to accommodate all these things into its fold. Consequently, no history, however factual it may be, can be fiction-free. An element of value judgment is bound to enter into every historical narration. Even the best effort of the most learned historian cannot get us to absolute objectivity in the sense of eternal verity. The highest premium that one can think of paying for "insuring" historical objectivity, for minimizing the mis-effects of relativism, is neither *pure* narration nor suspension of judgment, but openness to criticism.

Before I conclude this brief survey of *Itihasa* and history as two distinct concepts, it is perhaps clear that their relational overlap is unavoidable. It is true that history in its modern sense was not there at the centre stage of human civilization before the eighteenth century or so. At the same time, it seems from the available records and their interpretations that every group of human beings, including even the wandering nomads, have their race memory, more or less distinct self-perception and myths and legends.

In a way the past of a people is retained in its language in the extended sense. Neither the objects of the past nor those of the present are grasped in their purity by us. Both biologically and psychologically in our apprehension of the world around us our self-consciousness enter in a more or less constitutive way. In other words, we do not passively receive the ready-made world of the past; we endow it with something of our own mind. This reflective nature of our mind makes it difficult for us to be absolutely objective, no matter how earnestly we try. At the same time, because of this reflective ability we are not lost in the details of the objective world, nor overwhelmed by the innumerable neural intake that we receive from outside. We can select from among what we receive and this selection presupposes judgment.

The role of the historian in knowing the past is akin to other human ways of knowing the world. In the background of the minds both of the historian and the common man in every age, in every culture, there is a web of beliefs, a mix-up of facts and fictions, which colour their understanding. It is true that all human beings, all historians, because of their inherent freedom, are not identically shaped by their circumstances, past and present. Nor the contents of their imagination about the past and the future are identical. The gift of freedom largely explains the diversity, both cognitive and emotive, of our world-view, of our historical views. In a very serious sense both *Itihasa* and history are brought into existence by the concerned professional's judgment-cum-imagination.

This is not to suggest that our freedom makes it impossible for us to grasp what is objective. It is a verdict both of common sense and of sophisticated science that we more or less commonly share the world in our thought and action. In terms of abstract laws of science we know the predictable structure and sub-structures of the world. In terms of practical success we become and remain reasonably sure about the knowledge of our environment. The scientific views of the world are corrigible by both reason and fact. Somewhat similarly the difference in our historical views, given research and time, can also be substantially corrected or narrowed down by evidence and reasoning. After all, history is a learning process and perhaps Dionysius of Helicarnassus was right in observing that history is "philosophy learned from examples". History is philosophical because of its reflective character marked by *general principles*; and *particular* examples are important for it because of the concreteness it imparts to our understanding.

FLUX IN WEST AND EAST

Joseph Margolis

I am not quite sure how to characterize the essay I am now beginning. I should have liked it to be an appreciation of some aspects of
Nagarjuna's thought, but I am still nearly illiterate in Indian Buddhism. On the other hand, I should have liked to explore in a tact-
ful way some small convergence between my own views and what I
understand of Nagarjuna's, but my sense of the translations of
Nagarjuna's texts and the disputes about what to take them to mean
warn me against doing so. Some students and colleagues whom I
know to be familiar with my own views and who are better informed
about Nagarjuna's assure me that I have indeed moved in his direction,
but if I have, I have done so without benefit of explicit tutelage.

I have worked for many years to bridge the difference between
Anglo-American and continental European thought. I daresay I now
have the sense of the likeliest grounds for a rapprochment between
them. But I have always worried that I should never have the time,
mastering this complex matter, to consider the further possibility of
a rapprochment between Eastern and Western thought. The idea
that whatever I have in a reasonably responsible way worked out as
my own philosophical conception[1] might bear comparison with
Nagarjuna's *Mulamadhyamakakarika*[2] or with the Taoist texts of *Chuang
Tzu*,[3] which I have also been urged to review along the same lines,
fills me with a certain lighthearted pleasure. I have no illusions, of
course, about what I might discover in the way of detailed comparisons. I have no zeal for anything of that sort. But what I understand of early Buddhism and Taoism does indeed suggest that my
own theme—if I may call it that—namely, that there is no demonstration that reality or thought is necessarily invariantly structured
(and that *that* too is only a philosophical "bet" against the claim, not

---

[1] See, particularly, Joseph Margolis, *Historied Thought, Constructed World: A Conceptual Primer for the Turn of the Millennium* (Berkeley: University of California Press, 1995).

[2] Nagarjuna, *The Philosophy of the Middle Way* (*Mulamadhyamakakarika*), trans. David
J. Kalupahana (Albany: SUNY Press, 1986).

[3] *The Complete Works of Chuang Tzu*, trans. Burton Watson (New York: Columbia
University Press, 1968).

another claim of the same sort), might benefit from even an impoverished reading of these grand materials.

I am persuaded that, in the West, Protagoras must have been attracted to a doctrine of the sort I favour—the doctrine of the flux—and that Plato (in *Theaetetus*) and Aristotle (in *Metaphysics*, Gamma) have either deliberately misrepresented what Protagoras meant or simply misunderstood him completely. My reason is a lawyer's reason: Protagoras had the reputation of being a skilled debater, but the account assigned him by Plato and Aristotle makes him out to be a fool. The few teachings that remains hardly show the inevitability of the ancient reading, and modern commentators have done no better.[4] Heraclitus is too obscure for my money. He seems to have favoured the flux, but also the Logos that controls the flux; and no one can be sure how, in Heraclitus, the two are to be reconciled. Also, although we have more of his "fragments" than nearly anyone else among the Presocratics, most of what we have is plainly unusable.[5] Anaximander is even more problematic. For, although the *Apeiron* may bear some comparison with *sunyata*, what we can guess of Anaximander's intention does not seem altogether promising.[6] Furthermore, the interest of modern commentators in Anaximander (Nietzsche and Heidegger in particular) is already influenced by an interest in Indian and Buddhist thought.[7] It is also rather startling to find that the Buddhists of the Kyoto school, discoursing on *sunyatta*, sound for all the world like Heidegger.[8] All in all, therefore, I am drawn to making a series of unguarded reflections more or less in the direction of sensing rather than of demonstrating affinities.

---

[4] See, for instance, Myles F. Burnyeat, "Protagoras and Self-refutation in Plato's Theaetatus", *Philosophical Review*, LXXXV (1976).

[5] See Charles H. Kahn, *The Art and Thought of Heraclitus* (Cambridge: Cambridge University Press, 1979).

[6] See Charles H. Kahn, *Anaximander and the Origins of Greek Cosmology* (New York: Columbia University Press, 1960).

[7] See Martin Heidegger, *Early Greek Thinking*, trans. David Farrell Krell and Frank A. Capuzzi (New York: Harper and Row, 1984).

[8] See, for instance, Keiji Nishitani, *Religion and Nothingness*, trans. Jan van Brugt (Berkeley: University of California Press, 1982); and Kitaro Nishida, *Intelligibility and the Philosophy of Nothingness*, trans. Robert Schinzinger (Honolulu: East-West Centre Press, 1958).

I

I begin by stating and explaining a number of "theorems" that I am prepared to defend:

(1) that philosophy and science are presuppositionless;
(2) that the doctrine of the flux is coherent;
(3) that world and language, or cognized and cognizer, or objects and subjects, are symbiotized;
(4) that thinking is historicized; and
(5) that natural-language inquiries are reconcilable with (1)–(4). They make a tidy set.

Consider theorem (1). Some say that if you make any beginning—if you enter philosophical dispute at all—you must have done so on the strength of some presupposition. It is certainly true that there "must" be in play a practice of linguistic exchange and inquiry, even of dispute and argument, however inchoate or tacit, by the exercise of which you do indeed make a start and continue. But that is to say *you* make a start. Doing that remains presuppositionless if it cannot be demonstrated: (*a*) that there is or must be (must have been) a uniquely right beginning, a first or "originary" condition that can now be stated, which is the *sine qua non* of all inquiry aiming at what is true or real regarding rational understanding and whatever may be found in the world; or (*b*) that there is a criterion that can be stated, or a self-evident ground discerned, by the use of which whatever is thought to be necessarily true or conceptually necessary, or even an approximation to it, may be decisively and reliably shown to be so, or (*c*) that there is some *a priori* constraint on truth or reality, that can be stated, which it is impossible to deny or displace, without producing incoherence or contradiction or irresolvable paradox. The (*a*)–strategy invokes the "originary"; the (*b*)—the "apodictic"; and the (*c*)—what is "necessary *de re*" and/or "*de dicto*". Each and all together invokes the "totalized" (the presumption of the systematic closure of the domain in question), so that each and all is taken to be exceptionless. What I call the doctrine of the flux, theorem (2), is, effectively, then, the denial of all that.

To subscribe to theorem (1) is not to deny that discourse exhibits a discernible structure or to affirm that the context in which discourse is uttered is altogether without structure; it is only to claim that whatever is affirmed in this way is affirmed without implicating any modally necessary conditions. Philosophy is presuppositionless if, in beginning an inquiry, there are no fixed determinate preconditions that it must meet if it is to reach its mark. Speaking or thinking is not (in the relevant sense) a presupposition of rational inquiry: it merely marks the space in which presuppositions may be found. Of course, it is a "condition" of philosophical inquiry that the words one utters make sense. But, for one thing, that holds even if what you say is discernibly false; for another, speaking in accord with our habitual practice is "sufficient" for beginning our reflection, without having any idea of what we "must do" to meet or depart from any putative presupposition; and, for a third, if there are presuppositions, if there are any fixed necessary conditions for understanding ourselves, our world, and our thought, *they* must be located *there*: it is not enough to concede the usual regularities of ordinary discourse and perception.

This seems to be the sense in which Wittgenstein, in *Investigations* sections 201–202, concedes that, in speaking, we "follow a rule"; for, although we "follow a rule", *there is* (Wittgenstein advises) no rule *that* we follow. Here, for convenience, I distinguish between *indicative structures* and *modal invariances*: the first signifies whatever, contingently, spontaneously, "naturally" (that is, in accord with practice), or at any rate without presuming necessary invariance, we affirm or report or unguardedly say we find, which—equally unguardedly—appears to sustain our inquiry and discourse. Language and life itself (and of course philosophy) are presuppositionless if we simply support our practice according to our lights, if we do not insist on and cannot demonstrate a Cartesian "beginning" of any sort, or if no one can demonstrate that there is a determinate, even if tacit, principle that we cannot fail to conform to in exemplary inquiry. The mere viability of language and life is not proof of any particular presupposition or that any must obtain. A presupposition in the sense intended is an inviolably necessary second-order condition on first-order affirmations that aim at truth, the structure of reality, conceptual coherence, rationality, or the like.

Any philosophy that adopts presuppositions in the sense defined may be said to be a First Philosophy. The best-known specimens in the West are Aristotle's and Descartes's; but Kant's and Husserl's doctrines are also First Philosophies. Aristotle's thesis is a version of the (*c*)–condition: what is real as opposed to what is merely apparent is, Aristotle affirms, invariantly structured (*essentialism*). The denial leads "somewhere", Aristotle claims, to self-contradiction; even appearances cannot be consistently assigned to anything unless what they are assigned to possesses a fixed nature. To entertain the denial (the doctrine of the flux) is not equivalent to admitting that what *is* invariant may be open to change.[9]

One sees the presumptive force of Aristotle's claim. But the counter argument is stunningly simple: once the principles" of noncontradiction and excluded middle (on which Aristotle relies) are disjoined from his own metaphysics, it becomes impossible to demonstrate that the denial of Aristotle's "first principles" (or presuppositions) *is* self-contradictory. (And, of course, to say that it is "impossible" is not to advance another modal claim but only to make a philosophical "bet" that no one will succeed in defending the first claim or any pertinent alternative.) For, modal claims are false if their denials are not self-contradictory or incoherent.

Three further weaknesses beset Aristotle's argument. For one, nothing can be individuated by reference to "natures" alone; for natures are predicables and predicables are inherently general—multiply instantiable if instantiable at all. Secondly, Aristotle has no account of how to individuate particulars of any kind in such a way as to facilitate identifying and reidentifying them numerically. (*Hyle* does not serve the purpose, and the theory of *ousiai* presupposes rather than entails the answer.) Thirdly, contradictions obtain only in interpreted contexts; and no first-order (interpreted) claims can be shown to be pertinently inviolable if their denial is not self-contradictory or if they can be amended without contradiction. The "principle" of noncontradiction is not in play until interpreted, and the denial of excluded middle is plainly not self-contradictory.

Now, it is true that, in principle, one may commit a contingent error in discerning or in reasoning from or about a necessary truth.[10] Hence, it is "possible" that Descartes's *cogito is* a "first principle" in spite of the fact that there are good reasons for believing that it is vacuous (or trivially "true") merely because it *is uttered* by an existent agent (so that even if one affirmed, "je ne pense pas", it would still "follow" that "je suis"—whether that was affirmed or not). Descartes's

---

[9] See Aristotle, *Metaphysics*, BK. Gamma, in *The Complete Works of Aristotle*, (*The Revised Oxford Translation*), Vol. 2, (ed.), Jonathan Barnes (Princeton: Princeton University Press, 1985).

[10] See Susan Haack, "Fallibilism and Necessity", *Synthese*, XLI (1979).

alternative is meant to be a version of the (a)–option, or a bridge between the (a)–and (b)–options, but we see that disputes about its standing can hardly rely on appealing to it as a version of the (b)–option. Presumably, that was the point of Descartes's appealing to God's benevolence, a variant of the so-called principle of sufficient reason for relying on other signs of truth or on the application of the *cogito* itself to other would-be signs of truth. Certainly, there is no non-vacuous way to go from "je pense done je suis" to the finding that *I am a res cogitans*—something utterly different from a *res extensa*. The trouble with Descartes's option is that it does not supply a visible and viable discipline of reflection within the terms of which determinate necessary truths can be discerned to be such or shown and known to be progressively approached by whatever we do affirm.

That, if I may say so, is the locus for the supposed contribution of Husserl's method of "eidetic variation". Husserl's is a variant of the Cartesian *cogito* that transforms the (a)–option into the (b)–option, but it rests on the necessity that if there are any seeming conceptual regularities or fixities there must also *be* (in the modal sense) ideal conceptual invariances in accord with which we think about (or "constitute") the intelligible world as we do (*irrealism*). Husserl nowhere successfully affords a determinate characterization of such a reflexive power, one by which we may be assured, first, that there must be a determinate ideal that sets ineluctable limits to sheer conceptual intelligibility—an operative constraint on whatever we suppose is real or known or conceivable; and, second, that we actually *do* discern such invariances (by the eidetic method) or approximate the same. If the contingencies of language and the historical *Lebenswelt* can and must be overcome by more profound powers of thought, Husserl does not actually identify the necessary grounds on which to make the leap.[11] And if there is a principled sense in which the work of the "transcendental ego" (addressed to the alleged invariances required) is suitably distinct from our "naturalistic" cognitional powers but somehow common to mankind, then Husserl was the first to realize that *he* had not yet demonstrated its necessity.[12]

In any event, Husserl's First Philosophy is clearly a paradigm of

---

[11] See Maurice Merleau-Ponty, "The Philosopher and Sociology", *Signs*, trans. Richard L. McCreary (Evanston: Northwestern University Press, 1964).

[12] This is the point of Eugen Fink's critique of Husserl and the collaboration Husserl invited. See Eugen Fink, *Sixth Cartesian Meditation: The Idea of a Transcendental Theory of Method*, trans. Ronald Bruzina (Bloomington: Indiana University Press, 1995).

the form First Philosophy should take, if First Philosophy is to be recovered at all in the modern world. Aristotle's thesis (*c*) is a *de re* claim that can be denied without contradiction. Descartes's thesis (*a*) is a primitive instance of a cognitively focused condition that cannot satisfactorily escape the threat of vacuity or an inherent incapacity to provide a reflexive procedure for discerning and demonstrating further necessary truths. Husserl's "phenomenological reduction" grasps the option that is wanted—if any might succeed; but, for all its care, it never makes the case. Husserl's essential claim is that "pure" eidetic reflection is entirely "separate" from "natural" rational and empirical reflection. But then, it is not irrelevant that when Husserl first formulated his conception of the reflexive analysis of consciousness, in the *Logical Investigations*, he still construed it within the terms of natural and empirical reflection (*Investigations* V). Later, Husserl insists on completely "separating" an "*a priori* science" from *any* "dealing with 'nature' as a fact". Perhaps the following passage may be cited to give a proper sense of the boldness of Husserl's claim to distinguish what he offers from the efforts of both Aristotle and Descartes:

> In conformity with its origin [the discovery of "pure generalities" or "pure possibility"] in the method of free [pure eidetic] variation and the consequent exclusion of all positing of actual being, pure generality naturally can have *no extension consisting of facts*, of empirical actualities which bind it to experience, but only an *extension of pure possibilities*. On the other hand, eidetic generality must always be posited in relation to admitted actualities. Every color occurring in actuality is certainly, at the same time, a possible color in the pure sense; each can be considered as an example and can be changed into a variant. Thus, in the realm of arbitrary freedom we can lift all actuality into a plane of pure possibility. But it then appears that even arbitrary freedom [variation relative to the pure possibilities bearing on an *eidos* rather than an actuality] has its own particular constraint. What can be varied on into another, in the arbitrariness of imagination (even if it is without connection and does not accord with the understanding of a reality conceivable in the imagination) bears in itself a necessary structure, an *eidos*, and therewith *necessary* laws which determine what must necessarily belong to an object in order that it can be an object of this kind. This necessity then also holds for everything factual: we can see that everything that belongs inseparably to the pure *eidos* color, *e.g.*, the moment of brightness, must likewise belong to every actual colour.[13]

---

[13] Edmund Husserl, *Experience and Judgment: Investigations in a Genealogy of Logic*, revised

From this it follows that "eidetic [or] transcendental phenomenology" is "primary philosophy" (in the sense of fixing the "universal ontology or the logic of [possible] Being"), whereas "empirical philosophy of the factual", including intersubjectivity, is "secondary philosophy".[14] Hence, Husserl cannot suppose that he begins in a "presuppositionless" way. It is true, however, that, in his last years, Husserl called this relationship into doubt and began to reconsider the inseparability of eidetic possibility and actuality.[15] In an eccentric sense, therefore, Husserl may well have wished to say that he nowhere *begins* with the presupposition of a First Philosophy, but rather discovers the necessary dependence of the conceptual structure of actuality on eidetic necessity. But he cannot have it both ways: if the eidetic discipline is grounded in naturalistic conceptions, then perceived necessity cannot escape being an artifact of history and ethos; and if it is "prior to" and separable from the naturalistic, then we appear to be forced back to a doubtful Cartesian confidence in *its own* self-evident or apodictic standing. Here, in his usual mode, Husserl says: the fact that *"knowledge of 'possibilities' must precede that of actualities (Wirklichkeiten)* is, in my opinion, in so far as it is rightly understood and properly utilized, a really great truth".[16]

I conclude from these considerations that, first of all, the defeat of Aristotle's modal claim is elementary and provides the clue to affirming (as a philosophical "bet") my original theorem (2); second, that discerning Husserl's failure to ensure the separable and demonstrably apodictic competence of eidetic reflections provides the clue to affirming theorems (3) and (4) as additional "bets"; third, that Descartes's claim is vacuous or, for trivial reasons, without any modally necessary consequence; and, fourth, that the defeat of all three strat-

---

and edited by Ludwig Landgrebe, trans. James S. Churchill and Karl Ameriks (Evanston: Northwestern University Press, 1973), p. 352.

[14] This comes close to the essential "motto" (Husserl's own term) abstracted from nearly all of Husserl's mature work. I had in hand a passage from Husserl in which the distinction is made in much the same terms, but I have misplaced the reference. The wording here is drawn from another version of the same motto abstracted in Rudolf Bernet, Iso Kern, and Eduard Marback, *An Introduction to Husserlian Phenomenology* (Evanston: Northwestern University Press, 1993), p. 131. One can readily test its validity by applying it to particular studies: see, for example, Edmund Husserl, *Phenomenological Psychology*, trans. John Scanlon (the Hague: Martinus Nijhoff, 1977).

[15] See, for instance, Rudolf Bernet *et al., An Introduction to Husserlian Phenomenology,* p. 234. I have benefited from this scrupulous review.

[16] Edmund Husserl, *Ideas: General Introduction to Pure Phenomenology,* trans. W.B. Boyce-Gibson (New York: Collier Books, 1962), 79 (p. 113); italics added.

egies provides the clue for affirming theorems (1) and (5). The argument is inconclusive, both because I do not (and cannot) canvas all possible variants of (*a*)–(*c*), or related options, and because I do not (and cannot) show why there *cannot* possibly be a successful demonstration of the sorts instanced or alternatives. To have succeeded in doing that would have been to lose by winning, since I should have validated a First Philosophy by which to disallow all further First Philosophies.[17] One can see why, if Husserl fails, Kant must fail as well; and, if Descartes fails, Locke must fail as well; and if Aristotle fails, then (say) Reichenbach and Hempel fail. But the salient lines of argument remain clear. That is why the counterstrategy is a "bet" and not a First Philosophy. Furthermore, if you grasp the conceptual elision that runs from Aristotle and Descartes to Husserl (by way of Kant), you see why it hardly matters whether we speak of what is indubitable in a "naturalistic" or a "transcendental" mode. They are locally different options, of course, but the underlying strategies are ultimately less dissimilar than would appear. I offer all this as a sketch of a strong argument, not as that argument itself. I am merely explaining why I subscribe to theorems (1)–(5). I am preparing the ground for an appreciation of Nagarjuna in Western terms.

II

I apologize for going on at length about Husserl. But my reason is that Husserl offers what may well be the single most courageous and sustained attempt to demonstrate the necessity for admitting First Philosophy and what, on Husserl's own conception, First Philosophy yields. I have the greatest regard for Husserl's labour. We are surely in his debt. But the ultimate demonstration is nowhere provided and there are no compelling reasons for believing that any variant of phenomenology could succeed or do better than Husserl does. All the difficulties that beset Husserl's account are inexplicitly captured in the worry both Heidegger and Merleau-Ponty raise—to the effect that the phenomenological method cannot *ever* free itself from the intrusive consequences of socially perspectived experience, linguistically

---

[17] See, in this connection, Carl Page, *Philosophical Historicism and the Betrayal of First Philosophy* (University Park: Pennsylvania State University Press, 1995), particularly Ch. 2.

structured thought, historically formed concepts, all developed (I should say) within the terms of our initial enculturation as the apt selves we become and are.

In an extraordinary intuition, Wittgenstein hits on the same puzzle in an abbreviated way when he says, speaking against philosophers: "what *we* do is bring words back from their metaphysical to their everyday use".[18] What Wittgenstein means is plainly opposed (in sense, but not explicitly) to Husserl's conception. For Wittgenstein insists, in bringing "words back . . . to their everyday use", that we do *not* ordinarily *have* rules, criteria, assurances of common exemplars at any point or through any interval of change to govern or guide our usage: "When I obey a rule, [he says,] I do not choose. I obey the rule blindly".[19] (Wittgenstein does not satisfactorily explain what he means— except negatively, against all forms of cognitive fixity and privilege.) You may suppose (with Husserl) that the precise work of eidetic reflection (which, apparently, does not depend in any essential way on language) rightly applies to fixing the ideal limits of the inherent variability of concepts.[20] But if Wittgenstein is right in affirming: (i) that there is no conceptual precision of any invariant or apodictic or necessary sort to be found in natural-language discourse, and (ii), nevertheless, ordinary discourse is successful in a communicative way, then Husserl must be completely mistaken.

The force of the implied argument collects by stages. For one thing, it cannot be shown that Wittgenstein's conjecture is incoherent or paradoxical. Second, it cannot be shown that there is any recognizable form of reflexive or critical reason that is free of linguistic structure. Thirdly, it cannot be shown that linguistic and conceptual structures ("noematic" structures, if I may coopt Husserl's own idiom) are not artifacts of the historical experience of diverse societies altered as a matter of course in their actual use. (I concede that Wittgenstein was not particularly interested in the problem of history though he recognized, in effect, the horizonal nature of understanding the language and customs of one society and another;[21] and I take note,

---

[18] Ludwig Wittgenstein, *Philosophical Investigations*, trans. G.E.M. Anscombe (New York: Macmillan, 1953), I. Section 116.

[19] Wittgenstein, *Philosophical Investigations*, I. Section 219.

[20] See Edmund Husserl, "The Origin of Geometry", *The Crisis of European Sciences and Transcendental Phenomenology: An Introduction to Phenomenological Philosophy*, trans. David Carr (Evanston: Northwestern University Press, 1970).

[21] See, for example, Wittgenstein, *Philosophical Investigations*, II, Sections i, xi, (for instance, at p. 223).

in passing, that Hegel's phenomenology, as opposed to Husserl's, is, however difficult to fathom, favourably disposed to all the elements of the argument I bring against Husserl. In fact, speaking informally, the objection to Husserl's phenomenology ultimately derives from Hegel's phenomenology.)

The key to the entire puzzle remains, as before: that is, the pretended force of modal necessity. If you grant that you cannot extract from what is phenomenally or historically contingent what, *sans phrase*, is necessarily invariant *de re, de dicto*, or *de cogitatione*, (and that that applies as much to Kant's as to Husserl's transcendentalism), then Husserl's argument cannot succeed—*if*, for instance, Wittgenstein and Merleau-Ponty are right about the encumbrances of thought. I hasten to add that the argument is a *faute de mieux* argument, not an article of First Philosophy, and I acknowledge that Hegel speaks mysteriously (in the *Phenomenology*) of "necessities" internal to the process of *Geist*.[22] Nevertheless, the upshot is clear: it is not possible to demonstrate that there is any (or what is the) discernibly ideal limit, or "essence", that belongs to any concept in actual use—to which that use is conceptually bound. The "validity" of our conceptual practice is entirely *lebensformlich*, openended, subject to extension by improvisational changes within the terms of actual use. That is the import of that famous puzzling remark of Wittgenstein's (which Wittgenstein applies with equal conviction to mathematics and ordinary language): "If language is to be a means of communication then there must be agreement not only in definitions but also (queer as this may sound) in judgments. This seems to abolish logic, but does not do so".[23]

You must bear in mind that we are not obliged to demonstrate that Wittgenstein was right and Husserl wrong in their respective claims. No, the argument turns rather on the fact that Wittgenstein's thesis is coherent, plausible, relevant, adequate, more economical than Husserl's, and entirely apt, *and* that Husserl's claim cannot dislodge it. Grasping that, we see why Husserl's version of the (*b*)–strategy implicates something like Descartes's version of the (*a*)–strategy or something like Aristotle's version of the (*c*)–strategy, or both. In any case, the coherence and pertinence of Wittgenstein's proposal suggest why the admission that reason depends inseparably on the

---

[22] See, for instance, G.W.F. Hegel, *Phenomenology of Spirit*, trans. A.V. Miller (Oxford: Oxford University Press, 1979), particularly "Absolute Knowing".

[23] Wittgenstein, *Philosophical Investigations*, I. Section 241.

contingencies of language, ethos, history, experience, *Lebensform* or *Lebenswelt* mortally wounds phenomenology at its Achilles's heel. I subscribe to Wittgenstein's thesis (if I understand it rightly), but I argue only that it cannot be defeated by the fiat of foundational or transcendental claims. I also acknowledge that Wittgenstein's intuitions did not carry him far enough along the lines I wish to explore. (That has still to be shown.)

In the *Investigations*, as opposed to the *Tractatus*, Wittgenstein proceeds in a presuppositionless way. I don't say he proceeds without prejudice or conviction, but he nowhere posits a modal principle that he claims cannot be opposed in the ways Aristotle, Descartes, or Husserl believes must fail. According to Wittgenstein, it's the sheer *viability* of our consensual practices that is all that remains "foundational" in the success and fluency of those practices: there is nothing else to appeal to! Count that the linchpin,—in effect, item (iii) for the tally begun a little earlier,—of Wittgenstein's implicit argument against foundationalism and transcendental inquiries, Here, I suggest, stalemate is as good as victory. Wittgenstein's argument brings us to the edge of the decisive evidence. (Remember: the argument is a *faute de mieux* argument, a "bet" against First Philosophy.) For there are considerations that stand a very good chance of outflanking all First Philosophies. If they do—in the spirit of Wittgenstein's intuition (as explained)—then my original theorem (2) will be vindicated; and if it is vindicated, then the others stand a good chance of being vindicated as well; and if they are vindicated, then the relevance of Nagarjuna's analysis will glide into view.

The point at issue is this. *If*, as I believe, all thought and argument are linguistically encumbered or, secondarily, if all forms of mental, intelligent, or rational processes ascribed to prelinguistic children, sublinguistic animals, theoretical or unconscious mentation, machine analogues, transcendental reasoning, and the like are "anthropomorphically" modelled on human—that is, linguistically competent—natural-language exemplars, then, *if* the analysis of reference and predication precludes the use of powers like those invoked in strategies (*a*)–(*c*), the philosophical "bet" of theorem (2) (*a fortiori*, the "bet" of the other theorems as well) cannot be ruled out *a priori* or foundationally. That is as close as we are likely to come to a knockdown argument against foundationalist and transcendental claims regarding the necessity or indefeasibility of *any* form of cognitive privilege. I shall sketch the argument, but I draw your attention, in advance, to the fact that, as I understand their views, Protagoras and Nagarjuna adhere to strong forms of the doctrine of the flux—and for not dissimilar reasons. That is my charge. If this doctrine holds, then I will have succeeded in demonstrating how to bring the entire history of Western philosophy into a promising alignment with certain leading themes of Asian philosophy opposed to modal invariance. I should be happy to vindicate such a finding.

III

The argument is entirely straightforward though strenuous. I confine myself to a sketch of the principal considerations.[24] Regarding predication, I begin with two curious facts. One is that there is no evidence that Plato ever subscribed to the theory of Forms, although he certainly introduces and airs its uses and philosophical prospects (most notably, in *Parmenides*). But there can be no point to the theory of Forms if we lack any assured epistemic access to them; and, on Plato's argument, it is clear that either we lack such access or we cannot demonstrate that we have it. If we agree that it makes no sense to claim to have knowledge if we cannot demonstrate that we have knowledge, or if it is an intolerable paradox to claim that we have knowledge but do not know that we do, then, on the interpretation (of Plato's account) here offered, we must abandon the theory of Forms. Q.E.D. the second, the other, fact is that the medieval theory of real Universals (in the various realist or conceptualist forms familiarly espoused) is a conceptual disaster—is, at the very least, a family of theories that depend on an argument identical with what Plato requires or an analogue of the same; *and* that the nominalist alternative, which rejects Universals, is as much a disaster as the "realisms" it opposes. Wittgenstein, I suggest, shows us a way to solve the problem of predicative generality, though he does not go far enough.[25]

The puzzle of predication comes to this: natural languages clearly rely on the spontaneous extension of *general predicates* to new instances not yet introduced by anything that might count as their original

---

[24] I have given a more pointed account in a number of places, but especially in *Historied Thought, Constructed World*.

[25] See Renford Bambrough, "Universals and Family Resemblances", *Proceedings of the Aristotelian Society*, LX (1960–61).

exemplars. Are there, then, real *general predicables* ("real generals", in Charles Sanders Peirce's idiom)[26] that our predicates designate; and how (if there are) do we discern them? Plato's theory of Forms and the medieval realist and conceptualist accounts of Universals introduce invariant *tertia* functioning epistemically between our perceptions and thoughts and the genuinely predicable features of actual things. The trouble is, no one has the slightest idea how we discern—or how we may reliably know or show that we discern—the fixed forms by which we can (as a consequence) perceive that even inconstant or accidental predicables *are* variant instantiations of the Forms. Aristotle, of course, coolly pretends that we simply possess the powers of *nous* by the exercise of which, instantly and spontaneously, we cognize the essential "forms" of independent *ousiai*.[27] But that is the puzzle, hardly its solution. (It is also a conceptual scandal.) Husserl's (*b*)–strategy, you may guess, is a valiant attempt to provide an honest solution. That is what, as I say, Wittgenstein's thesis discounts—discounting the *need* for such a provision—when he advances the notion of the *lebensformlich*. (I admit that you cannot capture the full import of the "lebensformlich" on textual grounds alone; you must go beyond Wittgenstein's words.)

I understand the matter—naively—in the following way. Regarding general predicables—"red", say—we cannot, first, actually see a changeless generic RED in all the variable particular instantiations of what we are prepared to call "red" in ordinary experience; second, we are ordinarily prepared to allow or tolerate the extension of the term "red" to newly encountered "instances" in openended contexts of familiar use; and, third, *our* tolerance is a function of our sense (not a criterion of any sort) of the consensual tolerance of our society regarding *its* practice of extending such usage in familiar contexts of use. Imagine a newly manufactured line of lipsticks designated as variant forms of red. Our practices of manufacture and marketing already prepare us to "allow" particular specimens to count as "red" even if we do not know how they were originally introduced: the entrenched practice of designating new lipstick colors, or

---

[26] For a detailed sense of Peirce's account of "real generals", see Joseph Margolis, "The Passing of Peirce's Realism", *Transactions of the Charles S. Peirce Society*, XXIX (1993).

[27] See Aristotle, *On the Soul* (*De Anima*), trans. J.A. Smith, in *The Complete Works of Aristotle* (*The Revised Oxford Translation*), Vol. 1, (ed.), Jonathan Barnes (Princeton: Princeton University Press, 1985), particularly BK. III.

the colors of cars and clothes, is congenial enough in terms of our linguistic habits—habits not ordinarily baffled or puzzled by similarly informal tendencies to extend the use of competing predicates. We are spontaneously disposed to tolerate such informal extensions without untoward dislocations in the play of natural-language communication and whatever depends on it. We can always arrest the practice (if we wish) and impose—within a narrower gauge *but in the same consensual way*—more careful constraints on our predicates. But note: we succeed only consensually, never on the basis of discerning an invariant *tertium* of any kind.

For his part, the nominalist (Nelson Goodman, preeminently) fails as completely as the "Platonist". For the nominalist denies that there *are* general predicables (in denying that there are existent Forms); he holds instead that the extension of general predicates proceeds by conventional agreement or conventionally restricted criteria or the like, but he fails to see that *that* also implicates real "general predicables". He cannot explain his own success; it cannot be done without admitting "real generals".[28] So the realist and conceptualist (about Universals) fail because they have nothing to say about the essential epistemic role of predication; and the nominalist fails because he cannot escape a *reductio* of his own invention. What I claim is that Husserl's immensely important proposal—which I now regard as a metonym for all predicative strategies that mean to recover the epistemic *tertia* wanted (if the "Wittgensteinian" solution is to be offset or bettered) is subject to the same dilemma as the realist's (or conceptualist's) and the nominalist's options. I cannot see how that can be gainsaid, though it is hardly more than a *faute de mieux* manoeuvre.

If you grant the force of this, then it is no more than a step to grasp as well that, as with predication, denotation and reference (apt for fixing numerical identity and ensuring reidentifiability in epistemic terms) *cannot* be determinatively achieved by any algorithmic, principled, rule-governed, or criterial means. The reason is elementary. First of all, nothing can be individuated or reidentified (numerically) in predicative terms alone, for predicates are "general", that is

---

[28] Goodman actually makes the fatal admission but does not see that he does. See Nelson Goodman, "Seven Strictures on Similarity", in Lawrence Foster and J.W. Swanson (eds.), *Experience and Theory* (Amherst: University of Massachusetts Press, 1970).

multiply instantiable if instantiable at all. Secondly, if we suppose
(*per impossible*) that, in principle, every "particular thing" does indeed
instantiate a unique predicable, then no human could identify anything uniquely unless (as God is said to be able to do) a human
subject could identify everything conformably; but no one can actually do that in real-time terms. And, thirdly, such a predicative strategy would still remain subject to the difficulties already adduced in
defeating the realist and the nominalist. The fact is that W.V. Quine
has offered the very solution I have just deemed unworkable.[29] Leibniz
had long ago seen its futility: in effect, Leibniz's point was that a
policy like Quine's could never satisfactorily appeal to the principle
of noncontradiction alone but only (conceivably) to the principle of
sufficient reason (to God's benevolence, for instance); but Leibniz's
theology hardly satisfies our own needs and hardly satisfies Quine's.[30]

If, now, you put these two arguments together—regarding predication and reference—you see at once the full force of the argument
I mean to draw from Wittgenstein: the conditions of effective predication and effective reidentification of particulars lie *not* in our subjective criteria or in the independent world but *in the symbiotized
fluency of our lebensformlich practices, in our collective consensual tolerance of
predicative extensions and context-bound reidentifications.* We cannot *know* that
we succeed, predicatively or referentially, in any stronger way. We
succeed "pragmatically", if I may suggest a term. *Knowledge,* on the
argument, is a dependent artifact of the *lebensformlich* process. (By
"symbiotized", I may add, I mean that we cannot provide a principled disjunction between the "subjective" and the "objective", between the "realist" and the "idealist", between language and the world.
Language is "worlded" and the world is "languaged": in the context
of our "form of life", there is no distinction between analyzing language [addressed to the world] and analyzing the world [that we
access through natural language].)[31] Success in reference and predication is entirely consensual—read in a holist and noncriterial sense,

---

[29] See W.V. Quine, *Word and Object* (Cambridge: MIT Press, 1960), Sections
37–38.
[30] See *The Leibniz-Clarke Correspondence*, (ed.), H.G. Alexander (Manchester: Manchester University Press, 1956), particularly Leibniz's fifth letter.
[31] The most recent concession along these lines appears in Hilary Putnam, *The
Many Faces of Realism* (La Salle: Open Court, 1987), Lecture II. Putnam, I may say,
has not yet fully fathomed the implications of his admission—which, I suggest, completely undermines his confidence in truth as a *Grenzbegriff.*

read in a sense in which the work of would-be criteria is itself consensual. If, now, you concede: (i) the coherence and adequacy of
such a model, (ii) the failure of all would-be algorithmic resolutions
of the referential and predicative puzzles, and (iii) the insuperable
skeptical import of any principled disjunction between the subjective
and the objective, then you instantly concede the collapse of First
Philosophy. But that is precisely what the doctrine of the flux affirms.

IV

I wish to signify, finally, that (and in what sense) Protagoras and
Nagarjuna are exemplary advocates of the flux. Nagarjuna we may
discover in his own words; Protagoras we must reconstruct. There is,
of course, only one way to reclaim Protagoras: by inventing a plausible reading of his doctrine "man is the measure", and his adherence
to an idiom of "appearances" in the setting of avoiding the *reductio*
Plato (in *Theaetetus*) and Aristotle (in *Metaphysics*, Gamma) provide for
him. The strategy for escaping both traps is the same: merely postulate a flux (the denial of modal invariance) in which the admission of
denotata and predicables does not entail the admission of any principled distinction among *denotata* or the modal fixity of our referential or predicative criteria. Nowhere does Plato (at least, in the voice
of his spokesman, Socrates) or Aristotle (explicitly) demonstrate that
these options are neither coherent nor viable. But if, as I have already
argued, modal claims fail if there denial may be shown to be coherent and nonparadoxical, then it seems quite easy to recover Protagoras.
The irony is that, in doing that, we anticipate a rapprochement
between Western and Eastern philosophies. For Nagarjuna actually
offers a version of the general strategy now barely sketched.

The decisive postulate is this: discourse invokes an *external* relationship between cognizing subjects and cognized world; but the avoidance of cognitive privilege and skepticism and the resolution of the
puzzles of reference and predication entail that the external relationship holding between subjects and objects (and whatever that brings
in its wake) should also be an artifact *internal* to the interpretation of
an antecedently encompassing, symbiotized, and holist world. The
doctrine is a postulate, not a theorem, in the sense that it is the fruit
of a philosophical "bet". But it is a postulate that also fits (is made
to fit) the confirmation of particular theorems like those already

mentioned: for instance, the defeat of Aristotle's or Descartes's or Husserl's particular proposals.[32]

If you think carefully about this postulate, you will see that it is the generic form of the doctrine of the flux; for, on its assumption, all referential (or denotative) and predicative resources remain in place but are now construed as provisional, "pragmatic", adjusted to our salient interests, transient and contingent, open to plural uses, and the like. In short, the resources of the flux are more inclusive than those of invariance, for the only constraint that must be abandoned (within the terms of the flux) is that of modal necessity or modal fixity (which is in any case incompatible with the flux but nowhere demonstrated to hold true); and, even there, merely *apparent* (or "horizonal") invariances, relativized to historical experience, may readily be admitted. I take that to be the import of Foucault's ("archaeological") notion of the "historical" *a priori*[33] and, also, a fair sign of the doctrine's resilience.

In any event, the doctrine of the flux postulates that the inclusive "universe of discourse" or the inclusive "context of all contexts" is a "space" that we cannot inquire into—seeking to learn what is true of "it" as such; it is a space that lacks determinate structure *in that sense*; it postulates that all truth-seeking discourse is contexted and that discursive contexts are similarly contexted—without end. We may still conjecture how best to picture the "relationship" between what we discourse about and the indiscursible "universe". The flux is that postulate that (I suppose) best collects *whatever* our truth-claim addresses—in the face of the failure of First Philosophy. Flux, therefore, is the postulate that human inquiry is "presuppositionless", not bound to take as necessarily true—or as a first principle—*any* claim about the invariant structure of a world or thought or language. Alternatively put, First Philosophy is entirely discursive, entirely contextless.

The thesis does *not* require that whatever structure we impute to the determinable things of the world are illusory in any sense. Not at all. All it requires (or, rather, permits) is the rejection of modal necessity or invariance; and it does that—in contrast to the claim of

---

[32] I provide a more sustained account of this manoeuvre in my *Historied Thought, Constructed World*, but as a theorem within a larger argument.

[33] See Michel Foucault, *The Order of Things: An Archaeology of the Human Sciences*, trans. (New York: Vintage, 1970), Ch. 10.

First Philosophy—as a supreme "bet" (that is, against further First Philosophies). If I am not mistaken, this is precisely what Nagarjuna affirms in verse 8, Chapter 4 of the *Karika*:

> When an analysis is made in terms of emptiness, whatsoever were to address a refutation, all that is left unrefuted by him will be equal to what is yet to be proved.[34]

Nagarjuna uses the expression *sunyataya vigrahe krte* rather than the term *sunyata*—which is to say he speaks of "an analysis in terms of emptiness" rather than of "emptiness" itself. In the context of the entire chapter, it is reasonably clear (and his translator takes it to be clear) that the doctrine has a positive cast, is not intended to discount as unreal what we experience and what we take to have causal efficacy. On the contrary, it is meant to pit the "analysis" offered in terms of *sunyata* to *any* analysis of the world in terms of (what I call) modal invariance. Hence, I trust it will not be viewed as more than an open usurpation of Nagarjuna's notion to suggest the following theorem: *sunyata = flux*.

This comes as a surprise, since it is so simple and straightforward. I have no doubt that *sunyata* has a deeper meaning in the context of Buddhist spiritual exercises. I have nothing to say about that, being, frankly, ignorant of the tradition. I am suggesting no more than a minimal conceptual bridge between the two philosophical traditions. But the idea requires a second thesis. I have already stated it in the postulate I proffered earlier: the external relations that hold between discoursing subjects and discursible objects are the interpreted, "mythically" conjectured *relata* internal to our holist or symbiotized universe of discourse. There is no discourse without subjects and objects; to speak about anything implicates the logical structure of subjects and objects. The partisans of the flux—Protagoras and Nagarjuna, on my reading—contend that subjects and objects are contingent but obviously useful discrete nominalizations of *whatever*, on the postulate, belong to the prediscursive world from which *all our conceptual distinctions arise together*. They "arise together" in the sense that: (i) none is entitled to epistemic, alethic, or ontic priority; (ii) none functions except in the company of the others; (iii) there is no uniquely correct set of such distinctions; and (iv) even the flux makes no sense except as

---

[34] Nagarjuna, *The Philosophy of the Middle Way*, pp. 144–145. See Kalupahana's helpful glosses, pp. 145–146.

that which is postulated as that within the space of which our categories have application.

Protagoras conveys the sense of (i)–(iv) in advocating a "world of appearances"; Nagarjuna conveys it in speaking of what counts as "dependent arising" (*pratityasamutpada*).

My own suggestion is that we construe the determinate distinctions between individuated things, between subjects and objects, between reference and predication, and the like, *as* nominalizations (answering to our interests) of whatever ("mythically") we conjecture are the *relata* (within the flux) that we must sort out for discursive purposes. To treat the world in terms of independent elements of some sort risks all the possible variants of (*a*)–(*c*) that I am here opposing. To speak of *relata* rather than *denotata* or *elements* is merely to remind ourselves of that danger and the import of the last tally (i)–(iv) just offered. Nothing more. There *are* no primal *relata* just as there *is* no primal flux. But we do speak, of course, and we do act on the strength of whatever we discern linguistically. We must warn ourselves, therefore, of the possible bewitchment of our conserving habits. That is the point of what I call the "mythic" use of language. It preserves the sense in which all discourse is contexted *and* the sense in which we cannot complete the nesting of contexts. Discourse is openended, therefore, and we are bound to conjecture about how best to picture the "relationship" between provisional contexts and the "context of all contexts". Mention of the *relata* that belong to that (or our best) interpretive picture provides the "mythic" (non-truth-bearing) feature *of* truth-bearing discourse.

I find the sense of my tally (i)–(iv) adumbrated in verse 8, Chapter 13 of the *Karika*:

> The Victorious Ones have announced that emptiness [*sunyata*] is the relinquishing of all views. Those who are possessed of the view of emptiness are said to be incorrigible.[35]

The point appears to be that *sunyata* itself can be transformed into an invariant reality—which I take to be a confirmation of the notion of a philosophical "bet". This captures the sense of item (iv). The rest of the tally, which Nagarjuna appears to pursue in a notably uncompromising way, runs through all the principal forms of the familiar metaphysical categories: identity, causality, predication, existence,

---

[35] Nagarjuna, *The Philosophy of the Middle Way*, p. 123.

action, self. They are all analyzed in the self-same way: by invoking "dependent arising", that, if I understand the argument rightly, is the gist of (i)–(iii).

One remark that I find particularly strategic appears at verse 2, Chapter 5:

> An existent that is without characteristics is nowhere evident.[36]

I take this to mean that, first, there *is* nothing that exists in any integral isolation from all else, possibly unchanging for that reason; and, second, that whatever exists, exists in a way that cannot but be predicatively characterizable and that what is real in the way of being predicable is such in the sense (only) in which it actually qualifies whatever existent thing it qualifies. I cannot see how this can be meant in any way but as roughly equivalent to Protagoras's "world of appearances": hence, as incompatible with both Aristotle's and Plato's (apparent) doctrines. For, on Nagarjuna's view, there are neither invariant substances nor invariant Forms (ideal *tertia* that mediate, ontically and epistemically, between our experience and the predicable attributes of things).

I must break off here, lest I attempt more than I am entitled to say. I came to these views quite independently, I believe. I first discovered that I found the usual contemporary readings of Protagoras (which follow Plato and Aristotle closely) to be utterly uncompelling. Now, I find myself persuaded that Nagarjuna's doctrine is sympathetic to Protagoras's, though also very different in its explanation and purpose. I cannot treat the matter in textual terms, though I should like to have a confirmation of my reading. Beyond that, I am persuaded that the doctrine of the flux has far better resources than the doctrine of invariance. I have assessed its power in Western terms; but, if I can, I should like to pursue its larger prospects among the Asian philosophies as well.

---

[36] Nagarjuna, *The Philosophy of the Middle Way*, p. 148.

SATISFACTIONS AND OBSTACLES IN PHILOSOPHIZING ACROSS CULTURAL BOUNDARIES

Frank J. Hoffman

> The philosophy, which ought to be comparative, should not take man, or human reason, but the different types of humanity or reason, for its subject: and, the more these types differ, the more fruitful can we hope their confrontation will show itself to be—Paul Masson-Oursel, *Comparative Philosophy*, p. 33.

> The aim of comparative philosophy is to find out which problems of life are solved in which ways in the several traditions, and which aspects of life, when treated as basic hard facts, give rise to which philosophical problems and which kind of solutions. If man is so completely unlike in the East and the West as some suppose, then it is futile to attempt to understand each other. But if we are to understand each other, what is the common denominator for the various philosophical traditions? The same common denominator has to be chosen as the aim of comparative philosophy. If it is full and complete human life, then man becomes the common denominator.—P.T. Raju, *Introduction to Comparative Philosophy*, p. 291.

I. INTRODUCTION

This paper emerges out of a state of philosophical perplexity as to how to answer the question: what is "comparative philosophy"? Speaking personally for a moment, I have been doing something like "comparative philosophy" without directly espousing an allegiance to something so ambiguous as this for much of my philosophical life. And yet those of my generation and training have seldom if ever been provided the opportunity to study the idea of comparative philosophy as such, and were given to understand from our mentors that this was something best learned in the doing of it. What satisfactions can one find in it, and what are some obstacles to it? Answering these questions involves one in answering the question "what is comparative philosophy?

Could there be a taxonomy of human types or reasonings revealing a confrontation of ideas, as Masson-Oursel observes in the quotation above? (Would such a taxonomy inevitably be contrived,

wooden, and stereotypical, or could it be conceptually sophisticated?)
Or could there be a "common denominator," such as "full and
complete human life" as Raju states above? (Would such a common
denominator be describable in language such that philosophers from
a variety of viewpoints could accept it?) Juxtaposition of the Masson-
Oursel and Raju quotations above stimulates many such philosophical questions and reflections.

Descriptively speaking there are several logically possible forms that
philosophizing across cultural boundaries can take. In describing these
forms attention will be given to the motivation involved in cross-
cultural philosophy. One might philosophize across cultural boundaries in order to achieve understanding for its own sake, to attack,
or to defend. In doing one of these (or some coherent combination)
one might also engage in comparison and/or contrast. Seen in this
way, comparative philosophy is only one among various possible modes
of philosophical encounter with other cultures. In comparative philosophy at its best, comparison in comparative philosophy is something one does *in* the course of doing something else: comparison is
not something done for its own sake. To focus on "comparative
philosophy" as does this paper is to focus on one of the possible
modes that philosophizing across cultural boundaries can take.

One view sometimes heard among proponents of comparative philosophy is that all philosophy is necessarily comparative. (This might,
for instance, be used to cut off inquiry as to what is comparative
method.) It is open to proponents of the "necessity of comparison
thesis" to argue that philosophy in an evaluative sense (philosophy at
its best) is necessarily comparative, but it is dubious that philosophy
in a descriptive sense must necessarily be comparative.

The enterprise of comparative philosophy involves both significant
satisfactions as well as difficult obstacles. This paper is about these
satisfactions and obstacles and how they arise in the process of philosophizing across cultural boundaries. In this paper it is not my
main purpose to *encourage* anyone to do comparative philosophy, but
only to attempt to *understand* some conceptual issues concerning the
idea of comparative philosophy. As a by-product, I shall not be
unhappy if someone takes to the idea of comparative philosophy as
a partial result of reading this or other similar papers (provided that
they do so with imaginative sympathy and critical acumen), but
encouraging them to do so is not my objective.

II. Understanding, Comparison, Contrast, and Apologetics

A. *Understanding for Its Own Sake*

If one accepts the view that knowledge is an intrinsic good, then it is not necessary to provide a special justification for comparative philosophy as such. For even in its descriptive moment (leaving aside its evaluative moment), the process of engaging in comparative philosophy can lead to the acquisition of knowledge. Consequently, if knowledge is in itself good, knowledge of a comparative sort is also an intrinsic good. This line of thought is clearly parasitical upon the production of a philosophical account of the intrinsic/extrinsic distinction.

But what if the thesis that knowledge is an intrinsic good is not accepted? Are there ways to justify comparative philosophy on an instrumentalist account by showing that comparative philosophy is a means to some good? If, as a matter of fact, comparative philosophy really does increase world understanding, then it is a means to some good (assuming that an increase in world understanding is of value).

In my view it is probably true that comparative philosophy in education can make a positive difference (however difficult it may be to quantify the difference) in the outlook of tomorrow's leaders. If anyone doubts this, then they are invited to mentally compare what the world probably would be like with a prior exposure to the beliefs of other cultures (of which comparative philosophy is one component) when negotiation is to take place on practical matters and what it probably would be like without such exposure. Since one component of successful negotiation is compromise and since compromise requires that one be able to identify and understand the interests of the other, it is likely that comparative philosophy will help in this regard.

However, a persistent critic of the value of comparative philosophy may be supposed: a sort of Cartesian "evil genius" bedeviling comparative philosophers, a spirit as powerful as deceitful, making comparative philosophers think that they are something when they are really nothing (in either some ontological or, more interestingly in the present case perhaps, an axiological sense of "nothing"). According to this comparative-fixated evil genius, comparative philosophers are so grandiose that they cannot see how mistaken they are in believing that they are doing the world a favor by philosophizing in a comparative manner.

The *cogito* will not rescue the comparative philosopher from the clutches of this particular evil genius, however, for it is not existence but value that is mainly at stake. Perhaps nothing can. Perhaps the mistake lies in the skepticism itself. For it should be clear that doubt requires grounds for doubt. So what are the grounds for doubt that comparative philosophy is valuable? Put in this way, the burden of proof shifts, and it is not clear that the skeptic has an answer.

B. *Attacking Asian Philosophy by the Use of Comparison and Contrast*

Those who follow what Edward Said has called "Orientalism" will tend to do comparative philosophy (or comparative art history, comparative religion, *etc.*) by exerting power over the other, where the other is construed by negation (*i.e.* as lacking some good-making properties), through the use of texts as instruments of codification and, by extension, control. This "Orientalism" may take the form of blatantly biased apologetics for a competing worldview such as Christianity or it may take subtler forms by describing the other in varying degrees of deficiency.

C. *Defending Asian Philosophy by the Use of Comparison and Contrast*

Sometimes comparative philosophy amounts to little more than a defence of one's own (or adopted) cultural perspective against all comers. When does one explain and when does one defend? There is a lot of overlap between these two, for one may explain in such a polemical manner that the explanation amounts to a defence.

D. *Combination Strategies*

Can one coherently attack and defend at once? Yes, by turns, and this dialectical understanding is likely to be more true to the facts than wooden attempts to freeze the phenomena in a diachronic ("pie-slice") view. It need not result in inconsistency, for the points attacked and defended will be different ones in a consistent employment of the approach. The combination strategy is a type which attacks and defends by turns, depending on the terrain, and is not driven by an overall urge towards either vilification or apotheosis.

E. *Is all philosophizing necessarily comparative?*

When one values something it is tempting to think that everyone else must do so as well. Thus one finds in the work of Paul Masson-Oursel the sweeping claim: "All judgment is comparison: every comparison is an interpretation of diversity by way of identity".[1] In this way the comparative philosopher is tempted to say that everyone else (surreptitiously or not) must be doing comparative philosophy. But this is an error. Wittgenstein in the *Tractatus* or Descartes in the *Meditations* do not have to turn out to be crypto-comparativists for one to find these works valuable.

Masson-Oursel has argued that progress in the sciences occurs when studies become comparative, "so philosophy cannot achieve positivity so long as its investigations are restricted to the thought of our own civilization".[2] Part of this is right—the emphasis on the potential value of comparative philosophy to enrich philosophy itself—but what is dubious is the underlying conception of philosophy as a positive science. One must ask: "is the acquisition of certainty possible or desirable in this matter?" An adequate understanding of the limits of philosophy will deflate pretensions of its becoming a sort of super-science. But Masson-Oursel does not share this understanding of the limits of philosophy, and that is why his contribution is not as important to those studying comparative philosophy as it would have otherwise been.

From Masson-Oursel's viewpoint, however, there is the danger that comparative philosophy might become a matter of "individual phantasy".[3] Here he seems to be arguing from a scientific view of philosophy against the spectre of Idealism. Raju also wishes to safeguard against fantasy, for in one of the two lead quotations with which this paper began, Raju states:

> The aim of comparative philosophy is to find out which problems of life are solved in which ways in the several traditions, and which aspects of life, when treated as basic hard facts, give rise to which philosophical problems and which kind of solutions.[4]

---

[1] Paul Masson-Oursel, *Comparative Philosophy* (London: Kegan Paul, Trench, Trubner and Co., 1926), p. 31.

[2] *Comparative Philosophy*, p. 33.

[3] *Comparative Philosophy*, p. 42.

[4] P.T. Raju, *Introduction to Comparative Philosophy* (Lincoln: University of Nebraska Press, 1962), p. 291.

In speaking thus of "basic hard facts" Raju, like Masson-Oursel before him, hopes to avoid making comparative philosophy an exercise in fantasy. But one might wonder whether (a) there is any neutral point of view from which to articulate such basic hard facts; (b) there is not already a distinction between writers of fantasy and philosophers— one that is built into the very process of being educated as a philoso- pher, such that it is in practice highly unlikely that a philosopher would lapse into fantasy rather than express considered viewpoints.

In short, perhaps both Masson-Oursel and Raju want something that cannot be had, i.e. (a) above; and are overly scrupulous in wor- rying about something that is an unreal doubt, i.e. (b) above. A cor- ollary of this is that comparative philosophy should be seen less as a science getting at the putative hard facts of the matter than as an art—more exactly, as an exercise in critical and creative thinking done by a particular individual with his or her own cultural moor- ings and background.

Eliot Deutsch has clearly seen that last point (called a corollary in my argument above). In the Preface to *Studies in Comparative Aesthetics*[5] he writes that aesthetic theory has often been pretentious in claim- ing or implying that aesthetic theory is not bound by its own histo- rical placement and is applicable to art-works wherever they are found. Deutsch observes that it is especially evident in the works of non-Western cultures that the big aesthetic theories (expression- communication and the like) are only adequate to explain one of art's possibilities and not the way art must always be.

III. SATISFACTIONS AND OBSTACLES

A. *Some Satisfactions of Comparative Philosophy at Its Best*

I am not here defending the view that comparative philosophy in a wholesale descriptive sense yields satisfactions, but am maintaining that at its normative best it may indeed yield satisfactions.

1. *Discovery—of Other and of Oneself*
That in discovering the other one discovers oneself in the process is a truism in comparative philosophical research. Some dangers or

---

[5] Eliot Deutsch, *Studies in Comparative Aesthetics* (Honolulu: University Press of Hawaii, 1972), Monograph of the Society for Asian and Comparative Philosophy, No. 2.

obstacles involved are that one spends so much time discovering the other that the other becomes oneself—loss of critical distance such that there is no longer any object of study and hence no academic inquiry; alternatively that one becomes immersed in a pseudo-scientific false neutrality which does not allow for the development of philosophically authentic selfhood; or that one lapses into either a totally negative or unduly optimistic view of the other which is one-sided and not dialectically true to life. Provided that one can conquer such obstacles it is indeed possible to have one's own assumptions illuminated by comparison and contrast with those of persons in other cultures. Worldview analysis can then occur with greater insight than before.[6]

2. *Knowledge*

Regardless of whether or not one holds that knowledge is an intrinsic good, acquiring knowledge through the study of comparative philosophy is one of its satisfactions. For it is surely satisfying to have and share knowledge, both for its own sake and instrumentally. Apart from any possible practical gain, there is just an in-itself value in comparative philosophy at its best.

3. *Affective Values*

There are also affective values: seeing students grow in conceptual horizons and self-understanding is one of them. Another is seeing colleagues or friends with whom one has a special intellectual rapport develop their ideas in comparative directions. Even the prospect of being a big fish in a small pond might be an affective value motivating one to become involved in the enterprise of comparative philosophy.

B. *Some Obstacles to Comparative Philosophy*

1. *The Problem of Translatability of Concepts*

It is clear from the fact that philosophy may be taught in a particular language such as English but be about Greek, German, French, Indian, Chinese, and Japanese philosophies (to mention but a few of the rich philosophical traditions of the world), that translatability of concepts in fact does occur. (It is not a precondition of comparative

---

[6] Ninian Smart, *Worldviews, cross-cultural explorations of human beliefs* (New York: Scribner's, 1983).

philosophy that every idea in one language has a precise linguistic equivalent in another.) The question, however, is not whether it occurs, but how exactly it does occur. More precisely, what are the conditions under which understanding the philosophy of another culture is possible? Linguistic competence is one such condition, but another is sensitivity to the context in which the ideas are expressed. Without sensitivity one has only a "wooden" over workman-like pedantic translation devoid of cultural depth and feeling. But what is meant by "context" here? Not just linguistic context of what phrases or words occur before and after a particular word or phrase; something more like "environment" must be fathomed—in that sense understanding "context" is essential for understanding the philosophy of another culture. This is so in one important sense of "understanding". And here again there is complexity, for there are degrees of understanding of the cultural environment of ideas. The question of to what degree understanding the environment of ideas is requisite for comparative philosophy is interpretive, difficult to quantify objectively, and hence does not admit of any precise once and for all resolution.

2. *The Problem of the Meaning and Identification of "the Same Problem"*
Eliot Deutsch shows an approach to comparative philosophy which I find attractive in *Studies in Comparative Aesthetics*. In three essays on particular points in the aesthetics of India, China and Japan Deutsch demonstrates how "the same problem" crops up in each of these Asian traditions when compared with Western ones. This is one of the most fruitful approach to comparative philosophy articulated to date. It has the merits of being tradition specific. Yet even here the issue can be raised: how does one know that one has "the same problem"—at which level of generality does one have to speak in order to avoid the extremes of such a high level of generality as to be vacuous or such a specific level as to have nothing to compare? And why does comparative philosophy appear uni-directional in Deutsch, with the West always learning from the East?

3. *The Problem of Making Significant Cross-cultural Judgments*
One problem is how to formulate significant cross-cultural judgments without letting bias dictate judgment (*i.e.* without reductionism). In the relevant sense, bias here is the prepossession of some object or point of view such that one does not respond impartially to whatever is presented in relation to that object or point of view. So if one

must find a particular "ism" in a form of Asian thought regardless of whatever counter-evidence exists in the texts—counter-evidence which, if taken seriously, would open up other and divergent vistas of inter-pretation—then one's perspective is indeed biased. But it is easier to describe bias than to root it out, and the idea that one has a totally unbiased perspective is itself a radical form of bias. So the objective should not be the illusory one of getting to some neutral, totally objective point of view (whatever exactly that would be like in human understanding), but rather to be as free as possible from contrived points of view that are overridingly biased.

C. *How the Satisfactions and Obstacles Mentioned Arise in Comparative Philosophy*

The satisfactions arise when one is most keenly sensitive to the indig-enous texture of the worldviews studied and at the same time applies critical thinking in ways that illuminate rather than distort the philo-sophical system being studied. To be a true aesthetician, one should be a discriminating *sahrdaya* (lit., "one of similar heart"). In Buddhis-tic context, what this means is to be found exemplified in Nolan Pliny Jacobson's *Buddhism: the Religion of Analysis*; in Hindu context, it is to be found in Ramakrishna Puligandla's *An Encounter with Aware-ness*. These works are among the worthiest works of our time in South Asian comparative philosophy.

IV. CONCLUSIONS

In this paper I have defended the view that comparative philosophy is only one form that philosophizing across cultures can take; that attacking, defending, and doing both by turns are all possible forms of comparative philosophy. But I stop short of maintaining that all philosophy is necessarily comparative. The satisfactions of compara-tive philosophy include discovery, knowledge, and affective values. Obstacles to comparative philosophy include translatability, the mean-ing of "the same problem," and forming significant cross-cultural judgments without overriding biases.

The juxtaposition of the lead quotations with which this paper began—quotations from Masson-Oursel and Raju on comparative philosophy—invite philosophical reflection on method. Both the confrontational taxonomic approach of Masson-Oursel and the synthetic common denominator approach of Raju have difficulties. The problem-oriented approach of Deutsch is preferable, provided that there is no assumption that the direction of philosophical gain is always necessarily from East to West.

Although it is too much to claim that all philosophy is necessarily comparative, it is probably true that comparative philosophy in the curriculum can make a positive difference (however difficult it may be to quantify the difference) in the outlook of tomorrow's leaders.

Provided that one can conquer the obstacles discussed in this paper, it is indeed possible to have one's own assumptions illuminated by comparison and contrast with those of persons in other cultures. Worldview analysis can then occur with greater insight than before and the satisfactions of comparative philosophy may predominate.

Comparative philosophy is like a dangerous frontier sport for big game hunters who go beyond parochial boundaries. It is not for all philosophers. But neither is truth in all its fullness. Comparative philosophy is a safari into the hinterlands of consciousness, an excursion fraught with dangers, but one capable at its best of expanding conceptual horizons by an openness to the other. Comparative philosophy opens up a conceptual space, distinct from Masson-Oursel's dreaded "individual phantasy", wherein the philosophical problems of the other may not be so different from one's own as a superficial look might suggest. In the end if both East and West can approach philosophical issues with a readiness to consider with care both the phraseology of the problem and all manner of solutions, then the human world of intellectual inquiry will be enriched.

As some sectors of philosophy coalesce with Asian ways of thinking near the close of the 20th century (to take but two examples, Buddhist feminism and animal rights ethics), comparative philosophy will probably continue to find new sources of inspiration from the East while selectively drawing upon Western philosophical traditions as well. Going back to the juxtaposition of quotations with which we began, it may be asked whether comparative philosophy results in a confrontation of ideas (Masson-Oursel) or the discovery of a common denominator (Raju)? My position is that neither stalemate nor homogenization is the necessary outcome of comparative philosophy if one thinks of it as a problem-oriented enterprise in which both imaginative sympathy and critical acumen are at work.

UNDERSTANDING THE SELF'S OTHERS

Richard Shusterman

I

The quest for a better understanding of the culturally other, even
when it is quite sincere, often contains the further (and sometimes
primary) desire of better understanding oneself. My paper will concentrate on this idea of understanding the other as a necessary means
of understanding oneself. Since the concepts of self and other are
interdependent, I think it could also be conversely argued that a
knowledge of oneself is necessary for understanding the other. For
example, we must know (at least some of) one's cultural prejudices
and points of view in order to grasp the other more accurately and
better assess both her similarity to and difference from us. We understand anything in terms of a field, and the self is as much the background field of the other as the other is that of the self.

In choosing to concentrate here on knowledge of the culturally
other as a means of knowing oneself, I realize that this choice may
suggest the narcissism of contemporary American culture (philosophy
and myself included). But it also expresses the Delphic injunction "to
know oneself" that set the entire course of Western philosophy. I readily confess, however, that the idea of searching for self-understanding
through understanding of the other characterizes my current philosophical and existential project, indeed my actual life-conditions. I
am writing this paper in Berlin, where I have come to learn (once
again) a foreign language and culture, that for all its painful otherness (which I suffer daily), is helping me to discover who I am.

What is perhaps most interesting is that the discovery of self through
comprehension of the other proceeds not only by way of contrast
but by way of integrative participation. In short, we come to understand ourself better by discovering the cultural others in our self.
Sometimes these others are already deeply there in one's cultural self
and just need to be uncovered, but sometimes they are lurking more
in the margins as potential dimensions waiting to be incorporated
into the self. It should be clear from these remarks that I view the

self not as a fixed, universal entity but as something always in the process of change, whose unity derives not from an unchanging static core but from stability and coherence in transformation.[1]

It should also be clear that I think that speculation about problems of understanding the self and other should be illuminated through concrete empirical experience of the self in encounter with others, and not from merely abstract, formal philosophical analysis. This is why I allow myself to speak from my personal experience.

There is a prejudice in academic philosophy about talking about such concrete details, since they are contingent while philosophy is often alleged to deal only with the necessary. Though this repudiation of the personal and contingent may be justified in certain domains of philosophy, it hardly seems wise to preclude personal experience from informing our philosophical inquiry into questions of self-understanding. Even if it is banished on the level of explicit discourse, it surely motivates us beneath the surface. Why engage in the philosophical question of the cultural understanding of self and other, if not out of the personal experience of inadequate understanding and the desire to prove our understanding not only in theory but in personal concrete practice?

II

1. I begin, however, with the abstract point of the conceptual interdependence of the very identity of self and other, whose result is that knowledge of the self presupposes some understanding of the other. Through the logic of complementarity—whose recognition in the West goes back at least as far as Heraclitus and whose greatest modern champion is surely Hegel—anything or everything is defined by its others. The limits of any entity, hence its individuation, are determined by what lies outside those limits, by what constitutes the environing field in which these limits can be constructed. To understand oneself as self implies a knowledge that there is something outside the self, an other, in contrast to which the self can be defined and distinguished.

---

[1] My account of the self and its (often problematic) unity through transformation is developed in Ch. 9 of *Pragmatist Aesthetics* (Oxford: Blackwell, 1992), and in *Practising Philosophy: Pragmatism and the Philosophical Life*, forthcoming from Routledge.

Our environing fields are social and cultural as well as spatiotemporal. They are neither very precisely nor rigidly defined, but rather change with the changing elements in the field, the field being as much a construction of its elements and their varying positions as those elements are a function of their place (*i.e.* their interrelations with other elements) in the field. The result is that one's self-definition and sense of self are differently constructed in different contexts in light of the distinctive nature of the others who constitute the self's field. One is more conscious of being a man when one suddenly finds oneself in a group whose other members are all women. This logic of complementarity and contextuality also seems to govern one's cultural definition.

I know this from personal experience as an American-Israeli binational. Since English was my mother tongue, I was defined there as being of "Anglo-Saxon" origin, while in America I am defined as Jewish in contrast to Anglo-Saxon ethnicity. As an Israeli, one is geographically Asian, though culturally very close to Europe. Hebrew, however, is far from a European language. In the East/West division of culture—a division as false as most binary oppositions, Israeli culture seems to inhabit (and suffer) the punctuating slash.

As a student at Oxford, I would vacillate between seeing myself as an Israeli and as an American, though a close Sikh friend of mine had a third view of my ethnic identity. As only a second-generation American, whose parents came from Eastern Europe, I was neither American nor Israeli but an Eastern European. This shows that the contextuality of the field in which both self and other are reciprocally constituted (and hence reciprocally understood) can be historically as well as synchronically constructed. The number of different possible contexts is thus greatly multiplied. In a world where rapidity of physical transit and of information flow enables (and compels) us to shift our contextual fields quite rapidly, it is not surprising that our sense of identity has become more problematic. This problem, often discussed in terms of the disintegration of the subject, is a salient theme in postmodern thought.

2. Beyond the purely logical point of the complementarity of self/other and its argument that self-understanding requires the other because the very definition of self does, there is a second, more concrete way in which understanding the other is a necessary tool for understanding the self. The other provides a medium or dialogical partner through which the self can see and test its limits. This

theme is known throughout the fictional literature of diverse cultures, where the protagonist, in order to find himself, must venture into foreign lands or into the wilderness (a *natural* other which by being other to one's indigenous culture and so requiring different behaviour amounts to being a *cultural* other as well).

But philosophy also recognizes how the encounter with the culturally other is needed to awaken and enrich one's sense of self. Gadamer, for instance, insists on this point in discussing our prejudices, which he treats as enabling as well as limiting (and even enabling because they are limiting). "It is impossible to make ourselves aware of [our prejudice] while it is constantly operating unnoticed, but only when it is, so to speak, stimulated." An encounter with a culturally other, which for him includes "the encounter with a text from the past, can provide this stimulus" and so "make conscious the prejudices governing our own understanding" and constituting our self".[2]

But encounter with the culturally other, including the textual other, does not simply define the self and promote self-understanding by mere contrast. It also does so through accretion of absorption. In other words, the self does not only determine itself against the contrasting other but reshapes and enriches itself by assimilating or appropriating aspects of the other and consequences of the interchange with her. Through this process of self-definition and self-development by self-transformational absorption of the other, an individual (in Nietzsche's phrase) "becomes what one is". In this role, as well, the culturally other can be represented by a text as well as a "real-life" encounter, even if the familiarity of textuality (particularly through the medium of translation into a familiar language greatly reduces the degree of the encounter's otherness). We can take T.S. Eliot as a witness of how one's self is defined and transformed through wide-reading in alien cultural worlds, which can also include the very different historical cultures involved in the history of one's own cultural tradition.

In trying to fully understand a literary work (as in trying to fully understand another person), one must to some extent identify with the other and project oneself into her point of view. As Eliot describes the act of reading a powerful author, "you have to give yourself up, and then recover yourself; but the self recovered is never the

---

[2] H.G. Gadamer, *Truth and Method* (New York: Crossroad, 1982), p. 266.

same as the self before it was given".[3] When we are immature and read a powerful author, Eliot explains, "what happens is a kind of inundation, of invasion of the underdeveloped personality by the stronger personality" of the author. But the more experience and wider reading we assimilate, the more well-rounded, tempered, and sturdy our belief structures become, and thus the less likely we are to be one-sidedly possessed by any one author or foreign culture.

Moreover, since the views of different authors (or different cultures) are often incompatible, digesting a variety of them makes us critically compare and weigh their opposing views. This not only develops and sharpens our critical consciousness and power, but elicits the formation and expression of our own selfhood in our comparative assessment of and ordering of the different views. Wide reading and experience of the culturally other are valuable, therefore, "not as a kind of hoarding" or accumulation of information, but "because in the process of being affected by one powerful personality [or culture] after another, we cease to be dominated by any one or by any small number. The very different views of life, cohabiting in our minds, affect each other, and our own personality asserts itself and finds each a place in some arrangement peculiar to ourself."

In short, our encounter with the culturally other not only enlarges the self with the experience and beliefs of others but, by providing a rich and articulate background of comparison an contrast, enables us to form, define, and assert our own distinctive identity with greater richness and clarity. Hence Eliot insists that "we make the effort to enter those worlds of poetry in which we are alien" so that we can better understand the world and culture we identify as most our own, but do so without falling into a parochial, cultural chauvinism.

Eliot practiced what he preached. A native of St. Louis Missouri, he absorbed himself deeply in French as well as Indian culture, before thoroughly projecting himself into English culture which he eventually made his own by being naturalized as a British subject and

---

[3] The quotations from Eliot here come from Stephen Spender's "Remembering Eliot", in A. Tate (ed.), *T.S. Eliot: The Man and his Work* (New York: Delacorte Press, 1966), p. 56; and from T.S. Eliot, *Essays: Ancient and Modern* (London: Faber, 1936), pp. 102–3; and "Poetry and Propaganda", *Booman*, 70 (1930), p. 602. For a full discussion of Eliot's views on reading and culture, see Richard Shusterman, *T.S. Eliot and the Philosophy of Criticism* (London and New York: Duckworth and Columbia University Press, 1988), and "Eliot and Adorno on the Critique of Culture", *Theory, Culture & Society*, 19 (1933), pp. 25–52.

converting to Anglicanism. Eliot's fascination with Indian philosophy is particularly interesting with respect to the issue of understanding self and other through projection into the culturally alien. His example suggests that there are practical limits beyond which one's understanding and absorption of the other threatens to destroy one's stable, familiar sense of self. Eliot claims to have given up his study of Indian philosophy because the task of bringing himself to understand it in its utmost depth would have involved transforming himself into a very different person, which for practical and personal reasons he did not wish to be.

Self-expanding, self-testing encounters with the other are thus not only enriching but can be dangerously destabilizing. What is easy and limitless in theory is often painfully stressful and decapacitating in practice. This is a lesson that refugees in culturally alien cultures could teach us. My conclusion is not to eschew cultural travel but simply to recognize its risks and limits, so as to make the travel made most useful. This is a pragmatic way of putting what can also be aesthetically formulated. We should only seek cultural variety for enriching and defining the self to the extent that such variety can be held in a satisfying unity. As with other aesthetic questions, no fixed rules can be prescribed for the ideal balance. Taste, if not also a certain measure of genius, will be required to find this optimum.[4]

III

I come now to a third way in which understanding the culturally other promotes a better understanding of the self: not by mere conceptual or concrete contrast nor by enrichment through incorporation of the other and its means of comparative expression of the self. This third case is where our cultural selves are in fact actually composed of elements of the culturally other that we have so far failed to recognize or realize in their otherness and thus have not fully understood. Here by coming to understand the other we come to understand ourselves by understanding that other in ourselves.

Typically, we take the "selfness" of the self for granted (*i.e.* its purity, unity, and homogeneity) ignoring that our cultural self is often

---

[4] I analyze the diverse methods and problems of the aesthetico-ethical project of self-construct in *Pragmatist Aesthetics*.

partly constituted by elements of what we all too simplistically take as the radically cultural other. We fail to realize the cultural others in ourselves in two different ways: either by simply failing to recognize the culturally other dimension of these elements or failing to redeem the richness of this dimension even when we recognized its otherness.

To clarify these points let us consider some examples. Western philosophy tends to distinguish itself sharply from both Asian philosophy and from African philosophy (to the meagre extent that it is even ready to acknowledge and respect this latter). Yet it can be argued that Western philosophy is deeply indebted to Asian and African philosophical traditions, and thus already has these radical philosophical others incorporated within. I am not here claiming the truth of the "Black Athena" theory and other theories that seek to trace the origins of Western philosophy to non-Western sources. My point is simple that if they are true, we have a case where failure to recognize these cultural others in one's own Western philosophical tradition constitutes a lack in one's own cultural self-understanding. Moreover, even if the case for origins cannot be made, a clear case can be made for the Indian influence not only in modern continental philosophy but also in early Greek philosophy. Diogenes Laertius, for example, suggests that Democritus learned not only from the Indian Gymnosophists but also from the Egyptians.[5]

For an example far outside the realm of philosophical culture, consider American "Country Music". Frequently expressing the most patriotic and chauvinistic sentiments, it regards itself as pure, "all-American" music and sharply distinguishes itself from Black Music and other ethnic music. However, Country Music is in fact deeply rooted in the black musical tradition of the United States. Most of its early, influential stars, like Jimmy Rogers, learned their skills and style from black performers. This was originally so evident that Country Music was initially classified in record stores and in the professional music magazines as ethnic music along with black music. The steel string guitar sound, regarded by fans as characteristic of "pure country", was in fact imported from Hawaii as late as the 1940's.

It has taken very little time for these foreign ethnic roots to be

---

[5] Diogenes Laertius, *Lives of Eminent Philosophers*, Vol. I (Cambridge, Mass.: Harvard University Press, 1931), p. 445.

completely forgotten by those who identify themselves as country fans
and protectors of the country tradition. They have been erased in
popular consciousness not simply by time but by the drive to create
a model of authenticity based on an imaginary cultural pureness,
rather than pursuing a model of authenticity based on the actual
fruitful facts of cultural interpenetration. Underlying this drive for
pureness is the false assumption that cultural identity cannot tolerate
the inclusion of elements from another culture, an assumption that
logically excludes both the very idea of hybrid culture and the simple
historical fact that most cultures are hybrid and historically constructed
and defined through dialogue with each other.

A fuller self-understanding of someone committed to the Country
Music cultural tradition requires realizing its foreign roots or its
incorporated elements of the culturally other. The same, I would
argue, goes for our self-understanding as Western philosophers. Realizing the other in our cultural selves can simply mean recognizing
the historical fact of these other elements. But such bare recognition
does not seem sufficient for a true understanding of the other in
ourselves and hence of ourselves. We need to rcognize the other not
simply to acknowledge but to learn and assimilate that other, to grasp
and redeem consciously what previously belonged only blindly and
implicitly to us. This calls for a personal discipline of cross-cultural
study, whose limits seem ever expanding.

I am currently engaged in that discipline and the quest to redeem
the culturally other in myself. As an American pragmatist philosopher,
I recognize how much American pragmatism incorporates German
philosophical culture and how closely it relates to the work of the
Frankfurt School. As a Jewish intellectual, I recognize how much of
this cultural identity has been constituted and informed by German
culture. Even my family name bears a German cultural imprint,
though I have no known German ancestors. While I long regarded
German culture as not only foreign but hostile, it has undeniably
marked my cultural identity in many ways, even in something as
personal as my proper name. To give these markings clearer meaning
requires a fuller knowledge of the culture and language that left these
marks. To know myself means learning that culturally other. This
can be a difficult and painful process. But the philosophical quest for
self-knowledge has never been perceived as effortless and trouble-
free, even if its end is often seen as peace and tranquility.

CULTURAL OBJECTS

Kalyan Sen Gupta

I

What are cultural objects? Are they natural objects but only different in guise? Or, have they any identity of their own as distinct from natural objects? All such broodings invite some quibbles about "culture" in order to locate cultural objects in their proper setting. And here R.A.D. Grant's elegant analysis may come to our great benefit.[1] Roughly Grant has identified the following distinct, though related, meanings of culture:

(a) Culture, generically, is the distinctive characteristic of man as opposed to animals. It implies the whole pattern of human thought and behaviour which is not genetically but socially transmitted. Animal behaviour or interaction is more or less rigid or species-determined and biologically adaptive response to a relatively constant environment. Human behaviour, on the other hand, has indeed a biological foundation (humanity being an animal species), but this does not mean that human behaviour can be explained biologically. For man, as Rabindranath puts it, is an angel of surplus,[2] possessing a dimension of self-conscious meaning and purpose, and so his behaviour is not a mere rigid, mechanical, biological response to his environment but shows infinite variability. Through his diverse interaction, man continually modifies his environment and in this process continually recreates himself. Taken in this way culture is *nurture* as contrasted with biological needs, refinement or reformation of human nature through manifold interactions with environment.

(b) Cultures, specifically, as defined by their differences not from nature but from each other denote a distinctive historic group—a society—sharing a specific order of rules, goals and symbols circumscribed by a tradition. In other words, a culture means a specific

---

[1] R.A.D. Grant, "Culture" in *A Companion to Aesthetics*, (ed.) David Cooper (Oxford: Basil Blackwell, 1992), pp. 99–104. Incidentally I have extensively used this *Companion* for my paper.
[2] Rabindranath Tagore, *The Religion of Man* (London: Allen and Unwin, 1970).

society of men "with all its tools, possessions and characteristic ways of and conceptions of life". In this sense, every culture has a distinctive flavour of its own not shared by other cultures. Thus cultures are to be judged only with reference to their avowed or implicit aims, goals and purposes.

(c) Culture underlines the ideational component of a society (*i.e.* ideas, beliefs, sensitivities and values shared by all the members of a society) as opposed to its political, economic and technical structures.

(d) Culture also means the "arts" and the "higher" aesthetic realm. High culture in this sense is fundamentally "a quality of taste and sensibility", "a product of an appropriate education, formal and otherwise", "an unending process of development both in the individual undergoing it and in the collective product", "a thing unavoidably local in its immediate origin and perhaps in its ultimate loyalties, but generally outward looking". This high art has often been held in high esteem since the Romantic period as providing unity, meaning and value in experience that was once the prerogative of religion, before it was disrobed by the disenchanted world outlook of science.

In this paper I am going to pick out "culture" in sense (d) as referring to the aesthetic realm of art. To put my stance in the words of Rabindranath: "It is art that defines or characterizes the domain of human culture. It is here man fundamentally expresses himself and becomes himself".[3] Obviously cultural objects, as I take it, are art objects like painting, music or poetry which depend on the existence and distinctive activity of human beings. This does not, however, disown the other related meanings of culture. For art objects are expressions of surplus in man, and are informed by traditions, beliefs, practices, sensitivities and values that the members of a society share jointly. As John Dewey presents it:

> Works of art are inescapably located within the historical and cultural contexts of their appreciators as well as of their creators ... (so that) instead of pointing to a timeless realm, they reveal human historicity.[4]

---

[3] Rabindranath Tagore, *Sahityer Pathe, Rabindra Rachanabali*, Vol. 14 (West Bengal: West Bengal Government Publication, 1961), p. 444.

[4] T.M. Alexander, *John Dewey's Theory of Art, Experience and Nature* (New York: State University of New York Press, 1987), p. 188.

II

After this preliminary about cultural objects (or what we have identified as art objects) we may return to the question on their status vis-a-vis that of natural objects. Our response will take the following shape. Art objects may be rooted in natural objects; but the forms of nature do no more than stimulate the artist to create a new world.[5] It will be a grave mistake to think that the formal ordering of the art object reproduces the order of nature. Art objects have their special harmony of lines, colours, meanings, life and movement not to be confused with the order of nature. They are not *found* but *created* or transformed into human imagery through constant touches of the artist's sentiments and imagination. Moreover, we may ascribe stylistic qualities to them, but such an ascription to a natural object will be at best metaphorical. A brute tree has no style, though a picture of it may have, since it is a creation and not a mere representation or an imitation.

To continue our point in a slightly different way, we may invoke Rabindranath's celebrated distinction between "reality" or "truth" of art and fact. A fact is one we know or perceive dispassionately by standing apart from it. But the reality or truth of art is infused with human involvement, his in-depth feeling, imagination and intimate experience or realization. Let us hear it from Rabindranath himself:

> What we call literature and fine arts are imbued with the profound joy of human realization. . . .[6]

Or:

> Actually speaking, art is encounter with the form of nature not as it is, but as it is constantly taking shape within human heart. Art is the music that nature evokes in man.[7]

---

[5] Perhaps it is obvious that I have taken natural object to mean any object, physical or biological. Now even if we assume that art object is only an alternative way of seeing natural object in order to narrow down the distance between the two, the point still remains that the content of the two is different. This is admirably put by Rabindranath in the following words: "The admission of a donkey into a drawing room is violently opposed; yet there is no prohibition against its finding a place in a picture which may be admiringly displayed on a drawing-room wall". This is a quotation from *The Religion of Man*, p. 55.

[6] Rabindranath Tagore—*Sahitya, Rabindra Rachanabali*, Vol. 14, p. 353.

[7] Rabindranath Tagore—*Sahitya, Rabindra Rachanabali*, Vol. 13 (West Bengal: West Bengal Government Publication, 1961), p. 739.

The point of Rabindranath is that art reveals not the world's physical structure, but its human significance. Its truths are enacted and confirmed in our consciousness. In other words, we take nature as the mere given; culture as the humanly contrived. Consider, for example, (a) chair, and (b) Van Gogh's famous painting, Yellow Chair. In a sense both (a) and (b) are given, but the ways they are given are completely different. (a) is a concrete thing which gives itself completely and gives itself to my awareness as it is. Similarly (b) is also given but not in the same sense as (a). What is given in a painting or a song does not stand apart from the way or manner it is given. A natural or physical object like a chair may also exist in a non-relational context. But Van Gogh's famous Yellow Chair "exists" or acquires meaning only in the context of the artist's intense experience or realization. A simple chair out there is transformed into an art object "only when", in the words of Dewey, "it lives in some individualized experience".[8] We do not ordinarily look at our familiar chair or table as though we see in it some indepth mystery or light that was never on earth before. But the artist sees in it a possibility or significance in his creative involvement in the object. It is quite meaningless to speak of possibilities with regard to an ordinary chair, though we can meaningfully talk about the possible ways of using them. And this makes the difference between our ordinary experience of natural objects and our aesthetic experience. An art object like a painting has no readymade unchanging essence but "is revealed everytime it is aesthetically experienced".[9] Its meaning changes and it is shot with different possibilities under the impact of sensitive and imaginative attention. Even the artist himself finds different meanings in it at different days and hours and in different stages of his development. An art object unlike a natural object exists not because of any core of "monotonous identity" but because of its capacity to renew itself under the imaginative gaze of the artist. Thus an ordinary chair is only given to our senses as such; but it is not anchored in any creative involvement that discerns several possibilities in it. On the contrary, an art object is given not as such but only in the context of emergent possibilities or meanings under contemplation of varying degrees of acuity and intenseness.

Another way of presenting the distinctive profile of art object may

---

[8] J. Dewey, *Art as Experience* (New York: Capricorn Books, 1958), p. 108.
[9] *Art as Experience.*

go on in the following way. We have a certain picture of the world as consisting of brute facts where the paradigm of knowledge is knowledge of brute facts. This paradigm ranges from "This stone is next to that stone" to "Bodies attract with a force inversely proportional to the square of the distance between them and directly proportional to the product of their mass". But they share the common feature that the concepts which constitute the knowledge are essentially physical. Natural sciences represent the model for systematic knowledge of this kind, and knowledge of this kind is generally concerned with empirical observations recording sense experience.[10] In contrast art objects are sustained by what Joseph Margolis would call a *covering institution*,[11] *i.e.* their existence presupposes the existence of certain human institutions or certain cultural (artistic) traditions. Around every work of art there is a tradition or an artistic context. We recognize some work of Picasso done in the cubist style only against the background of the whole range of cubist paintings. What sanctifies Guernica and other works in its class is the tradition around them. Hindusthani classical music with its various acts of selecting, discovering and arranging exists within the well-defined musical tradition of *sruti*, *svara* and *melah* on which *ragas* are based. In fact, no art object can be identified independent of its continuity and significant resemblance in many respects with other art objects of a particular tradition. Hence it is futile to see any painting or music in isolation from its surrounding. That is why creation of appreciation of art objects depend upon upbringing, schooling, formal or informal in the tradition from which they stem.

Nonetheless we should remember one crucial thing. A tradition has no fixed and compelling structure which an artist is to follow blindly. This will impede creativity and originality. In fact, there have been periods in the history of art when artists have felt the need of dispensing with existing tradition and starting afresh, creating a new tradition thereby. Thus Picasso as a founder of cubism gave birth to a new tradition. Lecorbusier explicitly advocated an architecture based on the mathematical and geometrical purity of the "house machine" by eliminating all "dead" concepts with regard to the house. And this enables us to see some reason in a post modernist's urge for

---

[10] J.R. Searle, *Speech Acts* (Cambridge: Cambridge University Press, 1970), p. 50.
[11] Joseph Margolis, *Culture and Cultural Entities* (Dordrecht: Reidel, 1984), p. 98.

fluidization which speaks not in favour of one, but of multiplicity of culture or art traditions.

There is also another related way to formulate the distinction between natural and art objects. Any art tradition is rooted in a social milieu; and art objects are always addressed to a receptive or appreciative community of persons. In his art, the artist expresses not only himself but also his society. His attitude and response to life, his sense of value which stimulate his creation are more or less influenced or sustained by the practices and beliefs of his society. This, however, should be taken with some caution. A society is not manifested in cultural or art object directly in the form of causal relationship. This becomes evident when we find that we have not only objects of A type but also of B and C types in the same society X. For example, in the bourgeois social system we have not only sexual or dialectical art but also religious or mythological art. Thus the relation between a society and art is not causal. Nor should we entertain with Millard Meiss a general formula regarding the emergence of a form of art under the impact of a particular social condition. Meiss wanted to show that religious art flourished in Florence and Vienna in the 14th century because of the various social catastrophes in those two areas from 1340 to 1350. Similarly, war, famine and communal riot left their conspicuous mark on Bengali literature in the 1940's. Examples of this sort can be multiplied; but it is difficult to ascertain whether such examples are accidental or really confirm the general formula (theory) of Meiss.[12] Nevertheless some influence of society on the artist cannot be denied. And this social feature, we may say, has no counterpart in the world of objects.

III

When however, we talk about *cultural* or art object, the obvious implication is that we insist not so much on the creative person as on his product. Of course, it is not that the creative person can be delinked from his product. Indeed, as we have pointed out earlier, art object cannot be isolated from the imaginative involvement of the artist. But the question is: which one is logically prior—the artist

---

[12] Cf. Debiprasad Chattopadhyaya, "Artist Art Object and Society", *Rupa, Rasa and Sundara* (Calcutta: Riddhi—India, 1981), pp. 1–13.

or his product? And if we do not raise much dust, we can see that it is the art product which is logically prior. The reason is not far to seek. We cannot identify a creative man and his creative process independent of the object he has created. On the contrary, the person is a creative one and his intention is also a creative one only in the light of our assessment of the product itself as a creative product. A person is creative only because he has succeeded in creating an object that is accepted by people to be creative. This point gains its strength and substance from the following observation of Rabindranath:

> . . . the person who only looks at the sky but remains silent like it can hardly be called a poet. Poetry is nothing but *expression*: what one has in one's mind matters little to us. It is said that people desire sweets, but they do not find much pleasure in guessing what sweets are stored for them inside. It is more urgent that they should have the sweets directly.[13]

Thus what counts more is the product and not what is going on within the mind. If Rabindranath and Keats were mute, if Beethoven was deaf and dumb and without his immemorable symphonies could we reasonably call them creative giants?

Now if the above account works well, we are again confronted with another question: if an art object is not identified via the artist, how to identify it? The answer is that we can explain and identify the creativity of an art object only against the background of prior art objects by evaluating whether it resembles in important respects with the prior products, or whether it has filled up the gap that was lacking in the prior products. This also accounts for the emergence of a new tradition. The artist sees in the prior products a gap, a possibility that was not taken care of in the tradition in which they figured. Thus begins a new tradition that breaks, in important ways, with the tradition out of which they grow. And this interaction with the pre-existent tradition, this way of capturing an unrealized possibility, it should be pointed out, involves active imagination which ensures the real possibility of human freedom.[14]

Now we turn to a crucial problem, the problem of convergence between the defacto plurality of artistic modes or traditions. It is conspicuous that the artistic tradition of Madhubani paintings in Bihar

---

[13] Rabindranath Tagore, *Rabindra Rachanabali*, Vol. 13, p. 740.
[14] Cf. Larry Briskman, "Creative Product and Creative Process in Science and Art" (*Inquiry*, 23).

is different from the tradition of Rajasthani style of painting; and both these traditions are different from the Western tradition of cubist paintings as pioneered by Picasso. Similarly the tradition of music of North India is different from that of South India; and both these traditions are unlike a music tradition of the West. Art objects depend on the norms and practices of different cultural horizons. One thing is clear from this. We live in a world of cultural pluralism, and we cannot simply overlook the variety and richness of different historical strands of culture. And this recognition is very crucial, since it leads to the demonopolization of any particular cultural or artistic tradition, and prevents us from acting in an imperialistic manner towards art traditions other than our own. This pluralistic scene makes us modest seeking not to impose the gamut of an Indian tradition upon an Western one, but to recognize and learn from each other in mutuality, respect and trust. But at the same time recognition of this pluralism makes the problem of appreciation more acute. In view of such an enormous plurality of traditions, how can we hope to appreciate or capture one tradition from another? How can we learn from each other?

One of the well-known strategies for inter and intra-cultural appreciation is what Lyotard, calls *meta-narrative* or *grand narrative* which appeals to something like *core self* or *human nature*. It is said that since artistic creations follow from some basic human structure or from some fundamental emotive and feeling patterns of man, there is a core which unifies the different traditions of art. Now if the different narratives of artistic compositions follow from premises which everybody will acknowledge, this will facilitate our appreciation of different cultural traditions. But this insistence on something which stands beyond history and institutions is not perhaps much rewarding for it ignores the phenomenological fact that what counts as a cultural tradition is relative to historical circumstances. In fact, it looks a bit extravagant to relate the historicity of art narratives to some unhistorical core without showing how this relation is possible. But then we face two options: (1) Either we escape relativism by cleaving to unhistorical human essence; (2) or else we buy a *Verstehen* approach at the cost of relativism. We do not espouse (1) since it denounces the historicity of art world which is derived from the practices of the members of a given society. But this denial of ahistorical or transcendental cultural platform does not mean that we espouse (2) or crude subjectivism of the plurality of art practices. We do not entertain the complacent belief that our cultural traditions are entirely incommensurable with others. Rather we would opt for an alternative stance.

First, we should note that the commensurability between different cultural traditions takes place not at the cognitive level. For the artist does not intend to state a proposition. Even if he is influenced by the men, situations and events of his time, this informative or propositional content does not explain why his creation is a work of art. So appreciation of his work of art is not understanding or getting the factual content right—the factual content that may influence or activate his work of art. Communication as we normally understand it is not applicable to art. That is why Langer observes:

> ... the concept of art as a kind of communication. ... I think is a misleading notion.[15]

Therefore what counts more in art appreciation is not understanding but imagination. Unfortunately Western philosophers, being preoccupied by logocentric concerns were rather sceptical about imagination. Their attitudes toward imagination far from claiming it as the "Queen of the faculties" like Poe and Baudelaire range rather from distrust to disgust. In the face of this tradition of condemnation and neglect we should like to side with Vico and Santayana who insist on a more judicious treatment of imagination than it has usually received. Of course, this is not to affirm the rather extravagant claim of Anatole France that "to know is nothing at all, to imagine is everything". But we should acknowledge "the amplitude and intrinsic power of imagining" or recognize it as significant in its own right.

With this accent on imagination we may now point out that to appreciate a given work of art is not merely to perceive it passively as a spectator but to "extend", in the words of Casey, "our aesthetic experience from its initial perceptual base onto an imaginative plane". To give an example taking it from Casey:

> I am at the opera listening to Prokofieff's *War and Peace*. Although I am acutely aware of the perceived operatic spectacle, both auditory and visual, I find myself drifting in a state of mind that is qualitatively distinguishable from my perception of the sounds and sights before me. ... In this state I embroider in various ways on what I perceive:

---

[15] Susane K. Langer, *Feeling and Form* (London: Routledge & Kegan Paul, 1967), p. 410.

the Natasha that I see and hear on the stage becomes part of an invisible drama that carries on the actual stage production in imaginative terms.[16]

Similarly, we can appreciate a new art movement even in our culture, a new and different way of speaking other than one to which we are accustomed only by developing artistic sensibility and imaginative ability which enable us to see some significance, some possibility not belonging to our accustomed tradition. We find in a new tradition an answer to a problem inherent in the background but not answerable within the background. Likewise, appreciation of the cultural tradition of the West takes place when with our increased artistic sensitivity and imagination we capture in it a meaning or possibility not found in our tradition which helps to redescribe our tradition in a new light in terms of what it lacks. For example, Indian music, particularly Hindusthani classical music makes little use of harmony. For according to the fabric of Hindusthani music, every *svara* or note is beautiful in itself, and so it should not be swamped in the simultaneous playing of other notes. But this harmony is a distinctive feature of Western music. We can with profit introduce the beauty of this distinctive Western feature (amenable to acute artistic or imaginative awareness) in our tradition to fill up what it lacks. Rabindranath felt the need of this redescription when he holds: "We shall have to encounter the question whether harmony of European music can be incorporated into our music tradition. Our initial response may be against this incorporation. But ultimately this initial reaction is utterly dogmatic. This will be equivalent to saying that surgery prevalent in Europe since it is Western, cannot be applied to the body of a Bengalee".[17] Thus the goal of art appreciation is clear. It is, in the words of Rorty, "to seek ever new identities" and "not to get stuck with the one you started with".[18] It is the attempt to enlarge our imagination, to widen our self.

---

[16] Edwards S. Casey, *Imagining, A Phenomenological Study* (Bloomington & London: Indiana University Press, 1979), p. 140.

[17] Rabindranath Tagore, "Sangiter Mukti" in *Sangit, Rabindra Rachanabali*, Vol. 14, p. 901.

[18] Anindita Niyogi Balslev, *Cultural Otherness: Correspondence with Richard Rorty* (Shimla: Indian Institute of Advanced Study in collaboration with Munshiram Manoharlal, New Delhi, 1991), p. 19. Also R. Rorty, *Contingency, Irony and Solidarity* (Cambridge: Cambridge University Press, 1990). Moreover, I am indebted to Ranjan K. Ghosh, Director, I.C.P.R., New Delhi, for using some of his ideas in my paper.

SOME PHILOSOPHICAL DIMENSIONS OF THE WORLD CRISIS IN THE CONTEXT OF THE TRANSFORMATION OF THE WORLD*

Pranab Kumar Sen

The paper is divided into two parts. In the first, I begin with a preliminary characterization of the world (which is also human) crisis, or crises, and then make an attempt to understand their exact nature and their relationship, with a view to grasping their very essence. This understanding of what constitutes the essence of the crises inspires some immediate responses, suggesting some ways of resolving them. But these immediate responses themselves, though they may also be the right ones, are found to raise some deeper questions. In the second part of the paper, these deeper questions are traced to their philosophic roots—to some philosophical views regarding intercultural relationship, the relationship between language and the world, and between man and nature. These views are then subjected to scrutiny, and a certain attitude of the mind, embodied largely in the Indian philosophical and cultural tradition, is defined.

PART I: THE CRISIS

A. *A Preliminary Characterization*

The crisis facing mankind at the present time is mainly threefold: (a) the economic, (b) the political, and (c) the ecological. I do not mean that there are no other aspects to the crisis. One may say that besides the three I have mentioned, and people usually mention, there

* This paper was presented at the Fourth International Seminar on "Religion and Philosophy in the Tranformation of the World—World-views on World Crisis", organised by the United Nations University and Freie Universitat, Berlin, in July 1982. I have been greatly helped in writing this paper by my colleagues Professor D.P. Chattopadhyaya and Dr. Shefali Moitra, and my friend Dr. Kalipada Baksi, besides the UNU guidelines and Professor Wolfgang Haug's admirably clear and succinct statement of the theme of the seminar. In the preparation of the manuscript I have been helped by my daughter Manidipa. To all of them I am glad to record my gratitude here.

are others. They are the *moral* and the *spiritual* aspects of the crisis. But, perhaps, all these are not on a par, and it would at least be more convenient to begin with the economic, political and ecological aspects of the crisis, which are in any case the most palpable.

The economic crisis consists mainly, if not entirely, in poverty. It may be the poverty which divides men within a single community or nation, or nations themselves, into the rich and the poor. Nobody would perhaps maintain today that these two forms of poverty are unrelated to or independent of one another, that any of them could be tackled by itself. But still, in my discussions, I keep more in mind the form of poverty which manifests itself in the division of *nations* into the rich and the poor. The problem of poverty, we are told, is aggravated by two factors. One is the population explosion, and the other is the rapid depletion of all natural resources.

The political crisis, which is not so easy to characterize, may be said to inhere in the conflict of ideologies, as well as of interests. These two forms of political crisis are not, for sure, unconnected, and both of them are continuous with the military crisis, the armed conflicts which result in an ever growing danger of a nuclear war.

The untiring efforts of the ecologists and the conservationists have made us conscious of the nature and magnitude of the ecological crisis facing our planet. It is no less than a threat of a total ecological catastrophe caused by pollution and disturbance of ecological balance.

This being an initial statement of our problem, I must hasten to add that the division of the crises into three is not so neat as it appears at first sight. Of course, economic and political crises run into each other and both push us towards the ecological: economic needs lead to more and more extensive and intensive exploitation of nature, and that to pollution and ecological imbalance; political conflicts lead to armed conflicts and they, in their turn, demand more and more inventions and actual use, if in the form of "harmless" tests, of devices lethal to all life forms and to the nature which surrounds them.

This very intertwining of the problems makes it so very difficult to tackle them, both at the level of theoretical understanding and at the level of practical solution. We do not know how to proceed because we do not know where to begin: we do not know which problem to tackle first, and which problem to tackle next. But, on the other hand, there is a view according to which this very fact is a kind of advantage. *If* the problems are so intertwined, so "organically" related to each other, it does not matter where we begin. We can begin at any point we like, with any problem of which we may have a somewhat clearer perception, and then follow its inner logic leading us from problem to problem, eventually to cover the whole complex of issues.

It seems to *me*, however, that it is not possible to have either any genuine understanding of the problems and their relationship or any useful practical orientation with respect to them if we leave the problems at the level of the kind of preliminary characterization with which we have begun. What is of the utmost importance is that we have a correct *understanding* of the problems. If that is what we want, we have to probe deeper, to try and find out what they are in their fundamental nature; to discover, in other words, their very *essence*. It is only when we reach this level of understanding that we can entertain any hope for solutions. It is true that to understand a problem is not to solve it, it is not even to begin to solve it. But it is surely a *conditio sine qua non* of any solution, and in any case it is to this understanding, rather than to anything else, that a student of *philosophy* can perhaps make some contribution. So I ask the question: what is the essence of the world crisis, of the economic, political, and ecological problems at our time?

B. *The Essence of the Crisis*

I have a tentative suggestion to make: The essence of the crisis lies in *conflicts*, the conflict between man and man, and between man and nature, the second of these two taking two forms: the conflict between man and *inanimate* nature and that between man and *animate* nature. Look at the economic crisis, first, the problem of poverty. It obviously lies in a conflict between man and man, whether between individuals or between nations. The same conflicts, in the form of fierce economic competitions and arms race, leads to another aspect of the economic crisis of the day, namely, depletion of natural resources. The political crisis is more obviously a matter of conflict between man and man, either at the national or at the international level. Likewise, it seems to me, it is quite obvious that the ecological crisis lies in the conflict between man and nature, the animate as well as the inanimate.

When I put forward this tentative suggestion to my colleagues, some of them[1] told me that it was too simplistic, at least one-sided because it leaves out one very important feature of the crisis, the human crisis, which is a general *apathy*, especially among the younger generation, manifested quite so often in escapist trends in the form of pseudo-spiritualist movements and cults. Let us consider this objection for a while. It is true that one of the greatest problems of the day is this apathy. But what, and why, is this apathy? Apathy can take one of two forms, which, for the sake of convenience, I designate as (a) the practical, and (b) the theoretical. Apathy in its merely practical form springs, I suggest, from a sense of helplessness and a consequent sense of futility of all actions. This sense of helplessness and futility can, in the last analysis, only be due to a basic *distrust in others*, in a pervasive cynicism: I can not really achieve anything, solve even a single problem, *all by myself*; I need *cooperation* from others, and the others would not cooperate! If this analysis is correct, then practical apathy is no doubt a matter of human conflict in the broader sense of the term, in which it stands not only for active antagonism between people but also for passive, but positive, non-cooperation.

Apathy can also take a theoretical form in which it is no mere inaction in practice but a positive *doctrine*. This doctrine is that there is no *theoretical point* in striving for a solution to the so-called problems, since our very perception of the problems is illusory. The problems appear from a perspective, from a point of view, that is determined by our acceptance of some traditional values which are either intrinsically worthless, or meaningless in our age. This theoretical apathy, which would also lead to inaction in practice, poses a graver problem than the merely practical. In so far as it is a consistent doctrine at all, it would necessarily lead to a denial of all values, at least those values which may have any relevance to our living in this world. For, if it were just a matter of *replacing* the older values by some new ones, that would call for the same kind of striving for their realization and protection, and would not tolerate indifference and inaction.

If, thus, apathy is total rejection of, or, at least, indifference to, all values, then this problem of growing apathy in a section, apparently the younger section, of the society, poses a great threat to the future of mankind. And so this apathy has to be met, and met in its own terms, *i.e.*, at the philosophical level. It would not be possible for me to deal at length with this philosophy of *axiological nihilism*, if we may

---

[1] Especially Shefali Moitra.

call it so, in this paper. But I shall have occasion later to say something about one of its deeper theoretical bases, namely, moral and cultural relativism. Axiological nihilism, when it is something more than a mere rationalization of the practical apathy stemming from a sense of helplessness and futility, very often takes the dialectical route from relativism to scepticism, from scepticism to anarchy, and, finally, from anarchy to nihilism. For the present, we postpone any further discussion of axiological nihilism.

C. *The Conflict*

Let me now proceed on the supposition that the essence of the world crises, the economic, the political and the ecological, lies in conflicts, in conflicts between man and man, and between man and nature. What I should like to do now is to be clear about the true nature of these conflicts to reveal, if I can, their deeper roots. This I propose to do by first stating what may be called our initial response to the conflicts, and then identifying the various forces in us which frustrate this initial response and thus tend to perpetuate these conflicts. This would, I believe, be worth our while even if my thesis, that it is in these conflicts that the essence of the crisis lies, proves to be wrong. For, even if these conflicts do not constitute its very essence, there is no doubt that they constitute a very important aspect of the crisis. If we know what these conflicts are, and why they are what they are, we have a lever on our problems, many of the problems which I want to discuss.

An initial response to the conflict between man and man which manifests itself in poverty is this. We could end poverty by equal *sharing* of whatever we have or could have. It may be said, however, that we do not have as much as would remove poverty for the whole of mankind if what we have is shared equally, or even equitably, among all of us; because there is, on the one hand, the phenomenon of population explosion and, on the other hand, rapid depletion of natural resources. To this we may say that we need not take too seriously, at least not now or in near future, the alarmist views of scarcity of our natural resources—the words of the prophets of doom. The only thing which can happen when the haves share what they have with the have-nots is that all of us get little, far less than what our acquisitive culture has taught us to desire. So if we teach ourselves to be contented with little, we can share whatever we collectively have and thus bring poverty to an end. The twin principle of equal sharing and contentment with little is our answer to the problem of poverty.

To the conflict between man and man at the political level, *i.e.* to the conflict of ideologies and that of interests, an initial response may be as follows: We should learn to live with *difference without conflicts*. In case of any differences we should be content with reasoned dialogues and gentle persuasions.

An initial response to the conflict between man and nature, leading to the ecological crisis, seems equally forthcoming. We could believe that we are part of nature and that nature is our part. This belief would then lead to another, namely, that to hurt nature is to hurt ourselves, a belief which would motivate us more to preserve nature than to exploit it.

But, alas, these initial responses to the conflicts are easily thwarted. Consider the principle of sharing first. For the first thing, we do not all want to share, and, for the next—and this is more important, those of us who are prepared to share would not share in a way which would end conflict. To share is to part with something which is in one's possession. This we can do in the so-called spirit of "sacrifice", with the idea that the thing *originally* belonged to us, and we are now making a *gift* of it. But sharing conceived in this way would not end conflict, unless the recipient accepts that the thing did not *originally* belong to him, but it belonged to the giver. And this the recipient may not accept, and would not accept because this is *demeaning* to him. The recipient may want to believe that what he receives belongs as much to him as to the one who is sharing it with him, and it is not a *gift* with which he is *favoured*. So, if sharing is to end conflict it has to be done in a different spirit, in the spirit of giving up *possession* of what belonged no more to one than to the other.

Problems about sharing arise in another way too. One may seriously ask whether there could, or should, be complete sharing in the sense that all men share *equally* what there is to share. Do we really believe that every man *deserves* everything which any other man does? One may say no, and that may be the end of the very idea of sharing.

The principle of contentment with little does look vulnerable to an obvious objection. Is contentment with little really desirable? The life of the beast is a life of contentment. Are we, in the name of sharing or distribution of wealth, inviting man, the whole of mankind, to return to the state of animal existence? Is it not better that some people live, and live well, rather than the whole of humanity be reduced to a state of uniform frugality retarding the growth of all and every individual, of those who are as well as of those who are not capable of growth?

The initial response to the conflicts at the political level was that we should learn to live with differences without conflict. But can we do so? There may be a need to remove the difference as well. This need is partly theoretical—and man is a theoretical being, but it is only partly so, for some ideological differences lead to conflict of interests. To implement one ideology we have to come into conflict with the interests vested in another. In the face of this, one may make *practical compromises* without any change in one's ideology, or one may change one's ideology itself. To this second alternative, namely that of adjusting one's own ideology to that of the other, one may take one of the two alternative attitudes: The first one may be called the "religious"—any change in ideology is a kind of "sacrilege", one's ideology being something sacred. The second attitude is the more flexible—ideologies may change and, through change, come closer to each other, and close enough to push the differences below the threshold of conflict.

This second alternative, however, depends upon a belief in the possibility of *ideological dialogues*, and that again presupposes the possibility of genuine *communication*, which, in its turn, depends upon (a belief in) a *shared world*, a *shared truth*, a *shared idiom* (a common conceptual apparatus, if you want to call it so) and a *shared methodology*. On the other hand, the first attitude, which does not allow for adjusting one's ideology to others', is strengthened by a theoretical denial of the very possibility of ideological dialogues, along with all its presuppositions.

So it seems that alternative responses to political conflicts, pitting man against man, reduce to these two: either (i) we learn to live with differences without allowing them to develop into conflicts, by making practical compromises, or (ii) we start earnest ideological dialogues.

We have to think however whether the policy of practical compromises can be acceptable as a permanent solution. It seems to me that it cannot be. If this practical compromise is compromise of principles to needs—and the needs are as much of one's own as they are of the other, then men, at least some men, would eventually revolt against it. If the galling thought of sacrificing one's integrity is accompanied by a suspicion that the other is only *biding* time under a veneer of compromise, the whole exercise is lost. So it seems to me that while practical compromise is necessary when there is nothing else which we could do to prevent the conflicts, we have to seriously consider the other alternative of engaging ourselves in purposeful ideological dialogues. But this alternative is ruled out by some philosophical doctrines like conceptual relativism, incommensurability of systems, ontological relativity and impossibility of translation. In fact, if these philosophical doctrines are right, there can not only be an ideological dialogue, there cannot be any dialogue at all, not even the dialogue which is necessary for practical compromise.

An outcome of the political conflict, as well as the economic, stemming from clash of interests, is armed confrontations, always threatening to develop into a nuclear war. This threat of nuclear war is so great an aspect of the crisis that it demands almost an independent treatment: indeed it appears to have established itself as a kind of independent entity. We know why the danger is increasing, although the reasons are many and extremely complicated. One of the reasons is the very superabundance of nuclear weapons. (Russell's apprehension was that the nuclear system can any day be triggered by accident or mistake.) The huge armament industries both in the private and in the public sectors with their vested interests act as a tremendous pressure. We have to remember the simple truth that every industry depends upon the *use and consumption* of its products. If the nuclear industry is to survive, it will have to survive by creating a demand for piling up *stock*, if it cannot depend on actual use or consumption of its produce, and inevitably find its *raison d'etre* in *fear and distrust* among nations. But it is not only the case that the nuclear industry fosters this fear and distrust, it is also the case that they thrive on an independently existing, and sometimes pre-existing, fear and distrust.

What seems most important then is the question how we can eradicate this fear and distrust. We have first to realize that they *must* be removed and then have to believe that they *can* be removed. That is, we have to realize first that fear and distrust are the root of the crisis, and that they are, in the last analysis, self-stultifying: we have to live in order to entertain fear and distrust, and we cannot live on continual and unmitigated fear and distrust.[2] But they too can be removed through dialogue again, which, as I have already

---

[2] Recall David Hume's answer to academic scepticism.

pointed out, presupposes the possibility of communication and every-thing on which the latter depends.

So, to sum up, our initial response to all kinds of political conflict and its various proliferations is that we engage ourselves in purpose-ful dialogues. But the question remains as to whether such a dia-logue is possible at all. The question of the theoretical possibility of a genuine dialogue remains, even if we can satisfactorily dispose of some basic questions about the very *utility* of dialogues. Such ques-tions about utility are indeed of supreme importance, and so we have to spend some time on them here and wait for a consideration of the theoretical question until the second part of the paper.

One of the very conditions of honest dialogue—and, obviously, a dialogue is of no use if it is not honest—is that each of the parties in the dialogue accept right from the very beginning the *possibility* that the other party is right and it is itself wrong; and also has the willingness to be convinced by the other, and give up its own position. But unfortunately, more often than not, we engage ourselves in dialogues only to convince and win over the other, and break up the dialogue whenever there is a threat of ourselves' being proven wrong. An essential requirement of a meaningful dialogue is what Karl Popper has called "the attitude of reasonableness", which he characterizes as follows: "I think I am right, but I may be wrong and you may be right, and in any case let us discuss it, for in this way we are likely to get nearer to a true understanding than if we each merely insist that we are right".[3] In view of this, before engaging in any dialogue we should do a bit of heart searching, and find out for ourselves if we can take such a rational attitude at all. If we cannot, we should rather not open the dialogue at all.

Another way in which a dialogue may fail to serve its purpose is this. I may engage the other party in dialogue at the point of a gun, under threat (perhaps concealed) of dire consequences if the other party does not agree with me. Dialogue between those who are armed to the teeth with nuclear weapons and those who can depend only on obsolete and conventional arms may easily take on this character. If the whole purpose of a dialogue is removal of fear and distrust, a dialogue under threat is obviously useless.

There is yet another form of dialogue which is of no use. A dialogue

---

[3] Karl Popper, "Utopia and Violence" in *Conjectures and Refutations* (London: Routledge & Kegan Paul, 1963).

may be used as a surrogate for all action, as an excuse for total
inaction, and to block any change which will go against the interests
of the privileged.[4] If dialogue is only a reactionary ploy of this nature, it would be of no use. In fact, it would not for long serve the
purpose even of the one who uses it as a ploy. For, sooner or later,
that it is being so used would be detected by the other and that
would be the end of dialogue. That is why, the party which may
legitimately be supposed to benefit from inaction must display its
good will by matching actions with words, perhaps by taking some
antecedent actions which would produce conviction about the authenticity of its dialogic moves.

A realization of the futility of such dialogues would help us in
formulating the necessary conditions of a useful dialogue; and doing
this is indeed a very important task. But what I am more interested
in are the conditions of the very possibility of *any* dialogue, useful or
useless, *i.e.*, the conditions I have mentioned earlier, and these I shall
discuss in the second part of the paper.

Let us consider at last the prospects for our initial response to the
conflict between man and nature, the conflict in which, I have said,
lies the essence of the ecological crisis. The initial response is that we
view man as part of nature and nature as part of man, thus motivating us to preserve rather than to exploit nature. But there are ways
of conceiving the relation between man and nature, embedded in
much of traditional thinking,[5] which tend to thwart this initial response. Man is conceived as being *outside* of nature,[6] perhaps above,
because *superior to*, nature. Nature, if it is not a creation of the human
mind,[7] is nothing but formless and inert matter, which is meaningless,
the *surd*, being the limit of intelligibility;[8] knowledge of nature is of
value only because it gives us power, the power to control nature;[9]
whatever is of value is a matter of *culture*, and culture is the other of,
if not opposed to, nature;[10] the state of nature is the state of *savagery*,
and the human progress, the progress of the spirit, consists in rising

---

[4] Roy Edgley, "Reason and Violence" in Stephen Korner (ed.), *Practical Reason*
(Oxford: Basil Blackwell, 1974).

[5] More pronouncedly, I suppose, in the West.

[6] Perception is knowledge of "external" world.

[7] Kant.

[8] Aristotle.

[9] Bacon.

[10] The whole of Western anthropological and sociological tradition.

above nature;[11] nature is *hostile* to man, and man has to *protect* himself from the *dark forces* of nature;[12] man is the most *superior* of all animals; the law of the survival of the fittest reigns supreme in nature, and man is the *fittest* of all animals;[13] animals, the "sub"-human animals, are mere *automata*;[14] and so on and so forth.

All these ideas, beliefs and theories about the relationship between man on the one hand and animate or inanimate nature on the other are most definitely opposed to the kind of rapport which our initial response to the conflict between man and nature demands.

D. *The Basic Issues*

Let us now take stock of the problems which stand in the way of our acting upon the initial responses to the various conflicts constituting, on my thesis, the essence of the world crisis. We have found that the idea of sharing as a means to ending poverty seems to founder on the question of whether each man deserves equally everything that any other man does, and whether contentment with little can be an ideal for man. We have found that the idea that every difference and dispute should be removed through dialogue faces the scepticism that there cannot be any genuine dialogue at all. More recently we have found that the friendly gestures, which could put an end to the antagonism between man and nature, are ruled out by a whole way of thinking that pits man against nature, at least creates a cleavage between the two by placing man outside or above nature. So what thwart our initial responses are some ideas, views, theories, convictions, assumptions, attitudes or questions which, because of their generality and fundamental character, are all philosophical, showing once again why philosophy is important in our life and why philosophers can and should contribute to the solution of the problem of man's survival. I shall now turn to a consideration of these issues which may be said to give a true philosophical dimension to the present world crisis, the topic of this paper.

---

[11] The same as in 10.
[12] The dominant tradition in myths and folklores.
[13] Darwin.
[14] Descartes.

PART II: THE PHILOSOPHICAL DIMENSIONS

A. *Sharing and Deserving*

The question regarding equal sharing is whether all men *deserve* equally. It seems plausible that if *a* contributes more to the development of the society than *b* does, or *a* performs a task which is more important than the task *b* performs, or *a* performs the same task more efficiently than does *b*, or takes more trouble to qualify *herself* for the task, or *a* is more sincere in the discharge of *her* duties than *b* is, should we not grant that *a* deserves more than *b*, and is it not then *unfair* to apportion equal benefits to both? (Note that "*a*" and "*b*" can stand either for individuals or for nations in the above crucial question, *mutatis mutandis*.)

It is necessary to point out that the quantitative or qualitative superiority of *a*'s performance over *b*'s is often a function of the *opportunities* provided to *a* and *b*. So if we want to make a fair grading of individuals or nations in what we may call the "deserve scale", we have to make sure first that all those we want to grade in the scale were provided with equal opportunities to start with, and none had any initial advantage over the other. Another factor which determines the quality or level of performance is *aptitude*; and so we have to make sure also that each of *a*, *b*, and others, was asked to perform a task which suited to *her* aptitude. Until we are on a sure ground on these basic factors, we should refrain from grading if it is fairness which is our objective.

But it may be the case, and it is more of an empirical question than philosophical whether or not this *is* the case, than even after we had eliminated all initial relative advantages, some differences in actual performance would still remain. If it does so, we can have, and I am ready to accept that we can have, a fair grading in the deserve scale. But then this would mean that under the imagined circumstances there cannot be any strictly equal sharing.

But does it matter if there is no absolute equality in sharing? Recall that the idea of sharing was broached as our answer to the problem of poverty. Sharing would fulfil this purpose even if it was not absolutely equal but at least equitable, because, as we have every reason to believe, when those initial conditions were fulfilled, every man, and every nation, would deserve through actual performance enough for their emancipation from poverty.

It must be pointed out, however, that there is an aspect to sharing which should be delinked from deserving in that sense of deserving in which it is contingent on *earning*, the sense in which one deserves *only* what one earns. I want to put forward here an idea which seems to me to be of the utmost importance. It seems to me that in one sense of deserving there are certain items which everyone, irrespective of performance, deserves and deserves equally. That is, given this sense of deserving, things fall into two kinds: (a) those which all deserve equally and (b) those which all do not. In the first kind we may include the necessaries of life like food, shelter and clothing. We may say that these we all deserve equally because they belong to us all as the *natural inheritance of mankind*. The other things we may not all deserve equally; we would deserve them only if we could earn them.

It is this notion of natural inheritance of mankind that I want to emphasize and plead for. If we are born on this planet, then we have a right to breathe the air in its atmosphere, to drink the water in its rivers and springs, to eat the fruits on its trees and the corns in its fields, to take shelter in its caves and to cover our bodies with whatever nature may provide us. Our inherent and inalienable right such as these is what I call the natural inheritance of man. If progress of civilization has merely consisted in replacing these primitive items, in which the right of all would perhaps be accepted without question, by cultural commodities and sophisticated products in which all men cannot claim equal share, then that is the worse for civilization. In whatever form the society may provide for these basic needs to mankind, every man has an equal right to them as any other.

The rest of the goods available to man, given the equality of initial opportunities, may be a matter of deserving only by earning. But this idea of earning also seems to be fraught with dangers. The desire to earn breeds competition, and the more earnest the competition becomes the more fierce it tends to be. And, therefore, if the root of all our troubles lies in *conflicts*, we should be wary of the very idea of earning.

At this point, it seems to me, we are confronted with two alternatives, not necessarily exclusive of each other: (a) We may learn to accept that there are things which some of us do not deserve, because we are incapable of earning them, and realize that it is beneath our dignity to desire or ask for things which we do not deserve. (b) We may learn to be satisfied with earning things which need not be, and perhaps cannot be, shared with others; *i.e.*, we may learn not to regard goods and commodities to be our only rewards.

B. *Contentment with Little*

Our problem regarding the principle of contentment with little was roughly that an adoption of this principle was likely to lower the quality of life uniformly for all of mankind. My answer to this is related to what I have just described as a second possible attitude towards earning and deserving. Contentment with little should be understood only in terms of shareable commodities, especially those which can be produced only through relentless exploitation of nature. Centuries of enjoyment of material values have hardly taught us that the best way of ensuring quality of life is to seek our rewards in terms of consumer goods and things which money can buy. What our long hedonistic experience has taught us is that the quality of life does not inhere exclusively in the enjoyment of the senses. What is needed now is a new value-orientation, the spiritualistic, however pompous that may sound; or, rather a return to some older sets of values which the nineteenth and twentieth century materialism, with its endless sophistication, has taught us to decry and ridicule. Extolling values of the mind and the spirit in a world full of inequalities and inequities is indeed an "opium of the poor". But we are talking here only of a world from which these basic inequities are supposed to have been removed.

C. *Dialogue and Communication*

We have staked our hopes too high on the possibility of resolving conflicts through dialogues, especially ideological dialogue. But is such a dialogue possible at all? There are some philosophical theories which would in fact rule out this possibility. These views are conceptual relativism,[15] incommensurability of systems,[16] impossibility of translation[17] and ontological relativity.[18]

---

[15] Benjamin Lee Whorf, *Language, Thought and Reality: Selected Writings of Benjamin Lee Whorf*, (ed.), J.B. Carroll (Cambridge, Mass.: MIT Press, 1956). W.V.O. Quine, *From a Logical Point of View*, Second Edition, (Cambridge, Mass.: Harvard University Press, 1961), and *Ontological Relativity and Other Essays* (New York: Columbia University Press, 1969). Thomas Kuhn, *The Structure of Scientific Revolutions*, Second Edition (Chicago: The University of Chicago Press, 1969), and "Reflections on my Critics" in Imre Lakatos and Alan Musgrave (eds.), *Criticism and Growth of Knowledge* (London and New York: Cambridge University Press, 1970), and *The Essential Tension: Selected Studies in Scientific Tradition and Change* (Chicago and London: The University of Chicago Press, 1977).

[16] Paul Fyerabend, "Explanation, Reduction and Empiricism" in *Scientific Explanation, Space and Time: Minnesota Studies in the Philosophy of Science*, Vol. III (Minneapolis:

When I started to write this paper I thought that I would undertake a detailed examination of these views. But I now find that I have very little space left for this. So I have to invoke here too the principle of contentment with little. These views, however, have been made familiar and popularized in philosophical circles of our time by their very powerful exponents, although I doubt whether the tremendous implications of these doctrines for our problems at hand have been fully recognized.

Of all these doctrines, the doctrine of conceptual relativism seems to be the most basic. To think and talk about the world we make use of a conceptual scheme, a set of concepts, which determines our thought and language. The conceptual schemes used by different cultures, even perhaps different individuals of the same culture, are all radically different. A conceptual scheme constitutes a *total* response to experience or the world, and different conceptual schemes constitute such different total responses. In view of this, there is no possibility of setting up a one-one correspondence, a mapping, between two schemes. Since there cannot be any correlation between conceptual schemes, there cannot be any correlation between the languages either, and hence there cannot be any translation of one language into another. Also, the world, in so far as we can think and talk about it at all, is fashioned by our own conceptual schemes. Therefore, with our differing sets of concepts, we live in different worlds.

I shall restrict myself to making a few critical observations on this basic idea of conceptual relativism.[19] That people of different cultures, traditions, education, and even interests, differ in the concepts

---

University of Minnesota Press, 1962), and "Consolations for the Specialist" in Imre Lakatos and Alan Musgrave (eds.), *Criticism and the Growth of Knowledge*. See also, Kuhn, "Reflections on my Critics" in the same volume, 1970, pp. 266ff.

[17] Quine, developed over the period through 1960–69.

[18] Quine, *Ontological Relativity and Other Essays*.

[19] The most powerful critic of conceptual relativism is, I think, Doland Davidson. See especially Davidson, "On the Very Idea of a Conceptual Scheme", *Proceedings and Addresses of the American Philosophical Association*, Vol. XLVII (New York: The American Philosophical Association, Hamilton College, Clinton, 1974), reprinted in D. Davidson, *Inquiries into Truth and Interpretation* (Oxford: Oxford University Press, 1984). See also D. Davidson, "The Method of Truth in Metaphysics" in Peter French, Theodore Uehling, Jr. and Howard Wettstein (eds.), *Contemporary Perspectives in the Philosophy of Language* (Minneapolis: University of Minnesota Press, 1979), reprinted in Davidson, *Inquiries into Truth and Interpretation*. The best proponent of the thesis of the universality and stability of the basic conceptual scheme, however, is Peter Strawson. See P.F. Strawson, *Individuals: An Essay in Descriptive Metaphysics* (London: Methuen, 1959), and *Bounds of Sense: An Essay on Kant's Critique of Pure Reason* (London: Methuen, 1966).

which they employ is something nobody can deny. But the thesis that they have totally different and incommensurable conceptual schemes is an altogether different matter. My main objection to this thesis is very simple, so simple that it may not carry conviction. In any case, my objection is this: difference between conceptual schemes—both that conceptual schemes differ and that in which they differ—can be described and has to be described if the thesis of conceptual relativism itself is to go through. Such a description will have to be made in a language, embodying a conceptual scheme, a language which must be intertranslatable with those languages this third language compares and pronounces upon. If this be so, those two languages themselves cannot fail to be at least partially inter-translatable. In other words, those languages would embody conceptual schemes that cannot but overlap, although they need not coincide. To put the same point more bluntly, total divergence of conceptual schemes is not intelligible. Differences become intelligible only if there are some points of agreement from which divergence can shoot off.

At this point, I should like to comment on ethical relativism, the subject we came upon in connection with axiological nihilism and have left pending. If moral dialogue is possible at all—and it does seem to me that it is possible—then there cannot be any *total* dis-agreement on moral matters, however widely people or cultures may diverge in details. There must be some shared moral beliefs to serve at least as the common point of departure.

D. *Man and Nature*

We have said that the ecological crisis results essentially from conflict between man and nature, and that this conflict would be removed by establishing a rapport between man and nature, but that a whole tradition of thinking about the relationship of man and nature makes that extremely difficult, if not impossible. On this way of thinking man is pitted against animate as well as inanimate nature; at least a cleavage is created between the two by placing man outside, or above nature. So the remedy lies in challenging this tradition itself, and in changing our whole attitude. Much of the existing attitude of an-tagonism is due to ignorance of animate as well as inanimate nature. There are events and processes in nature which are hostile to life; but is it not the case that it is this nature itself which has produced and sustained life? Although there are life forms which do appear to be hostile to man, most of them are not, most of them would not hurt us if we left them alone, and even with regard to those forms which do appear to be dangerous and hostile it can be said that we do not really know whether there are ways, *unknown* to us, in which they too are serving the purpose of man's life on this planet. So advance in knowledge of nature, and dissemination of this knowledge, would certainly help in changing our attitude.

But knowledge alone is not sufficient. We must learn to view nature as an object of love and respect. If this is animism, let it be so. That would be a necessary corrective to the attitude of antagonism. And it is not doctrinaire animism which I am advocating, but only an attitude of the mind, or an *ethic*. If nature sustains us, why should we not love and respect nature? And talking of ethic, do we not have a moral obligation to other living beings? If we have an obligation to share with other human beings what I have called the natural inheritance of man, so do we have an obligation to share with other living beings what may be called the natural inheritance of all creatures on earth. The responsibility is all the greater here, because we are called upon to share with beings who cannot negotiate or bargain with us. Let us stop thinking that the world belongs to man alone, the fittest and the most superior of all creatures.

This attitude of love and respect for nature I have just adumbrated permeates the cultural tradition in which I have been brought up. Whether it is the ancient worship of nature's elements,[20] or the conception of the earth as the *mother* of which all creatures are children, or the still surviving practice of worshiping of different species of animals,[21] or the living folklores and cults with which millions of people live even today, or the ethics of non-violence[22] embedded in a vast network of most elaborate and sophisticated metaphysical systems, it is the same attitude of love and respect of nature which is manifested. We may find revolting its coarse and often repulsive exterior, the crudity of its theoretic content, or the extravagance of its imaginative flights, but we should not fail to appreciate the noble sentiments which form its core. Please let it be understood that I am speaking only for this sentiment, and not advocating the cults and rituals, not even the philosophical theories, at least not here.

---

[20] Polytheism and Henotheism in the Upaniṣads.
[21] The too well-known and much derided worship of cow.
[22] In Jainism, Buddism and Hinduism.

E. *A Summing Up*

I may now sum up by saying that the resolution of the conflicts which constitute the essence of the world crisis can be achieved, if at all, through

(i) an enlightened view of *sharing* with man and other living creatures;
(ii) a *value re-orientation* through shift of emphasis from the material to the non-material values;
(iii) *dialogues*, especially ideological dialogues; and
(iv) *love, respect* and *knowledge* of nature.

The observations made in this paper, not, I suppose, very original, are made with all humility which become an amateur. I shall be happy, however, only if I have succeeded in being clear about how some philosophical views and attitudes bear upon the present-day crises. If I am right about this, we should call upon the very best philosophers of our time, to whatever tradition they may belong, to direct their attention to them. But it seems to me that most of them do not attend to them. And this adds, to my mind, yet another dimension to the crisis.

GLOBAL DEVELOPMENT:
ALTERNATIVE VOICES FROM DELHI

Fred Dallmayr

I

Our age—all evidence shows—is "on the move". During the past several centuries, this movement has been the distinctive hallmark of European or Western civilization—from Enlightenment to industrialization and then to the information revolution. In the meantime, the momentum has been globalized. Into its farthest corners, the entire world today is in the grip of "development"—whose meaning or direction, however, remains obscure. The two Great Wars of our century have been fought to make the world "safe for democracy", but the sense of that phrase was ambivalent. According to some observers, there were several plausible and viable interpretations of the phrase: chiefly those of Western liberal democracy, of socialist "people's democracy", and of indigenous democracies in "developing" societies. The Cold War soon congealed or consolidated these options under the aegis of three competing international power blocs, thereby effectively splitting the globe into three antagonistic "worlds": the worlds of the liberal-capitalist West, of the Soviet East and of the so-called "non-aligned" nations (comprising most of the Third-World countries).[1]

All these divisions or demarcations have more recently been thrown into disarray if not entirely erased. The end of the Cold War has also meant the end of many previously cherished options or possibilities (of thought and action). In lieu of the cauldron of competing "worlds", our time is increasingly under the spell of "one-world" formulas—formulas backed up by the hegemonic status of Western societies and world-views. Although seemingly conducive to global peace, such formulas are bound to cause alarm among friends of

---

[1] Compare, *e.g.*, Irving Louis Horowitz, *Three Worlds of Development: The Theory and Practice of International Stratification* (New York: Oxford University Press, 1966). Regarding different models of democracy see C.B. Macpherson, *The Real World of Democracy* (Oxford: Clarendon Press, 1966); also his *The Life and Times of Liberal Democracy* (Oxford: Oxford University Press, 1977).

democracy. In the words of the dean of contemporary European philosophy, Hans-George Gadamer (hardly suspect of extremist leanings): "The hegemony or unchallengeable power of any one single nation—as we now have with just *one* superpower—is dangerous for humanity. It would go against human freedom".[2]

As one should note, Gadamer's indictment is directed not so much against liberal Western democracy as such, as against its erection into a uniform and universal standard—a standard imposed on all other societies with or without their consent (and thus possibly without popular democratic support). In both philosophical and political terms, Gadamer's comments challenge a univocal and one-dimensional conception of "world", that is a world without alternatives and diversity, one whose meaning is no longer open to questioning. Neatly streamlined and hegemonically managed, such a world—he correctly perceives—would also be a world without hope, without vision or excess, without (ontological) difference. As it happens, despite intensive efforts made by one-world protagonists, the nightmare of uniformity feared by Gadamer has not yet emerged or become fully entrenched on a global scale. Both in the West and the non-West, there are voices of dissent diverging from the hegemonic mainstream, sometimes in muted or confused, sometimes in sharply articulated ways.

Given the prevailing asymmetrics of power and wealth, dissent is a particularly urgent concern in non-Western societies (sometimes termed "South" or "periphery"), and especially among the under-classes in those societies reacting to conditions of economic and political marginalization. Thus, dissenting voices and movements can be found today in Latin America, Africa, the Islamic world, and in South and Far East Asia—and this quite apart from (and sometimes in direct opposition to) the more strident and virulent noises emanating from the upsurge of (what is called) "fundamentalism" or "communalism". In the present pages I want to illustrate this critical temper by drawing attention to a prominent locus of both intellectual and political ferment on the Indian subcontinent: the Centre for the Study of Developing Societies in Delhi. Established in 1963 by Rajni Kothari and some of his associates, the Centre during the past four decades has emerged as one of the most stimulating and clear-sighted insti-

---

[2] See Thomas Pantham, "Some Dimensions of the Universality of Philosophical Hermeneutics: A Conversation with Hans-Georg Gadamer", *Journal of Indian Council of Philosophical Research*, Vol. 9 (1992), p. 132.

tutions of academic and political non-conformism in South Asia (and in the "developing" world at large).

To be sure, my focus here is purposely restricted and not meant in any way to disparage or silence other expressions of dissent. As I fully realize, India is a richly diversified social fabric, a diversity which also surfaces in the variety of oppositional strands. One of the more prestigious oppositional strands is linked with the so-called "Subaltern Studies" project initiated by Ranajit Guha and his associates, a project that has already resulted in a string of publications offering critical new vistas on colonialism and post-colonialism.[3] Despite the undeniable merit of these endeavours, my decision here to bypass the project is prompted by several considerations. First of all, Subaltern Studies have been widely acclaimed and thus are relatively familiar to scholars and intellectuals in the West. Secondly, and more importantly, as inaugurated by Guha and his associates, the project was in many ways still closely wedded to traditional premises of Marxist political economy, premises which today have become questionable. (I shall return to this point at the end).

Even within the confines of the Delhi Centre, my presentation will necessarily have to be selective. Akin in many ways to the Frankfurt School of Social Research, the Centre from the beginning has been a collective enterprise of scholars from many disciplines, including the humanities, the social sciences, and psychology. Over the years, the studies sponsored by the Centre have been both empirical and theoretical in character and have dealt with a broad spectrum of issues ranging from the ethnic and social-psychological components of change to problems of rural development and ethno-agriculture to the role of science and technology in the modern world.[4] For present purposes I shall focus on two leading spokesmen of the Centre: Rajni Kothari, its founder and long-time director, and Ashis Nandy, one

[3] For a good introduction to the subaltern project see Ranajit Guha and Gayatri Chakravorty Spivak (eds.), *Selected Subaltern Studies*, with a Foreword by Edward W. Said (New York: Oxford University Press, 1988). The first volume of Subaltern Studies was published in Delhi in 1982; since then, at least six additional volumes have appeared.

[4] A brief introduction to the perspective and work of the Centre is provided by Rajni Kothari in "Towards an Alternative Process of Knowledge" in his *Rethinking Development: In Search of Humane Alternatives* (New York: New Horizons Press, 1989), pp. 23–43. (The book was first published in India by Ajanta Publications, Delhi.) The Centre issues periodic *Research Reports*, among which the most detailed and comprehensive was the report published in 1988 on the occasion of the Centre's Silver Jubilee.

of its senior members (and also one-time director). Following a review of some of their main works, I shall try to assess their contributions in the light of our contemporary global context.

More than ever before, critical intellectuals today cannot be neutral
spectators; according to an old adage: reflection without practical
commitment is empty, commitment without reflection is blind. Among
members of the Delhi Centre—and perhaps among Indian intellectuals at large—no one exemplifies this adage better than Rajni
Kothari. Trained both in India and the West, Kothari over the decades
has distinguished himself as an accomplished scholar, an institution
builder, and a political activist on all levels (local, national, and international) of politics. The establishment of the Delhi Centre in 1963
was designed both to facilitate broadly interdisciplinary research
and to reduce—and if possible to overcome—the theory-praxis hiatus
afflicting modern higher education.

While some of Kothari's early publications—like *Politics in India*
(1970)—still showed him strongly indebted to Western social scientific paradigms (especially functionalism), he soon freed himself from
such subservience in favor of more innovative and experimental modes
of inquiry. In 1974 he was instrumental in launching the quarterly
Alternatives, a journal which soon emerged as a leading forum for the
discussion of issues relating to social change and global transformation. Roughly at the same time, he became actively involved in the
Janata Party, a leftist movement which at that point was raising basic
questions about the direction of the Indian government under Congress leadership. During the period of the Emergency imposed by
Indira Gandhi (1975), Kothari surfaced as a vocal spokesman of the
anti-Emergency campaign and one of the chief leaders of the civil
liberties movement in India. Both his scholarly and his political talents
coalesced in 1980 when, together with other Centre colleagues, he
inaugurated "*Lokayan*" (meaning "dialogue among people") designed
as an arena for the meeting of scholars, policy-makers, and activists
concerned with local or rural grassroots initiatives. His moment of
greatest visibility came in 1989 when, following the defeat of Rajiv
Gandhi, he joined the Janata Dal-led National Front government as
a member of the national Planning Commission.[5]

---

[5] *Lokayan* in the meantime has become an autonomous institution with its own
statutes: six times a year it publishes a journal known as *Lokayan Bulletin* (in English
and Hindi).

In his capacity as a scholar and critical intellectual, Kothari has produced an impressive corpus of writings which so far (in the West) has not gained the recognition it deserves. The outlook pervading these writings is, broadly speaking, a radical democratic humanism— a perspective which does not fit neatly into any ideological blueprint or partisan programme. This outlook is already announced in the subtitles of many of his publications, especially those published in rapid succession during the past decade. 1988 saw the publication of two important volumes, titled respectively *State against Democracy: In Search of Humane Governance* and *Transformation and Survival: In Search of a Humane World Order*. These texts were followed a year later by three additional books: *Rethinking Development: In Search of Humane Alternatives* and *Politics and the People: In search of a Humane India* (the latter comprising two volumes). Although linked together by common thematic concerns, the books are differentiated by their distinctive accent or focus.

State against Democracy was written mainly in protest against the policies of Indira and Rajiv Gandhi whose regimes were denounced for their attempt to marshal state power against the democratic aspirations of the people. In large measure, the book was meant as a challenge to the relentless process of centralization which, during the post-independence period, was steadily moulding India into a uniform "nation-state" along Western lines. Buttressed by the resources of modern technology and corporate business, this nation-state—in Kothari's view—was erecting or deepening a structure of stratification or inequality which the struggle against colonialism had meant to erase. The situation was further aggravated by the progressive militarization of the state promoted in the name of "national security" interests. These and related factors conspired to produce a social-political crisis which, according to Kothari, was changing or rather perverting the character of the state: namely, from "being an instrument of liberation of the masses to being a source of so much oppression from them".[6]

The critique of state-sponsored accumulation of power was carried forward in *Transformation and Survival* into the global arena. Paralleling

---

[6] Rajni Kothari, *State against Democracy: In Search of Humane Governance* (Delhi: Ajanta, 1988), p. 60. As one should note, Kothari did not entirely condemn the modern state. In a progressive democratic vein, he endorsed the state provided it served as an "instrument" of democratization. Put differently: the state for Kothari was to be in the service of democracy and the people (not the other way around).

the bifurcation of domestic society into a propertied elite and impoverished, marginalized masses, the operation of the international state system promoted and, in fact, steadily reinforced a global structure of asymmetry: that between North and South, between "developed" and "developing" societies, between centre and periphery. As on the national level, this global asymmetry was compounded by the concentration of technological, economic, and military resources in the hands of hegemonic (developed) states. In their combination, this battery of forces for Kothari posed a threat to the natural environment, to international peace, and ultimately to the survival of humankind itself. As an antidote of those perceived dangers, the two volumes of 1988 formulated an alternative vision of human existence and social-political life, a vision that was not beholden to any of the reigning ideologies of the time. In fact, as Kothari insisted, it was necessary to move beyond both the liberal-capitalist and the classical Marxist paradigms, since both were "offshoots of the same philosophic pedigree of the Enlightenment and nineteenth-century (mechanistic) humanism" with their unlimited faith in progress abetted by technological mastery over nature.

In lieu of this "modernist" pedigree, the books invoked approvingly the legacy of Gandhi who, in writings like *Hind Swaraj* as well as in his political actions, had challenged Western imperialism while at the same time promoting democratic mobilization at the grassroots level; in his entire life-work, Gandhi thus had honoured "the moral imperative of treating people as a source in the recovery of a humane order". In addition to Gandhian teachings, the texts also drew inspiration from left-leaning modes of political radicalism wedded to the promotion of human freedom and social justice. As one should note, "freedom" here meant not only an act of withdrawal or negative abstinence but a capacity for social well-being and public participation. To this extent, human rights—a central concern for Kothari— denoted not so much private entitlements or privileges as rather basic constituents of a good social order. As we read in *State against Democracy*: "Human rights movements, ecology movements, women's movements, the peace movements are all about restoring the first principles of the 'good' and 'good life' in the conduct of human affairs".[7]

---

[7] See Kothari, *State against Democracy*, pp. 2–3, 151; also his *Transformation and Survival: In Search of a Humane World Order* (Delhi: Ajanta, 1988); pp. 6, 170–171. In the latter text, Kothari states his vision in these terms (p. 173): "My preferred world is one in

In the following I shall not pass in detailed review the successive volumes of Kothari's corpus; instead, I want to lift up some particularly instructive passages or sections in his recent work. My main focus here will be on *Rethinking Development* (1989) and on a more recent publication titled *Growing Amnesia* (1993). The opening chapter in the former provides important clues to his alternative vision. Entitled "Alternatives in Development: A Conceptual Framework," the chapter immediately zeroes in on the basic problem besetting "development" debates: the confusion regarding its meaning and direction. Both in mainstream literature and mainline policy planning, development has tended to be identified with unfettered economic and industrial expansion propelled by advances in modern science and technology. In Kothari's view, this outlook has not only engendered a deadly arms race and a wasteful, consumption-driven civilization, but also a pernicious class structure on both the national and the global levels: a structure pitting both the "developed" North against the "underdeveloped" South, and Westernized elites in the South against large marginalized masses of people. As a result, democracy is under siege both at home and in the world at large.

For Kothari, the trouble with the dominant "economistic" model is not only that it is difficult to implement due to various roadblocks, but that it is inherently flawed and mistaken. For too long, he notes, development has been fuelled by a faulty vision, namely, by the idea of a "uniform end product to be achieved by all societies", a goal characterized by "a state of urban, industrial affluence, managed by experts at the top running secular affairs through a 'rational' bureaucracy, and backed by a capital-intensive technology". The increasingly evident costs exacted by this model, especially in terms of human suffering, give impetus to an alternative vision, or alternative visions, of development. In Kothari's words, the notion of alternatives implies

> two considerations: that the world is becoming too uniform, too standardized, too dominated by a single conception of life and its meaning, with little scope for other available cultural and historical propensities

---

which the individual enjoys *autonomy* for his self-realization and creativity—what is generally known as freedom. This is my principal value. . . . The primary condition of freedom is sheer survival, a protection against violence—local, national and international violence, as well as conditions tending towards either annihilation of the properties of life or towards a deadening uniformity of all forms of behavior and social structure".

and potentialities: and that such domination of a single conception has
led to political and cultural domination by a single region of the world
over all the others.[8]

In proceeding to outline details of his own alternative vision, Kothari
right away cautions against some pitfalls or simplistic shortcuts: especially the pitfalls of a reactionary anti-modernism and a rampant
cultural relativism (following the "anything goes" maxim). Faced with
domestic and international inequities, he writes, the temptation is
great to launch into a virulent attack on the West or the "Western
model" or else to retreat into the shell of cultural narcissism or self-
enclosure. What these shortcuts neglect is the inextricable entwinement of North and South, that is, the fact that different modes of
social life and development inevitably condition each other in our
age. Although there may be radically different options and even
different "worlds", these options are still embedded in, and held
together by, our global (or globalizing) context. According to Kothari,
the philosophical principle that must guide us in such a setting should
"steer clear of both imperialist claims to universality and the normless
striving for relativity." Concretely, this involves a double gesture or
double affirmation which endorses both "the principle of *autonomy* of
each entity (human as well as social) to seek out its own path to self-
realization" *and* "the principle of *integration* of all such entities in a
common framework of interrelationships based on agreed values".

In terms of specific policies or development strategies, the chapter
offers a list of recommendations, among which I can highlight only
a few major points. One set of proposals has to do with the fostering
of alternative life-styles, in opposition to the high consumption patterns present among elites. Taking a leaf from Gandhi, Kothari here
advocates an "ethic of consumption" that discourages ostentatious
living in favor of a frugal limitation of wants. Closely linked with this
policy is the establishment of normative guidelines regarding "minima
and maxima" of income and wealth. Another set of proposals deals
with the "organization of space", that is, with the promotion of a
more equitable balance between urban and rural spaces, between
town and countryside, agriculture and industry; Gandhian-style de-
centralization here serves as a key to curbing the unchecked growth

---

[8] Kothari, *Rethinking Development*, pp. 3–5. The chapter was first presented as a
paper at a Pugwash Conference on Science and World Affairs held in Madras in
1976.

of metropolitan centres. In a sense, decentralization also animates Kothari's educational policy, dedicated to a "basic cultural attack" on illiteracy (with special attention given to villages and the education of women). All these items are rounded out by the demand for broad-scale popular participation both in economic production and in public life. As he states: "I am firmly convinced that it is only on the basis of a clear acceptance of a decentralized and highly participatory democratic structure that social justice can be realized".[9]

The contours of his alternative vision are further sharpened in a subsequent chapter titled "Alternative Development and the Issue of Environment." In examining the crisis features of our time, the chapter draws attention to recessed philosophical premises undergirding these dilemmas: specifically the post-Cartesian bifurcation of mind and matter and as a corollary, the ascendancy of human mastery over nature by means of science and technology. Buried in the myriad problems of our age, Kothari notes, lies a "dominant philosophical doctrine" that, although originating in Europe, is by now encircling the globe: namely, the "doctrine of modernity" according to which "the end of life is narrowly defined as to be within the grasp of all— progress based on economic prosperity". Fuelled by Enlightenment teachings, this doctrine presents social progress entirely as a matter of social engineering, superseding old-style beliefs. All that human beings and societies have to do in this model is to "discard tradition and superstition and become rational and 'modern'", all they need to learn are the "essential techniques" for procuring happiness for everyone.

A crucial backbone of this model is modern "science-based technology" or rather science in the service of technology. Subservient to technical needs, science (and knowledge in general) here becomes a mere instrument of power, that is, "an instrument of domination over the sinister and unpredictable forces of nature"—which later spills over into domination over "social forces and institutions" and, ultimately, over "relations between societies and between cultures and races". Echoing insights articulated earlier by Horkheimer and Adorno (regarding the "dialectic of Enlightenment"), the chapter queries:

> Isn't the theory of progress, as developed in the West, based on an anthropocentric view of nature and a positivist conception of knowledge

---

[9] *Rethinking Development*, pp. 7–21.

and science, which are responsible for a model of development spelling
domination and exploitation? And if these be the essence of Occidental culture and its contribution to human thought and values, shouldn't
we discard large parts of it, and look for alternative modes of thought
and values embedded in some other cultures?. . . . It is essential to come
to grips with this particular world view, of which science and technology are but means, that stands for steamrolling almost the entire world
into uniformity, reducing its rich diversity to a predictable and prede-
termined state.[10]

Given the deleterious effects of this worldview or doctrine of modernity, as shown in its domestic and global repercussions, the search
for alternatives had to be attentive to ideas or perspectives originating outside or at the periphery of the modern West, especially perspectives indigenous to developing societies. In forthright language—
bound to be shocking to radical modernists—Kothari at this point
refers approvingly to the cultural, including religious, traditions of
non-Western countries. "The religions and civilizations of India, of
the Islamic world, of the complex web of humanist thought that has
informed China, and of Buddhism," he writes, "provide major streams
of thought that could substantially contribute to the present search
for alternatives" (although this possibility is presently only latent or
embryonic). Possible contributions of these cultures extend to the
domain of knowledge and science, by offering an alternative to technological mastery. In Kothari's view, the major cultural regions of
the non-Western world had important traditions of science and human
learning; but what was common to them was a view of science as
basically "a search for truth" or "a means of self-realization and self-
control", not as "a means of bringing anything, least of all nature,
under domination."

As in the previous chapter, the turn to alternative cultural traditions is hedged in again by important caveats, having to do with the
lure of purely negative or reactionary sentiments. As Kothari emphasizes, modernity is not something that can simply be "wished away"
or ignored; to a significant degree, modernity is "not just Western or
Occidental" but is "part of us all," just as "the West itself is part of

---

[10] *Rethinking Development*, pp. 48–49, 51. The chapter was first presented as a paper
at a conference on alternative development strategies held in Bangkok in 1979.
Compare in this context also Max Horkheimer and Theodor W. Adorno, *Dialectic
of Enlightenment*, trans. John Cumming (New York: Herder & Herder, 1972).

us all." What needs to happen in our world is not a mutual encapsulation but a reciprocal openness and engagement, that is, an effort to relate the "presently dominant tradition" (of Western modernity) to "other civilizational traditions and meaning systems" and thus to evolve a "process of critical interaction" or dialogue between them. To promote such interaction, what must be avoided above all is "intellectual brainwashing" on all sides, especially the brainwashing which preaches that there is only one "uniform and homogeneous end product for all societies": that of an "all-encompassing modernity." Coupled with such reciprocal learning must be the critique of prevailing domestic and global inequities, that is, a shift from elitism to a popular and ecologically sensitive perspective. Such a perspective, Kothari concludes,

> must promote a view of human welfare that does not assume some linear progression on some uniform pattern but, instead, allows for autonomy and self-reliance in a variety of local contexts so that everyone participates with a first-hand knowledge of actual conditions.[11]

Growing Amnesia is separated from the developmental study by an interval of four years. That interval was marked by momentous historical events on a global scale: chiefly the dismantling of the Soviet Empire and, as a result, the termination of the Cold War between superpowers—which also meant the waning of a viable "non-alignment" policy (as sponsored by India and other Third World countries). Although widely hailed in the West as the dawn of a new "world order"—and even as the goalpoint or "end of history"— Kothari's book voices serious qualms and critical reservations about the emerging global situation. In his view, the turn of events signalled basically the triumph of capitalist market economics and corporate free enterprise—processes which augur ill for the cause of social justice and participatory or grassroots democracy. Given the concentration of power and wealth in developed countries (and multinational conglomerates), the existing gulf between North and South, centre and periphery was prone to be further deepened, while the

---

[11] *Rethinking Development*, pp. 50, 52, 54–55. Regarding ecology compare also the chapter "On Eco-Imperialism" (a critique of Garrett Hardin), pp. 107–117. The book contains an important chapter on "Ethnicity", pp. 191–224, where ethnicity is not merely castigated (as a possible ally of xenophobic communalism), but also affirmed and celebrated as a possible source of human empowerment and as an emblem of cultural diversity (against the encroachments of globalizing uniformity).

lot of underprivileged masses around the world was bound to be
abandoned to apathy or else consigned to "growing amnesia".

As the opening chapter observes, economic liberalism by itself is
unlikely to be a harbinger of democracy. In fact, the priority granted
to the market principles of "liberalization" and "privatization" puts
an entirely new slant on the notion of development: "Among other
things, the whole rationale of development as a reduction of poverty
and the promotion of equity goes. The whole focus shifts to deregu-
lation, mainly for foreign investors and multinationals." Thus, the
slogan of "liberalization" should not be confused with emancipation
or popular liberation. Sanctioned by global-hegemonic and multinational forces, implementation of the slogan "can and probably will
destabilize the democratic polity, put the masses under severe strain,
turn against labour and further marginalize the poor".[12]

While bemoaning the sway of liberalization, Kothari is far removed
from endorsing a communist-style planned economy under the auspices of a centralized state. As he is well aware, the Indian state—
once an engine in the struggle for independence—has itself become
an instrument of oppression by being captive to privileged elites. We
know, he writes, that the state and its various agencies "have increasingly become repressive and cruel vis-a-vis the poor and the
radical movements that support the poor". Yet, for Kothari, available options should not be restricted to the competing dystopias of
an unchecked market and a centralized state bureaucracy. Above all,
in developing societies, a viable agenda cannot consist in the simple
cancellation of the latter in favour of the former. Given the powerful
sway of globalization, such a cancellation means in effect the surrender
of national or local self-rule to hegemonic economic forces—which,
in turn, is a synonym for a form of neo-colonialism. As Kothari writes
bluntly, addressing himself to the post-Cold War leadership in India:

> They have quite blindly gone in for an erosion of the role of the state,
> for an acceptance of the market as the key mediator in the develop-
> ment process, and for globalization. In doing so, they have walked into

---

[12] Kothari, *Growing Amnesia: An Essay on Poverty and the Human Consciousness* (New
Delhi: Viking, 1993), pp. 8–9. As he adds (p. 26): "Quite apart from the decline
in the role of the state in preserving spaces for the underprivileged and protecting
peoples and cultures from globalizing trends, there is the danger of the whole normative framework of democracy being undermined. The assumption that the liberalization of the economy would lead to a more liberal policy and generate more
liberties for individuals and groups is thoroughly unfounded."

a trap laid by global hegemonic interests not just a debt trap but also a trap for recolonizing large parts of the world.[13]

In order to avoid this trap, what is needed is a move beyond both a centralized bureaucracy (the backbone of the traditional nation-state) and a mindless globalization (governed by hegemonic market forces). Kothari at this point formulates a Third World vision designed to fill the vacuum created by the "world without alternatives" (emerging in the wake of socialism and non-alignment). In this vision, the modern state is retained but sharply recast or redefined in a popular-democratic direction, namely, as the arena or space of democratic participation and self-rule. With this redefinition, the state ceases to be the monopoly of traditional elites; it also ceases to be the preserve of an upwardly-mobile middle class increasingly alienated from the broader community. The latter is particularly important in the Indian context. As Kothari notes, while previously a mainstay of Gandhian ideas and the movement towards a "humane and progressive" India, the Indian middle class has progressively adapted itself to the global bourgeoisie, in the process abandoning their social conscience in favor of a "vulgar consumerism" and the relentless pursuit of private wealth and pleasure.

Against the backdrop of these developments, Kothari's vision assigns to the state chiefly the role of "preserving spaces for the under-privileged" as well as "protecting peoples and cultures from globalizing trends." At least partially shielded by the state, peoples and cultures here emerge as sources of resistance to global hegemony—notwithstanding the danger of such cultures degenerating into xenophobic forms of populism or communalism. For Kothari, the basic issue is how to counterbalance the implacable sway of globalism and thus to salvage the mediating role of cultures in the crucible "between tradition and modernity" and hence "between external and indigenous structures and values." Only a properly democratic politics can accomplish this goal—where democracy means

> not just electoral politics but a politics based on critical interventions that will once again give a sense of hope and confidence to the poor and marginalized sections of society, generate a process of empowerment, a new realignment of forces and, out of it all, a new agenda for the state.[14]

---

[13] *Growing Amnesia*, pp. 17, 28.
[14] *Growing Amnesia*, pp. 22–23, 26, 28–29, 31.

Democratic politics, from this angle, requires a serious effort of de-centralization, both in the public-administrative and the economic spheres. In this context, Kothari again pays tribute to the legacy of Gandhi—without subscribing in every details to Gandhian programmes or policies (such as the programme of village autonomy). The basic point for Kothari is the need to build social and economic life from the ground up rather than from the top down, in a managerial or technocratic style. Contrary to centralized strategies (still favoured by traditional Marxists), *Growing Amnesia* starts from the ordinary life-world of concrete experience—guided by the commitment to take "people seriously" by "respecting their thinking and wisdom" and by fostering institutions and technologies that "respond to their needs." Only by following this maxim is it possible to counteract managerial elitism and to establish an economic system that, in Gandhi's words, "not only produces for the mass of the people but in which the mass of the people are also the producers".

The turn to the ordinary life-world also entails a certain respect for popular or indigenous beliefs, including religious and cultural tradition. As Kothari notes, some of the most intense conflicts and resentments arise from threats to "the cultural and social identity of a people". Although traditions and customary beliefs are certainly not immune from change or critique, Kothari's book strongly coun-sels a transformative approach which proceeds from within, and with the resources of, a given cultural context—this precisely as an anti-dote to chauvinism or aggressive xenophobia. As he writes in a pas-sage which deserves to be carefully pondered:

> If minority (or, for that matter, the majority) groups in this country are to be weaned away from the influence of fundamentalism, they must be made to feel socially and economically secure. Their culture and religion must be protected from external violence and from unneces-sary moralizing. It must be recognized that social transformation can only legitimately come from within a society or community. . . . Exter-nal threats to the identity of such communities only strengthen the traditionalists and fundamentalists within them, and marginalize the progressive forces.[15]

---

[15] *Growing Amnesia*, pp. 123, 134, 149, 151. As he adds at another point (p. 90): "Basically, without the deeper cultural base, it is not possible to achieve human well-being. Even if it is temporarily brought about through some administrative or technological means . . . it will soon disappear".

II

Kothari's insider perspective—or his view of the world "from the bottom up"—is also emphatically shared by Ashis Nandy, his senior associate at the Delhi Centre. Like Rajni Kothari, Nandy for a long time has been a spokesman of democratic politics and democratic transformative change—but a change which is popularly or locally legitimated rather than being imposed by hegemonic (colonial or neo-colonial) forces or else by self-appointed middle-class elites. If there is a difference between the two thinkers, it is one of emphasis and disciplinary focus: whereas Kothari centrestages issues endemic to political economy and sociology, Nandy—a trained psychologist and psychoanalyst—is more concerned with the psychic (or psycho-cultural) wellsprings of popular resistance as well as with the inner traumas of colonial oppression. One of his early publications, titled *At the Edge of Psychology* (1980), traced perceptively the intersections and cross-currents linking the domains of politics, culture, and psychology—especially as these intersections are experienced in non-Western societies. His next book, *The Intimate Enemy* (1983), probed this constellation more concretely by focusing on the psychic effects of colonial domination, primarily on processes of introjection or internalization of the colonizer's worldview—which, among the colonized, lead to a "loss of self" and an ensuing struggle for self-recovery. Regarding the latter struggle, Nandy in psychotherapeutic fashion sought to unearth submerged or suppressed layers of an "uncolonized mind," layers which might be mobilized as possible sources of resistance and self-transformation.[16] For present purposes I shall forego a general overview and rather concentrate on some of his more recent writings, especially writings which aim to spell out his political vision as an alternative or challenge to prevailing formulas.

In a relatively clear and concise manner, Nandy's alternative vision is articulated in *Traditions, Tyranny and Utopias* (1987), especially in the chapter titled "Towards a Third World Utopia." The chapter immediately takes its stand at the grassroots level, by viewing the world

---

[16] See Ashis Nandy, *At the Edge of Psychology: Essays in Politics and Culture* (Delhi: Oxford University Press, 1980); *The Intimate Enemy: Loss and Recovery of Self under Colonialism* (Delhi: Oxford University Press, 1983). Nandy has also been a prolific writer on the politics and culture of science. One of his early texts in this field was *Alternative Sciences: Creativity and Authenticity in Two Indian Scientists* (Delhi: Oxford University Press, 1980).

"from the bottom up". As Nandy emphasizes, the notion of the "Third World" is not a timeless, metaphysical idea; rather, it is a political and economic category "born of poverty, exploitation, indignity and self-contempt." Given this stark historical background, the formulation of an alternative future for non-Western societies must start from the experience of "man-made suffering"—not for the sake of inducing self-pity or self-hatred, but in order to permit a therapeutic "working through" of the traumas of oppression. My approach, Nandy writes, is guided by the belief that the only way the Third World can transcend colonialism—as well as the "sloganeering of its well-wishers"—is by "becoming a collective representation of the victims of man-made suffering everywhere in the world" and then by "owning up" the forces of oppression and "coping with them as inner vectors".

As helpmates in this process of coping and working through Nandy at this point invokes healing powers latent or buried in indigenous traditions—especially as such powers were mobilized in the Gandhian struggle for independence. A prominent resource of this kind is the relative distance of non-Western cultures from modern (Cartesian) dualisms or dichotomies, especially the dualism of subject and object, humans and nature—and colonizers and colonized. Appealing to the Gandhian notions of non-violence and non-cooperation, Nandy construes them as (therapeutic) exit routes from domination. For Gandhi, he states, the aim of the oppressed was not "to become a first-class citizen in the world of oppression instead of a second- or third-class one", but rather "to build an alternative world where he can hope to win back his humanity." With specific regard to colonial domination, Gandhi sought "to free the British as much as the Indians from the clutches of imperialism". Nandy sees here a parallel with forms of (non-orthodox) Marxism as well as Christian liberation theology; and he quotes a statement by Gustavo Gutierrez to the effect that "one loves the oppressors by liberating them from their inhuman condition as oppressors, by liberating them from themselves".[17]

---

[17] Nandy, *Tradition, Tyranny and Utopias: Essays in the Politics of Awareness* (Delhi: Oxford University Press, 1987), pp. 21, 31–35. The importance of Gandhi's legacy for the future of developing societies is spelled out with eloquence and subtlety in the book's concluding chapter, titled "From Outside the Imperium: Gandhi's Cultural Critique of the West", pp. 127–162. As one should note, in exploring therapeutic alternatives, Nandy did not postulate a latent Indian "essence" untouched by external intrusion. It is not easy, he writes at one point (p. 17), "to live with an alien culture's estimate of oneself, to integrate it within one's selfhood and to that self-induced inner tension. It is even more difficult to live with the inner dialogue

The publication of *Traditions, Tyranny and Utopias* coincided roughly with the appearance of one of Nandy's most well-known and widely discussed essays, titled "Cultural Frames for Social Transformation: A Credo" (in the journal *Alternatives*). The essay took its point of departure from the anti-colonial struggle in Africa, and especially from Amilcar Cabral's stress on popular or indigenous culture as a counterpoint to external oppression. In Nandy's view, Cabral's stance could be extended to other colonial or post-colonial societies; basically, the stance implies a turn to the lived world of people at the grassroots (and thus a perspective "from the bottom up"). As he writes, the emphasis on culture and cultural traditions signals a defiance of the modern (Western) ideas of intellectual and scientific "expertise", an expertise uncontaminated by popular customs or beliefs; it gives voice to societies and peoples "which have been the victims of history and are now trying to rediscover their own visions of a desirable society". In our post-colonial world, the issues of cultural resistance and self-assertion is by no means obsolete; on the contrary, it is gaining added significance and salience due to the relentless momentum of globalization or global standardization under Western auspices. Thus, the stress on "cultural frames for social transformation" constitutes in our time "a plea for a minimum cultural plurality in an increasingly uniformized world".[18]

An important objective of Nandy's essay is to sort out the spectrum of possible (ideal-typical) responses on the part of non-Western societies to the inroads of both colonialism and globalization. One such response is that of modernizing elites, especially urban middle-class professionals, entrepreneurs, and intellectuals. Having received much of their education and training in the West, these elites are basically committed to Western-style modernization—that is, "the values of European Enlightenment"—although they may be willing to fit selected fragments of native traditions into their modernist scheme. In contrast to this mode of "critical modernism", radical traditionalists are bent on repulsing and ostracizing all Western influences and hence on encapsulating themselves in native traditions—which in effect means to ossify or "museumize" the latter.

---

within one's own culture which is triggered off by the dialogue with other cultures because, then, the carefully built defenses against disturbing dialogues . . . begin to crumble". See also Gustavo Gutierrez, *A Theory of Liberation* (New York: Orbis Books, 1973), p. 276.

[18] Nandy, "Cultural Frames for Social Transformation: A Credo", *Alternatives*, Vol. 12 (1987), pp. 113–114.

Nandy's own sympathies are with neither of these options. Instead, his essay pleads for a different path, termed "critical traditionalism": one which seeks to marshal the resources provided by cultural traditions or inherited "cultural frames" for purposes of social and political transformation. The chief exemplar of this approach in the Indian context was Gandhi. As Nandy recalls, Gandhi's *Hind Swaraj* launched a "savage" critique of Western civilization and Western modernity (which Gandhi at one point did not hesitate to call "satanic"); but this critique did not in any way inhibit him from denouncing traditional abuses like the caste system and untouchability. In fact, Nandy writes, Gandhi's inveighing against untouchability was only "the other side of his struggle against modern imperialism"—which means that "neither of the two struggles could be conceived without the other". In contradistinction from radical traditionalists, he adds,

> Gandhi did not want to defend traditions; he lived with them. Nor did he, like Nehru, want to museumize cultures within a modern frame. Gandhi's frame was traditional, but he was willing to criticize some traditions violently. He was even willing to include in his frame elements of modernity as critical vectors. He found no dissonance between his rejection of modern technology and his advocacy of the bicycle, the lathe and the sewing machine. Gandhi defied the modern world by opting for an alternative frame.[19]

Elaborating further on the path of critical traditionalism, Nandy emphasizes the difference between this path and a backward-looking historicism retrieving the past for merely academic purposes. What is needed instead is a recollection of the role of cultural traditions in the lived experience of peoples; this, in turn, requires attention to the internal fissures in traditions, especially the fissures between oppressors and oppressed. In Nandy's words, critical traditionality invokes the memory of traditions in their embroilment with (overt or covert) modes of oppression. Differently phrased: to be valid or legitimate, recollection of traditions has to foster also "an awareness of the nature of evil", that is, of the persistence of "man-made *dukkha* or suffering" from the past into the present. Conversely, to be pertinent and intelligible, a theory or account of oppression has to be cast "in native terms or categories", that is, "in terms and categories used by the victims of our times".

The latter postulate militates against certain modernist theories of

---

[19] "Cultural Frames for Social Transformation", pp. 114–116.

oppression (including orthodox Marxism) which, couched in the idiom of post-Enlightenment rationalism, are disdainful of vernacular languages and experiences. Resorting to popular culture here means again to privilege the voice of the victims. In emphatic terms, Nandy insists

> on the primacy that should be given to the political consciousness of those who have been forced to develop categories to understand their own suffering and who reject the pseudo-indignity of modern theories of oppression using—merely using—native idioms to conscientize, brainwash, educate, indoctrinate the oppressed or to museumize their cultures. The resistance to modern oppression has to involve, in our part of the world, some resistance to modernity.... The resistance must deny in particular the connotative meanings of concepts such as development, growth, history, science and technology. These concepts have become not only new "reasons of state" but mystifications for new forms of violence and injustice.

These arguments lead Nandy in the end to articulate a "general skepticism" towards some key premises of Western modernity. All his doubts boil down to a general distrust of the ideas sponsored by "the winners of the world and their allies"—a distrust which prompts him to turn from mainline doctrines to "the faiths and ideas of the powerless and marginalized. That way lie freedom, compassion and justice".[20]

To round out this discussion of Nandy's writings I turn briefly to his recent book titled *The Illegitimacy of Nationalism* (1994). The book is a critical indictment of one of the key features of "Western modernity" namely, the centralized nation-state and as a corollary, the idea of "nationalism" seen as the driving engine of that state. Nandy follows Partha Chatterjee in perceiving the nation-state in India basically as a British import foisted on a more or less amorphous Indian society and civilization. Yet, whereas for Chatterjee—and for many "subaltern" as well as progressivist writers—the nation-state was merely a half-way house or obstacle on the road towards a more global vision (either that of a global free market or a classless world society), Nandy invokes indigenous cultural resources as critical buffers against the homogenizing effects of both nationalism and (Western-style) cosmopolitanism. In following this path, he expresses his strong indebtedness

---

[20] "Cultural Frames for Social Transformation", pp. 117, 123. Nandy's distrust of some key categories of Western modernity is evident in a subsequent volume edited by him under the title *Science, Hegemony and Violence: A Requiem for Modernity* (Delhi: Oxford University Press, 1988).

to Rabindranath Tagore, the great Indian poet and novelist of the pre-independence period. (A major portion of the book is in fact devoted to a detailed exegesis of some of Tagore's main novels.)

In Nandy's view, Tagore differed from many leaders of the independence movement by his ambivalent and quasi-dialectical attitude towards nationalism and the nation-state. Although initially willing to marshall nationalist sentiments in the struggle against colonialism, his more mature or seasoned work came to suspect nationalism as an accomplice of neo-imperialist modernization schemes. In Nandy's portrayal, many leaders of the independence movement saw nationalism as a "premodern concept" that functioned merely as a "pathological by-product of global capitalism". Once India and humanity at large had overcome the seductive charms of this "vestigial medievalism," nationalism and the nation-state were expected to "wither away" in favour of an "enlightened, secular universalism" greeted as harbinger of a "future One World". In opposition to this outlook, Tagore and a small band of dissenters regarded nationalism indeed as a by-product of the Western system of nation-states, but also and more importantly as an ally in the steadily accelerating process of globalization and global standardization. Shunning cultural relativism, the alternative vision of these dissenters was a global civilizational perspective, but one rooted in "the tolerance encoded in various traditional ways of life in a highly diverse, plural society".[21]

Among the band of dissenters in the independence movement, Nandy includes next to Tagore also Gandhi—notwithstanding some pronounced differences of emphasis and orientation. According to Nandy's text, the main difference had to do with the type of cultural resources mobilized in the anti-colonial struggle. Whereas Tagore was primarily attracted to India's "high culture" as represented by its classical traditions, Gandhi in his endeavors turned for support chiefly to the popular or folk traditions (both in India and the West). This difference is also linked with their general attitude towards Western modernity. Although starting out as a modernist, Tagore in the course of his life came to make "less and less sense of the modern world", Gandhi on the other hand, proceeding from the counter-modernism of *Hind Swaraj*, emerged as a major critical figure whose defence of

---

[21] Nandy, *The Illegitimacy of Nationalism: Rabindranath Tagore and the Politics of Self* (Delhi: Oxford University Press, 1994), pp. x–xi. Compare also Partha Chatterjee, *Nationalist Thought and the Colonial World: A Derivative Discourse* (Takyo: Zed Books, 1986; second impr.: Minneapolis, MN: University of Minnesota Press, 1993).

folk traditions carried "intimations of a post-modern consciousness."

What linked the two, in Nandy's account, was basically their assessment of nationalism. Both recognized, he writes, "the need for a 'national' ideology of India as a means of cultural survival"; yet both also recognized that, for the same reason, India "would either have to make a break with the post-medieval Western concept a nationalism or give the concept a new content". As a result, nationalism for Tagore became gradually illegitimate, while for Gandhi it had to involve an internal self-critique coupled with a critique of the nation-state. For both, the latter critique did not entail the endorsement of a bland globalism, but rather the need to strengthen cultural and popular sources of resistance to imperial or neo-imperial designs. For both also, such an accent was completely at odds with ethnic chauvinism or exclusivism, especially the notion of a "single-ethnic Hindu *rashtra*"; instead, whatever meaning India might have could only be the work of continuous interpretation and renegotiation, a process yielding fragile unity only "through acknowledgment of differences".[22]

III

My presentation in these pages has tried to offer glimpses, or highlight major accents, of the Delhi Centre for the Study of Developing Societies, by focusing on the work of Kothari and Nandy. As indicated before, my focus in this regard is limited and highly selective, given the multifaceted character of the Centre's activities. As an institution devoted to research on social policy issues, the Centre counts among its associates—in addition to Kothari and Nandy—numerous practioners whose leanings are more empirical or social-scientific in character, or else straddle empirical, theoretical, and practical domains; on several occasions, collaborative projects have also been undertaken by associates from diverse disciplines. In all these respects—as I mentioned earlier—the Centre bears a resemblance to the Frankfurt Institute of Social Research established by Horkheimer, Adorno and several others during the later years of the Weimar Republic. Curiously, the parallel between the two institutions breaks down when applied to the present period. While initially committed to the critical analysis of capitalist developments in the West—and hence also to an

---

[22] Nandy, *The Illegitimacy of Nationalism*, pp. 1–2, 6, 87.

investigation of the dark underside of modernity (or the "dialectic of enlightenment")—the Frankfurt School in recent decades has emerged as a chief protagonist of Western modernity and of the global process of modernization and secularization. To this extent (one might say), the Delhi Centre recaptures strands of the earlier Frankfurt program which have been cast aside or sidelined by recent representatives of that school.

Not being a neutral onlooker of global affairs, I find myself harboring a strong sympathy for the overall pattern (though perhaps not all the details) of the Centre's perspective. Above all, the Centre's accent on popular culture and folk traditions strikes me as preferable to a narrow political economy approach—an approach that has tended to characterize "Subaltern Studies" (at least during their formative years). For one thing, from the vantage of developing societies, political economy—especially when couched in a traditional Marxist idiom— is likely to be experienced as a Western import, that is, as part and parcel of the arsenal of conceptual frameworks (including the nation-state) bequeathed to subaltern peoples by colonial or neo-colonial policies. Moreover, in its orthodox-Marxist mode, political-economic analysis is prone to compress or streamline social life into a polar opposition of classes—in a fashion which ignores the complex welter of differentiated interactions and antagonisms prevalent in non- or partially industrialized societies. This problem has been duly noted by Edward Said, in his Foreword to one of the subaltern volumes. If subaltern history, he writes there, follows this polarizing strategy and construes itself as simple antithesis, it runs the risk of "just being a mirror opposite" of official historiography, and thus becoming "as exclusivist, as limited, provincial and discriminatory" as the "master discourses" of colonialism and capitalist elitism.[23] Finally and most importantly, in its bent toward secularist universalism, Marxist analysis rides roughshod over and thus homogenizes local experiences and

---

[23] Edward W. Said, "Foreword" in Ranajit Guha and Gayatri Chakravorty Spivak (eds.), *Selected Subaltern Studies*, p. viii. Since the time of the first volume in 1982, the Marxist and Gramscian moorings of Subaltern Studies have been transformed by a series of other influences, including structuralism and post-structuralism as well as British political sociology. To this extent, Said is entirely correct in noting (p. x) that "none of the Subaltern Scholars is anything less than a critical student of Karl Marx," and that today "the influence of structuralist and post-structuralist thinkers like Derrida, Foucault, Roland Barthes and Louis Althusser is evident, along with the influence of British and American thinkers, like E.P. Thompson, Eric Hobsbawm, and others".

traditions by subjecting them to a global design. Hence, futurist in orientation, such analysis strips oppressed people of their cultural memories just at the point when these are most needed as points of resistance.

Although in many ways partial to the Centre, I am not unaware of certain quandaries or unresolved issues besetting its perspective. One of the more troubling and recalcitrant problems has to do with the role of politics, particularly the role of the state. On this point, the writings of Kothari and Nandy reveal a notable ambivalence, and also a certain difference of emphasis. Both are opposed to the homogenizing threat of centralized power; yet Kothari seems unwilling to jettison the modern state entirely—at least in the absence of other mediating and policy-setting agencies. While moving away *Amnesia,* from an earlier progressivism (supporting the Indian welfare state), his recent work grants to the state at least a limited function— as long as it provides a protective shield for popular resistance to global or multinational pressures. As he writes in *Growing Amnesia,* there is a need not to allow the complete erosion of the state's "legitimacy"—for experience shows that, lacking alternatives "the poor and the marginalized have nowhere to turn other than to the state".

For Kothari, salvaging a properly chastized, transformed or "humanized" state also means salvaging a "democratic space" or a public forum for the redress of grievances. On this point, Nandy's position appears more adamant. In an essay titled "Culture, State, and the Rediscovery of Indian Politics", Nandy distinguishes between two basic approaches to politics: a "culture-oriented" and a statist or "nation-state-oriented" approach; whereas in the latter, culture serves merely as a tool for the promotion of state power, in the former the state is a handmaiden of culture (or for the "enrichment of culture"). Between the two options Nandy is not in doubt. As his essay asserts, it is imperative to abandon the primacy-of-state theory—adopted by India from the West—in favour of an outlook privileging culture or civilization. A basic premise of that outlook is the belief "that a civilization must use the state as an instrument and not become an instrument of the state".[24]

Nandy's position raises difficult questions regarding the relation

---

[24] See Kothari, *Growing Amnesia*, p. 95 ("Role of the State"); Nandy, "Culture, State, and the Rediscovery of Indian Politics" in *Interculture*, Vol. 21, No. 2, Issue 99 (1988), pp. 2–3, 8.

between culture and politics, questions for which there are no stand-ard formulas and hardly any very reliable guideposts. A central query might be formulated in this manner: how can culture "use the state as an instrument" or provide an agenda for state policy? Couched more briskly, the question comes to this: can culture be a "frame" (a cultural frame) for social transformation? I am fully in accord with Nandy's critique of the modern nation-state (as a totalizing project) and, more generally, of a narrowly "state-oriented" approach to politics bent on merely "using" or abusing cultural traditions. His critique, I believe, can be extended to a recently fashionable thesis according to which culture is nothing but a political product or artifact, hence something which can be wilfully constructed and "deconstructed" by political elites or agents. Although often propounded with fan-fare, the thesis can hardly stand up to scrutiny; simple hermeneutical sobriety should be sufficient to guard against this excess (of subjec-tivism and social engineering).

On the other hand, however, culture cannot be completely immu-nized or segregated from politics or policy concerns—as might be suggested by the notion of a "culture-oriented" or "primacy-of-culture" approach. To treat culture as such a non- or pre-political domain—a domain which only subsequently utilizes state policy—means to lapse into, or move in the proximity of, cultural "essentialism" or "foundationalism" (terms which today have a pejorative ring). As it seems to me, culture always requires interpretation (which, in a sense, is a political act); but it is also always in excess of any given inter-pretation—with the result that interpretations (and political "uses") remain contestable. To put matters somewhat differently: culture or the cultural life-world is a background which can never be fully "foregrounded"—although politics (as a project) consists in this fore-grounding attempt. These considerations point out the complex entwinement of life-world and policy, of culture and agency—where both are mutually implicated, thereby constraining and modulating each other.[25]

The privileging of culture raises additional questions to the extent that it implies a privileging of native or indigenous cultural resources—over against alien (mainly Western) cultural and political-economic

---

[25] On the relation of culture and politics see, *e.g.*, Margaret Archer, *Cultures and Agency: The Place of Culture in Social Theory* (Cambridge: Cambridge University Press, 1988); Gayatri Chakravorti Spivak, *In Other Worlds: Essays in Cultural Politics* (New York: Methuen, 1987); and Marshall Sahlins, *Culture and Practical Reason* (Chicago: University of Chicago Press, 1976).

influences. As has often been pointed out (especially by Western intellectuals), such a move conjures up the danger of cultural exclusivism or self-segregation—coupled perhaps with the utopian imagery of the "*bon sauvage*". Despite occasional overtures in this direction, Nandy's as well as Kothari's writings are on the whole remarkably free of this temptation of self-seclusion. As both have persistently emphasized, the voices of the marginalized and dispossessed in Third World countries can only be heard or come into their own when placed into the broader public forum of the emerging world community—provided they are not droned out by standardizing hegemonic refrains. In this connection, it is well to remember a passage in *Traditions, Tyranny and Utopias* where Nandy states that the issue is not to choose between Westernization and a static "reactive Indianness", but to find a path for cross-cultural encounter in the context of Western global hegemony.

Such encounter, he writes, inevitably succumbs to the hierarchy of power "unless the dialogue creates a shared space for each participant's distinctive, unstated theory of the other cultures". Cross-cultural dialogue, he adds, inevitably spills over at this point into intra-cultural dialogue, that is the "dialogue within each participating culture among its different levels or parts". This insight is corroborated by Kothari in his comments on the internal complexity and multivocity of Indian cultural life. By way of conclusion I want to cite a passage from *Growing Amnesia* which ably reflects his alternative vision for India—and possibly for the rest of the world:

> One of the continuing cultural traits of the Indian civilization has all along been in terms of its high tolerance of ambiguity. Only the modern hi-tech elite wants to regulate things, "resolve" contradictions along some rationalist calculus.... The age of these modernists... is fast coming to a close, here and elsewhere in the world. This does not mean any return to some pristine past as if such a "past" were ever there for us to "revive". This is then the ambience of a new awakening, a redefinition of Indian identity, one that is at once so uncertain about what lies in store and so pregnant with possibilities.[26]

---

[26] Nandy, *Traditions, Tyranny and Utopias*, pp. 16–17; Kothari, *Growing Amnesia*, p. 179. Compare also Nandy's comment, in "Culture, State, and the Rediscovery of Indian Politics" (p. 11): "Unlike the modernists and Hindu revivalists, those viewing Indian politics from outside the framework of the nation-state system believe it possible for a state to represent a confederation of cultures, including a multiplicity of religions and languages. To each of these cultures, other cultures are an internal opposition rather than an external enemy".

SEX DETERMINATION TEST IN INDIA:
REINFORCING THE BIAS AGAINST WOMEN

Krishna Mallick

India is one of the four countries in the world along with Iran, Pakistan and Australia where there are less women per thousand men. In the case of other countries male female ratio is the other way, namely, there are more women per thousand males and biological reproduction requires more women than men. In Australia the adverse sex ratio is a result of the large number of male migrants. In India, Iran and Pakistan, however, social reasons are the primary cause. In these countries, there is a strong preference for male children who are expected to support their parents in old age and also economically benefit the family. Women are culturally conditioned to accept the tragic fact that unless they bear a male child, they do not have any social worth. Women's choice is dependent on the fear of the society. Girl babies are considered to be an economic burden to the family because when they grow up, parents have to arrange for their marriage and pay the dowry to the bridegrooms's family.

In 1901, the Indian sex ratio was 972 females per 1000 males. More recently, the ratios were 930, 934 and 929 per 1000 men for 1971, 1981 and 1991, respectively.[1] This shows that there has been a steady decline of females through the 20th century. One of the reasons for the adverse sex ratio in these countries is the practice of aborting female foetuses detected through amniocentesis.

Of the methods of contraception available in India, abortion is the most widely practiced, with six to nine million women having abortions annually. The medical termination of pregnancy is legal in India, but only 5% of abortions performed are indeed legal. In 1980–81 a total of 385,749 legal abortions were performed, out of which 10.9% were done in Maharashtra, 9.4% in Tamil Nadu and Kerala and the rest were performed in the other twenty nine states and union territories in India. In many of these cases, abortion was sought because of the presence of a female foetus.

---

[1] Amulya Ratan Nanda, *Census of India, 1991*, Series 1, Registrar General & Census Commissioner, India, Statement 12, p. 51.

Amniocentesis is a test for detecting genetic disorders in foetus. A needle attached to a syringe is inserted into the amniotic sac that surrounds the foetus in the uterus. Twenty to thirty ml. of amniotic fluid is then drawn out into the syringe. This fluid is examined microscopically to determine the sex of the foetus. The test is done at the end of four months of pregnancy or 120 days after the last menstruation. In general, it is simple and medically sound.

In India, from 1978 to 1983 about 78,000 female foetuses were aborted after the performance of sex determination tests.[2] In Bombay alone, according to one recent report, there were 14,000 foetuses aborted in one year.[3] A second report noted that sex-determination tests have been conducted "since 1977 but gained nationwide notoriety only after the erroneous abortion of a male foetus in an Amritsar clinic in 1982".[4] It was after this that this issue of sex-determination tests became public.

Since these tests can be done at a cost of Rs. 80 or approximately $3.00 to Rs. 800 or approximately $30.00, it is affordable for poor people. A survey conducted in several Bombay slums demonstrated that many women had the sex-determination test performed and, after finding that the foetus was female, had undergone an abortion. These women justified their action by saying that it is better to spend Rs. 80 or Rs. 800 now than spending Rs. 80,000 later for dowry and marriage. It is also important to note that physicians were advertising the availability of sex-determination test with its low cost.

In the case of India, the sex-determination test through amniocentesis is an instrument of discrimination against the female foetus, since young mothers are conditioned by centuries of tradition to consider females as burdens to themselves as well as to society. Women's self-worth and value is often dependent on their reproductive functions. Due to cultural conditioning, women themselves go to great lengths to ensure a number of children as a result of pressure of the family and the society. Sons are viewed as economic, and ritual assets; whereas daughters are viewed as liabilities. Sons are considered as valuable sources of income. Sons often stay with the parents after they are married and thus, provide security for the parents in their

---

[2] *Times of India*, Editorial (June 1982).
[3] *The Hindustan Times* (December 8, 1990).
[4] *India Today* (January 31, 1988), p. 55.

old age. Among Hindus, sons are needed to perform rituals which protect the family after the death of the father. Daughters, on the other hand, marry out and cannot provide support for the families of birth. During daughter's marriage parents have to provide dowries to the bridegrooms's family. Daughters cannot perform the ritual after the death of the father.

Except in special circumstances, in Indian law abortion is a criminal offence at any stage. According to the Medical Termination of Pregnancy Act of 1971, at up to 12 weeks of pregnancy, one physician is required to issue a certificate to this effect; between 12 and 20 weeks two physicians are required to do so, since the risk to the mother is greater at this point; after 20 weeks, abortion is legal only if the child will be born seriously abnormal or the birth will endanger the life of the mother or her physical or mental health. Amniocentesis is performed in the 14th to 16th week of pregnancy, ostensibly to prevent injury to the mother's mental or physical health, but in actuality, the test is conducted for the purpose of sex selection, and can be legally performed. It is probable that it will become possible to predict the sex of the foetus at a much earlier stage.

The state of Maharashtra has legislated an act called "Maharashtra Regulation of use of Pre-natal Diagnostic Techniques Act". This law regulates the use of medical techniques for prenatal diagnosis.

This paper addresses questions like, should sex determination tests be condemned as a threat to Indian society? Should sex-determination test, as many have argued, be welcomed as a means of slowing down overpopulation in India? Are women in India choosing to have sex-determination test and then deciding to abort the female foetus out of their free choice? Is the Maharashtra legislation sound? Does it accomplish the objective of reducing sexual inequality which is pervasive in India? I answer these questions by analyzing the arguments related to the test and by examining the moral implications and effectiveness of the Maharashtra legislation. I will argue that the technology of amniocentesis has been abused to the extent of making the situation worse for Indian women in terms of sexual equality. Technology must be linked with the socio-economic and cultural realities. It demonstrates that legal measures can succeed in India only when supported by organized campaign of the people directed toward bringing about socio-cultural revolution, thus improving the status of women.

I. With female foeticide, the number of female would eventually decrease. This would be a socio-cultural perversion of a natural or biological requirement. Biological reproduction requires, in fact, more woman than men because a woman typically bears only one child at a time, whereas a man can impregnate many women. For the survival of a child, it is the female that plays the dominant role: carrying the baby in the womb, providing the foetus with the tissues and nutrients from her own body, and breastfeeding it after birth. It is tragic that Indian society does not value the being who contributes most to the continuation of the species.

If the female sex ratio continues to decrease, it ultimately could lead to the extinction of the race. Himachal Pradesh is a state in India where there are fewer women than men. This had led to polyandry, with as many as five husbands sharing one wife.[5] If this were to continue, though the number of women in the population will decrease it does not necessarily guarantee that the overall population will decrease. If that is not guaranteed, then it would be a negative increase in population.

There are other morally preferable ways to reduce the overpopulation problem than by reducing the number of girl babies being born. In India, it has to be an extensive programme of social change. The perceived need to have sons to help their parents in their old age can be reduced by basic reforms like improved medical care, by reducing infant and child mortality; by some kind of government funded social security for the elderly; by reducing unjust economic differentials through property and income redistribution. Providing educational opportunities for girls and women, delaying the age of marriage, educating women about family planning measures and improving the efficiency with which birth-control methods are employed; creating more job opportunities for women in general, a move toward more equal social, legal and economic status for women will help to change the perception that it is only sons who can improve the family's status. In this way, the need to continue childbearing until there are enough boys will diminish. To justify abortion of female foetuses to have the effect of reducing the problem of overpopulation is asking for a quick fix which cannot be morally justified, as stated above, because the predicted effect does not take place and also, it

---

[5] Lakshmi Mohan, "The sex-determination controversy continues", *Eves Weekly* (September 25, 1982), p. 13.

is morally wrong to target one gender as the cause of the problem without looking at the root cause of the problem. The objective is to achieve equal rights and equal justice for persons of both sexes. The method of aborting female foetus through sex determination test goes against this objective. In the case of India, instead of promoting sexual equality, the technology of amniocentesis has been abused to further deteriorate the situation of women.

Government and private practitioners involved in this lucrative trade justify sex determination tests as a means of population control. Women have always been the worst target for family planning policies. As Dharma Kumar writes, "Is it really better to be born and left to die than to be killed as a foetus?"[6] Her point is that the birth of millions of unwanted girls does not contribute to improving the status of women and it aggravates the issue of male/female sex ratio. She also notes that with the decrease in the number of women, females will be treated better by Indian society.

It must be asked whether this will really improve the status of women. Kumar's argument is based on the assumption that in the process of wanting to have sons couples will have more children. This assumption has limitations. Studies have demonstrated, for example, that the poor have more children because of the high infant mortality rate and because of the economic contribution of children. Therefore, to argue for the availability of sex-determination tests to allow people to have a balanced family and, at the same time, to ignore the changing socio-economic and environmental conditions, represents an unbalanced priority. What constitutes a balanced family is problematic and planned parenthood cannot be equated with the choice of the sex of the child. Further, India is one of only four countries in the world with an adverse female-male population ratio. This situation actually has worsened over the last six decades, yet it has had no significant impact on India's overall rate of population growth. The following chart demonstrates that the overall rate of population growth has not decreased.[7]

---

[6] Dharma Kumar, "Amniocentesis Again (Discussion)", *Economic and Political Weekly*, 18:24 (June 11, 1983), p. 1075.

[7] Amulya Ratan Nanda, *Census of India, 1991*, Series 1, Registrar General & Census Commissioner, India, Statement 2, p. 21.

Population of India: 1901–1991

Year	Population	Decadal growth Absolute	Average Annual exponential growth rate percent	Progressive growth rate over 1901 percent
1	2	3	4	5	6
1901	238,396,327	–	–	–	–
1911	252,093,390	+ 13,697,063	+ 5.75	0.56	+ 5.75
1921	251,321,213	– 772,177	– 0.31	–0.03	+ 5.42
1931	278,977,238	+ 27,656,025	+11.00	1.04	+ 17.02
1941	318,660,580	+ 39,683,342	+14.22	1.33	+ 33.67
1951	361,088,090	+ 42,420,485	+13.31	1.25	+ 51.47
1961	439,234,771	+ 77,682,873	+21.51	1.96	+ 84.25
1971	548,159,652	+108,924,881	+24.80	2.20	+129.94
1981	683,329,097	+135,169,445	+24.66	2.22	+186.64
1991	843,930,861	+160,601,764	+23.50	2.11	+254.00

The above chart shows that beginning in 1931, the population of India has increased steadily. There is a slight decline in the population between 1981 and 1991, but not at the same rate as the female sex ratio is declining.

Secondly, amniocentesis has potential complications. The risk of the needle piercing is relatively low, but if it occurs, an abortion can result. Also, the needle could damage the mother's abdomen. In rare cases, the test itself can precipitate an unwanted abortion. As Dr. Nandini Purandhare observes, "Developmentally, the male foetus is weaker than the female, and any interference could set off an abortion. Will the family condone the abortion of a third or fourth or fifth son? Whereas, from my own experience as a doctor I find that parents would sacrifice the third or fourth female child without a qualm".[8]

Another argument that has been put forth against the ban of amniocentesis is that women are choosing to have the procedure done based on their own free will. However, in a society where women are socially conditioned to accept the tragic fact that unless they bear

---

[8] Dharma Kumar, "Amniocentesis Again (Discussion)", p. 14.

a male child, they do not have social worth, a woman's choice is significantly influenced by fear. The so-called choices result from the powerlessness of women and their oppression. Though feminists throughout the world believe that women should have the right to choose to bear a child or not and have control over their own bodies, for India, the social, political and economic factors cannot be overlooked. Due to lack of food, economic security, clean drinking water and adequate health care facilities, a woman must have 6.2 children in order to have at least one surviving male child.[9] Since freedom is not absolute but always operates within a certain cultural, social, political and economic situation and since these situations, to begin with, are not conducive to sexual equality, it can be argued that it is not really freedom of choice. Individual right cannot be stressed without taking into consideration the conditions under which choices are made. Individual right and choice can be easily turned against women themselves.

Considering the pro-life and pro-choice debate in abortion, I take the side of pro-life, except in cases where the mother's life is in danger, when there is a possibility of a severely defective baby being born and when the pregnancy is the result of rape, as I believe that right to life of the foetus should be given priority over other rights because life has intrinsic worth. The woman has the responsibility to respect the right to life of the foetus and a responsibility towards her action. The woman does not have an absolute right to do whatever she wants with her body. With every right, there is a responsibility. Where the mother's life is in danger, or when there is a possibility of a severely defective child being born or when the woman is a victim of rape, abortion can be justified because in each of these cases, there is a severe threat involved, either to the mother, or to the foetus. In any other case, the right to life of the foetus should be respected. I do not take an absolutistic stand but at the same time I do not take a teleological standpoint also.

Carrying this middle ground between the two extreme views on abortion to the case of abortion after sex-determination, my argument is that late abortion, as a result of amniocentesis which can be medically done only at a later stage of pregnancy, is morally problematic because first, danger to the woman is greater medically and

---

[9] Neera Desai and M. Krishnaraj, *Women and Society in India* (India: Ajanta Publications, 1990), p. 225.

it is a morally relevant question to ask if a woman can be justifiably asked or advised to voluntarily terminate her pregnancy for a greater social good, *i.e.*, limiting population growth. Second, in the second trimester of pregnancy the foetus develops some capacity of sentience and though one might argue that sentient foetuses are not persons, yet I believe that the deliberate act of killing a foetus is still *prima facie* wrong or at least requires morally sound justification to show that it is not merely something that the woman has the right to choose but which she is right to choose. Late abortion can be morally justified to protect the health of the woman, or to avoid the birth of a severely handicapped infant. But late abortion because the foetus is female is morally wrong as it is an expression of the wrongful devaluation of all females.

Some people take a cultural relativistic standpoint and argue that late abortion of female foetuses is an accepted practice in India and it is working within the caste system, socio-economic and religious context in India and therefore, it is right. To this, my response is that though it is true that the cultural/socio-economic/religious context is important to understand the differences in the accepted practices of different cultures, yet respect for life is a right that should be followed always as it is moral no matter what the socio-economic or religious context is. Any accepted practice is not necessarily moral, specifically in this case, as it violates the principles of justice and equality. Through this practice, women's status is deteriorating rather than improving and therefore, cannot be morally justified. The general question about morality cannot be set aside due to socio-economic and religious background. In some cases at least, a commonly accepted moral viewpoint will lie beneath all local traditions. I am not suggesting that tradition, socio-economic/religious conditions are not at all important. They are, indeed, extremely important in our understanding of cultural differences. What is needed is cultural symbiosis without ignoring the morality of it. Inter-cultural understanding is crucial in the global context of today.

II. In 1988 an act was passed in Maharashtra called the "Maharashtra Regulation of use of Pre-natal Diagnostic Techniques Act." This is "an Act to provide for the regulation of the use of medical or scientific techniques of pre-natal diagnosis solely for the purpose of detecting genetic or metabolic disorders or chromosomal abnormalities of certain congenital anomalies or sex-linked disorders and or prevention of the misuse of these techniques for the purpose of pre-natal sex determination leading to female foeticide; and for matters connected therewith or incidental thereto.[10]

Under this Act, gynecologists possessing the prescribed qualifications at registered genetic centres can perform activities relating to the pre-natal diagnostic techniques with the help of procedures such as amniocentesis, chorionic villi sampling or any other pre-natal diagnostic technique only under the following conditions:

(1) the age of the pregnant woman is above 35 years;
(2) a history of two or more abortions or foetal loss;
(3) there is a history of exposure to potentially teratogenic drugs, radiation, infection or hazardous chemicals;
(4) there is a family history of mental retardation or physical deformities such as a spastic or deaf-mute child or any other genetic disease;
(5) any other condition as may be provided by the appropriate Authority.

The pre-natal diagnostic test can be performed only to detect abnormalities, such as chromosomal abnormalities, genetic metabolic diseases, hemoglobinopathies, sex-linked genetic diseases, and congenital anomalies.

On the commencement of this Act, the State Government shall constitute a State Appropriate Authority which shall consist of the Director of Health Services, the Joint Director of Health Services, two representatives of Voluntary Organizations, the Director of Medical Education and Research, a gynecologist, a medical Geneticist and a representative of the Indian Council of Medical Research.

On the commencement of this Act, the State Government shall appoint a State Vigilance Committee which shall consist of Secretary of the Appropriate Authority as Chairman and Convener, two representatives of Voluntary Organizations, the Director-General of Information and Public Relations or his representatives, a gynecologist, a medical geneticist and a Civil Surgeon or Chief Medical Officer. Also, a local vigilance committee shall be formed.[11]

There is no doubt that this Act is a significant achievement for public campaigning, but there are limitations and loopholes to this

---

[10] *Bombay Cases Reporter*, 20:3 (1988), p. 2.
[11] *Bombay Cases Reporter*, pp. 5–7.

Act. First, through this Act, all private genetic laboratories and genetic clinics are not abolished and this Act provides for the registration of these. If all these laboratories were monitored by the government, then the registration could have been prevented and checked. But as that is not the case, it is quite easy for someone to open a clinic for the purpose of sex-determination test.

In addition, the act is short-sighted in that it applies only to the regulation of the existing technologies and techniques. With more research in reproduction, new diagnostic techniques and sex pre-selection methods will be developed, and this legislation eventually will become obsolete. As the objective of this act is to stop the misuse of amniocentesis, in particular, female foeticide, it must have regulation against any other reproductive technology which would also lead to the problem of female foeticide. Otherwise, the objective of solving the problem of female foeticide will never be achieved.

Some argue that banning amniocentesis is only an irrational over-reaction. With the advancement of science and technology to the point where simpler and more effective ways of sex-determination will be discovered, the large-scale abortion of female foetuses will result.

Another issue is that if sex detection tests are banned and therefore defective babies are not aborted, the general quality of the population will be affected. The defective babies will turn out to be a liability to the society. This argument can be refuted by noting that the ban of amniocentesis for the purpose of sex-detection does not mean that amniocentesis will not be allowed. It simply means that the abuse of amniocentesis is not allowed. A ban on the misuse of amniocentesis does not necessarily exclude abortion for legitimate reasons.

Another related problem involves the enforcement of the legislation. The legislation does not guarantee that sex detection tests will not be performed. Even if this legislation is passed in all the states in India, unless it is enforced properly, abortion after sex detection tests will continue.

To answer the question whether legislation efforts will act as a deterrent, one has to answer the question whether legislative efforts have succeeded in controlling the crime against women. Various studies have demonstrated that crimes against women have increased over-all. For example, compared to 2,487 reported cases of rape in 1971, there were 4,300 cases reported in 1979. This latter figure amounts to 12 rapes a day or one rape every two hours. In Delhi, 619 cases of bride-burning were reported in 1982 compared to 421 cases in 1980. Unreported cases of such crimes can be, in some cases, 15 to 20 times greater than the reported cases.[12] It is important to emphasize that the offenders come from families with high social status and high income groups, such as lawyers, physicians and civil servants. Some political elites are opposed to this ban of the sex detection test because crime against it will increase. Thus, despite legislation, the practice will continue. Legislation against dowry and the Child Marriage Restraint Act have not achieved the desired objectives. Women against whom these crimes are committed always come from the lower socio-economic status.

In conclusion, I contend that in the context of India, legislation effort alone will not solve the problem of female foeticide. Along with the enforcement of legislative measures, a campaign must be launched to improve the status of women in India through government policy changes focused on the interests of women and through the involvement of more women in the political arena. Equally important are non-governmental measures such as an organized women's movement to improve the status of women through education. Efforts in this connection are taking place in India. Recently a national organization called the Forum against Sex-Determination and Sex-Preselection (FADSP) has been formed with local affiliates in Gujrat (Baroda, Amhedabad, and Valsad), Tamil Nadu (Madurai), and Karnataka (Mysore). Nationally it consists of thirteen leading women's organizations. FADSP is trying to convince the central government's Ministry of Health to take immediate action against Sex-Determination and Sex-Preselection tests. Women's group perceive the need for birth control and family planning in terms of women's choice and the right to decide the number of children they want as well as the method of contraception they would like to use. The women's movements have moved beyond the social and ethical realm to the political realm and it is my belief that only when resistance is reflected at all levels, social, ethical and political that a forward moving change will take place in relation to sexual equality. How long will it take to achieve this objective of sexual equality in India remains to be seen. I am optimistic as it is a step in the right direction. I end with a note of caution. As Nandita Gandhi and Nandita Shah write, "The

---

[12] H.C. Upadhyay, *Status of Women in India*, I (New Delhi, India: Anmol Publications, 1991), pp. 183–187.

diversity of perceptions coming from different ideological bases also becomes problematic as it suggests different political emphases and organizational priorities. The other danger of such slogans, as the women's movement has discovered, is their use by rightist and conservative forces. It is necessary to sort out these ideological biases so we can distinguish between different situations and resist manipulation and distortion by those opposed to the principles of the women's movement".[13]

---

[13] Nandita Gandhi and Nandita Shah, *The Issues at Stake* (New Delhi, India: Kali for Women, 1992), p. 136.

ON FREEDOM, POWER, JUSTICE:
FEMINIST PERSPECTIVES

Christina Schües

Feminist philosophy is practical philosophy: philosophy of liberating women from the system of patriarchy. As such it must be critical of that system and it must conceptualize an alternative project, that is a *vision*. Taking as guidelines for different forms of research the multiple exploitations, discriminations, and oppressions of women in different areas of life and the arguments of patriarchy which either defend or try to obscure such discriminations, feminist philosophy includes a variety of different approaches, perspectives and projects. Discrimination is not only an error about which men need to be enlightened; it is also a phenomenon which is to be found in every aspect of social life and which has, at least for the Western world, its social and cultural foundation in the tradition of the history of occidental thinking and in the social, economic and political history as such.

If women were to formulate simple "complaints" or demand revenge against the oppressor, then they would see themselves *only* as victims. However, firstly, being victim covers *only* a part—though an important part—of the story, and secondly, it does not lead beyond *her* story in *his*tory. I (woman) must begin to see the "reality", I must develop a *vision* of my way of seeing my "sex", *my feminine sexual difference*, as other to masculine fantasy, to androcratic[1] reality, to patriarchal and capitalist regulations, and to the "law of the father". Feminist researches must have the vision of liberation which does not just mean liberation of women from men, but includes the transformation of society into a more just living together. I envision a world of partnership[2] in which justice is meant for all people with

---

[1] Andro: man, crato: to rule.

[2] Eisler proposes for the partnership model the (rather artificial) term *gylany*. *Gy* derives from the Greek root word *gyne*, or "woman". *An* derives from andros, "man". The letter *l* between the two has a double meaning: it stands for the linking of the two halves of humanity. And it derives from the verb *lyein* or *lyo*, which means to solve or resolve (as in analysis) and to dissolve or set free (as in catalysis). See Riane Eisler, *The Chalice and the Blade. Our History, Our Future* (New York: Harper Collins, 1988).

respect for their gender, class, race, age, and other differences. I
envision a world in which the notion of "freedom" is not conflated
with the illusion of autonomy, in which power is not taken as violence or understood as a tool of domination, or demand of obedi-
ence obtained by force or the threat of force, and in which justice is
not founded upon an androcratic standard of abilities and prejudices.

LIBERATION

From early modernity, liberty has been understood as autonomy of
the (male) subject. The male was never born, he was alone in the
beginning. "Let us consider men . . . as if but even now sprung out
of the earth, and suddenly, like mushrooms, come to full maturity,
without all kind of engagement to each other".[3] This vision of men,
born of their own as mushrooms is the ultimate principle of autonomy. This principle frees the man from all human attachments and
dependencies, from his mother, his family, or any other. Even worse,
the other actually threatens the male self by her presence. Hegel
writes: "Self-consciousness is faced by another self-consciousness; it
has come out of itself. This has a twofold significance: first, it has
lost itself, for it finds itself as an other being; secondly, in doing so
it has superseded the other, for it does not see the other as an essential being, but in the other sees its own self".[4]

   History is the story of the threat of loss when confronted with the
other. In making up for this dramatic threat he confronts himself
and others with domination, fear, war, anxiety, and death. But the
drama is not getting out of hand (so it seems), he controls it, or tries
to control it by establishing a law. Having no mother and no father
the autonomous subject must freely establish (Kant) the universal law
in the light of his own self-image of rationality. Thus, in a way this
is even the destruction of traditional patriarchy. Not the father rules,
man rules himself; hence, the term androcracy is more adequate to

---

   [3] Thomas Hobbes, "Philosophical Rudiments Concerning Government and Society"
in Sir W. Molesworth (ed.), *The English Works of Thomas Hobbes*, Vol. II (Darmstadt:
Wissenschaftliche Buchgesellschaft, 1966), p. 109. This is also discussed in Seyla
Benhabib, "The Generalized and the Concrete Other" in Seyla Benhabib, Drucilla
Cornell (eds.), *Feminism as Critique* (Minneapolis: University of Minnesota Press, 1988).
   [4] G.W.F. Hegel, *Phenomenology of Spirit*, trans. A.V. Miller (Oxford: Clarendon Press,
1977), p. 111.

name this state of affairs. Of course, the law does not cure any anxiety, it simply helps to domesticate it; it eases and tames some destructive forces; it is also fundamental to modern consciousness. Brotherly love is then understood as a human experience in terms of impartiality and fairness, duties and rights are taken as means to negotiate conflict, sovereignty as means of conducting rational decisions:[5] delink yourself from the other, and regard him/her just as if the other would be like yourself. This is the male rationale of history, her story is either his story, *i.e.*, living up (or down) to the masculine principle, or women are simply what men are not. From early modernity, *i.e.*, from the 17th century onwards, woman is defined by negation and lacks, *e.g.* as nonaggressive, non-competitive, not public, but private. In short, woman is defined by a lack of autonomy. Under this paradigm, she is unfree, not free from her dependencies.

A further problem is that the dichotomies become fixed in a set of antinomies: the feminine is not only the opposite of the male but also the opposite par excellence. The problem is not so much that the feminine realm (associated with family and privacy structures, reproduction and the public) and the masculine realm (associated with laws, politics, production) stand in opposition or are supposed to function as a dynamic force in the evolution of society and culture. The problem is rather, firstly, that actually the feminine is regarded as taking care of the private sphere while being negligible or even destructive for the public sphere, and, secondly, that the symbolic structures bear direct reference to their empirical referents. The "masculine" is taken to be the exclusive property of biological males, the "feminine" is the monopoly of biological females—so that the symbolic opposition can be taken as the mark of a specific division of labour and evaluation between men and women.[6]

As man rises up from earth on which the mushrooms grow, he

---

[5] Since the rise of capitalism, rational decision making is inherently connected with utilitarian thinking: Under the paradigm of utilitarianism rationality uses cost-benefit logic by pushing forward criteria of necessity without honestly asking "necessary for whom?" or "necessary on the basis of what?" Utilitarian rationality follows ultimately the economic interest in profits by the most powerful which needs the dichotomy of subject and object, the fragmentation of reality and even human life. The utilitarian analysis of only parts of an object splits human lives and societies apart. See Maria Mies, *Wider die Industrialisierung des Lebens* (Pfaffenweiler: Centaurus-Verlag, 1992).

[6] See the essay by Rosi Braidotti, "Patterns of Dissonance: Women and/in Philosophy" in Herta Nagl-Docekal (ed.), *Feministische Philosophie* (Wien: R. Oldenbourg Verlag, 1990).

celebrates and dramatizes the passage from earth to heaven, from nature to culture. In this passage he is caught between his needs for the relations with others and sovereignty, between nurturance and autonomy, between ranking and linking with, between others and self. Thus, his "freedom", or "liberty", is essentially the drama of antagonism, whereby the other is most threatening to the disembodied, disembedded autonomous self, striving for freedom and unity. This autonomous subject however, is not free. Sovereignty is not freedom. And she, the "nobody", or the "object of his phantasies", is regarded as nature, matter, irrational *etc.*, that is, according to the social norm, she is regarded as that which has to be formed and controlled. Being controlled is not to be free.

The androcratic principle of characterizing the others by negation not only holds for sexual discrimination but can be extended also to cultural, ethnical, or racial discriminations. This does not imply that sexual discrimination is just paradigmatic for all other discriminations. Rather, discussion of one can be used to initiate discussions of others and link them up with discourses on the multiple forms of aggressive hierarchies and their forms of discrimination.

I argue in the following for the liberation of subjects who must not be afraid of the other or who must not dominate the other. Liberation can only be achieved by an embodied and embedded subject[7] in relation with, and in difference from, the others.

SUBJECT AND LINKING

In the last thirty years,[8] in the climate of a challenge to Western values and to the hegemony of the occidental tradition, we can observe the emergence, even at times merging, of two parallel phenomena: on the one hand, the re-emergence of the women's movement, and feminist theories with regard to women's status, roles, and discourses

---

[7] Theories of a sexed corporeality and the need for a body-subject are well discussed by Elizabeth Grosz in her book *Volatile Bodies, Toward a Corporeal Feminism* (Indianapolis: Indiana University Press, 1994).

[8] See, for instance, as an overview Jutta Ecarius, "Geschlechterverhältnisse" in H.-H. Krüger a.o., *Einführung in die Erziehungswissenschaft*, vol. 1 (Opladen, 1995); Uta Gerhard, "Differenz und Vielfalt—Die Diskurse der Frauenforschung" in *Zeitschrift für Frauenforschung*, Heft 1 + 2 (Kleine Verlag, 1993), pp. 10–21; Herta Nagl-Docekal, "Was ist feministische Philosophie"? in Herta Nagl-Docekal (ed.), *Feministische Philosophie*.

in science and society; and on the other hand, a struggle[9]—a form of dissolution—which is internal to contemporary European philosophy, and which has also influenced Anglo-American philosophy. The different strategies of deconstruction or destructuring attack the notion of rationality, which has been put forward in the history of occidental philosophy as being constitutive of human consciousness as well as of the human ethical ideal. These discussions focus on questioning, transforming and dissolving the dualistic thinking about say, male/female, rational/emotional, and also the implicit hierarchies which subordinate the second member of each pair under the first. Both emerging trends have the potentiality to transform philosophy into a tool of resistance, rather than using it as an offensive blade of "truth."

Along the lines of these two strands of thinking, two dangers could arise for the search for constituting a (feminine) subject: on the one hand, an oversimplified recourse to the idea of female role and essential characteristics such as to be found, for instance, in Carol Gilligan's[10] study which puts forward an ethics of a "care perspective" that is developed in relation to a specifically female life context. On the other hand, there is an opposite extreme which takes the deconstruction of the subject so far that at the end "nothing" or "nobody" remains except discursive functions and flows of information.[11] That is, if we just have manifold differences with only a tendency towards non-differentiation, then we have a manifold without priority, no direction, continuous relativism, indifference, and therefore, no political programs. But, in actuality, if we (women) are not developing a political programme of liberations, then men will develop

---

[9] Particularly from France came the radical critique of human subjectivity guided by poststructuralists: *e.g.* Foucault's notions of "genealogy" and "power", Deleuze's and Guattari's "productive desires", Derrida's deconstructive moves, Lacan's psycho analysis and Irigaray's consequent critique thereof.

[10] Carol Gilligan, *In a different voice* (Cambridge, Mass.: Harvard University Press, 1982). I do not want to say that her work itself is oversimplified. On the contrary, she advanced the women's movement substantially.

[11] Feminists have accused Butler and Cornell of getting rid of the subject; I do not think this is really true in either case, rather they used a Foucaultian or a Lacan/Derridian perspective with the goal of questioning and dismantling gender-identity in regard to their historical, specific, powerladen discursive regime or phallocentric symbolic order. However, political battles against oppression or exploitation cannot be fought with the help of poststructuralists.

(and have developed) their androcratic capitalist system for themselves and against us. This is the danger of extreme relativism.[12]

"It seems to me that contemporary philosophical discussions on
the death of the knowing subject, dispersion, multiplicity *etc.* have
the immediate effect of concealing and undermining the attempts of
women to find a theoretical voice of their own".[13] And they have the
immediate effect, as I like to urge, of undermining the attempts of
women to find a political voice and ways to act politically.

Politically speaking, contemporary philosophers need to be aware
of the historical dimension of the oppression of women. And then
they might wonder whether one actually can de-sexualize a sexuality
one has never gotten the authority of. Before women can deconstruct
the subject they must first have the authorization to speak as one.
The dispersion and fragmentation of the subject would result in the
same status which the "feminine" had before: a form of negation,
i.e., no standpoint. Hence, one cannot and should not deconstruct
the subject. Thus, the first step must be to find a positive alterity,
female subjects who are (making-) differences and who are born out
of transformation.

"Western culture has proven incapable of thinking not-the-same-
as without assigning one of the terms a positive value and the other,
a negative".[14] Thus, the first question is: can we think outside this
logic of domination and exclusion, without deconstructing the binary
into multiple, fluid "nomads" (Delueze/Guattari), "nobodies"? In other
words, can we think a subject who is not dominating an object, *i.e.*,
the other, and who is female or male regardless of whatever concept
of "feminine" or "masculine" one has in mind? I envision a feminine
subject who is capable of acting and who is capable of communicating with the others without the need to isolate herself or control the
other. I will argue that the capacity to act initiates a transformation
in such way that a "subject" can emerge who is not afraid of the
others and who can link with the others. It is my thesis that if we can
think in the context of an attempt at linking rather than ranking, we
can hope not only for "better" relations among human beings, espe-

---

[12] See Rada Ivekovic, "Die Postmoderne und das Weibliche in der Philosophie"
in Herta Nagl-Docekal (ed.), *Feministische Philosophie*, p. 130.

[13] Braidotti, "Patterns of Dissonance: Women and/in Philosophy" in Herta Nagl-
Docekal (ed.), *Feministische Philosophie*, p. 119.

[14] Alice Jardine, quoted in Braidotti, "Patterns of Dissonance: Women and/in
Philosophy", p. 110.

cially for women and children, but also for a better intra-cultural understanding. However, within the present androcratic capitalistic system, "linking" should not be understood as just "feminine work"; at this point it is a vision for the future. She, the other, is not reaching out (as she did so often) for the hand of the dominator.

Before I discuss the notions of "transformation", "power" and "justice", I like to address the notion of a "feminine subject" in regard to questions of identity and the capacity to act:

A. *Identity*

Simone de Beauvoir wrote:

> Now, what peculiarly signalizes the situation of woman is that she—a free and autonomous being like all human creatures—nevertheless finds herself living in a world where men compel her to assume the status of the Other. They propose to stabilize her as object and to doom her to immanence since her transcendence is so overshadowed and forever transcended by another ego (conscience) which is essential and sovereign. The drama of woman lies in this conflict between the fundamental aspirations of every subject (ego)—who always regards the self as the essential—and the compulsions of a situation in which she is the inessential.[15]

As much as I agree with many of Beauvoir's statements, concerning, for instance, her famous claims against "natural necessities" that women are not born but made, as little do I agree with her aspiration that woman could or should "live up to"[16] the subjectivity described by a free and autonomous subject. There is no sense, not even wish, to be like him. Human society does not need the other half of humanity to try as hard and to fall into the same drama of antagonism as described above and thereby renounce that which had always been considered as feminine, *e.g.* care, love, nurture. However, this does not mean that reason is not relevant for both masculine and feminine human beings. Women should not engage in conceptions which determine her as the other of reason. If woman would orient her identity exclusively on a picture which equates femininity with emotionality, then this would mean giving up the claim

---

[15] Simone de Beauvoir, *The Second Sex*, trans. H.M. Parshley (New York: Random Press, 1974), pp. xxxiii–xxxiv.
[16] See Drucilla Cornell, *Beyond Accommodation, Ethical Feminism, Deconstruction, and the Law* (New York: Routledge, 1991), pp. 193ff.

to participate in ethical, social, and juridical processes of decision-making. This would mean the affirmation of her exclusion from traditionally male oriented realms.

But should women actually search for their own identity? I shall argue that the search for their own identity determines perhaps the status quo at the moment, but it is not itself a political programme. The result of such searches is the affirmation of differences between the genders, races, ethnic groups, classes and, last but not least, between different individuals. At most, the acknowledgement of differences or identities leads to discussions (or fights) about ways of distribution of the goods within the present capitalist system. But it does not reach over and beyond the present capitalist androcratic system as such.

The search for one's own identity mostly arises out of a crisis, *i.e.*, the awareness of either the lack of identity or someone externally assigning an identity. In either case such searches are certainly valuable in terms of investigating questions of socialization, social structure and its implications, *etc.* But such search leads to a description of the role and status of a certain group or individual and, in the case of women, and rightfully so, to a complaint against androcratic strategies. However, the identity, say, as a white, middle-class, christian socialized woman (I am not even sure whether this is an identity) does not yet imply a political or philosophical programme. It is not a *vision*. The search for identity is, perhaps, important for finding out where we come from and where we stand now, and therefore, it remains in the present. However, the search for a vision is directed towards the future and is necessary to show us where to go, and how we can transform and change societies, rid them of injustice, violence, and discrimination for future generations. In other words, *differences between individuals and groups are not the problem*; the problem is how to liberate women and other oppressed groups from androcratic oppressive and exploitative strategies; how to transform the individual situation and the whole social, economic, and cultural system.[17]

The idea of identity stems from a metaphysics of presence which is grounded in a logic of identity whereby we can posit both equality

---

[17] Since capitalist system is ultimately guided by an utilitarian rationality which uses an economic calculation of cost-benefit, I do not believe that women's situation can improve substantially within it.

and difference. However, the logical meaning "A equals A" cannot be the same as the social meaning of "she equals me". The social meaning of identity might not mean equality in every respect, but rather "who is equal or similar with whom?" and "by which profound norms and standards do we (Who?) decide?". In these questions lies the tendency to conformism. Conformism means either one's own desire to conform and to be subsumed, or the need or strategy of the dominators to subsume others under certain characteristics and regulations. In any case, identity, *i.e.*, conformism, functions by subsumption and exclusion. Exclusion must take place when someone is not equal to someone else. Socially speaking, since she is not like him, she is defined by a negative definition, and such definitions are actually understood as devaluation; she is not as good, as valuable as he is. It can be some consolation that actually she equals her or him, but that might not even be the case because she probably does not subscribe to the norms and characteristics by which she is considered equal. Besides, can we ever find fixed characteristics which let us be equal to someone else? I do not think so. Even worse, under the doctrine of identity, or conformity, the antinomy between unequals is insurmountable; the result is isolation and the other becomes an enemy.

Identity in good times is not like identity in bad times, identity for women is not like identity for men because the perceptions and objectives of good and bad times are not the same. Disclosing one's identity in bad times, for example, in times of discrimination and persecution, leads to the call of privileging the collective over the individual developments. Many forms of identity cannot be hidden, many forms had (have) to be hidden because of threats. In good times the question of identity is usually not even asked.

Just the search for identity leads to defend oneself or to blame the oppressor, to the disclosure of the presently existing norms, and to the demand of equality within the system, as in the case of affirmative action. However, what is needed is more than that: a discussion with different voices (at least from the ones who can do it now) about their different visions, reaching over and beyond the present situation.

What is needed are feminine subjects who do not get stuck in conformism but who use their difference and their voice to speak up, who find a niche to begin to act, and who have a vision.

B. *In my vision feminine subjects have the capacity to act*

I mean by the capacity to act, the capacity to make a difference according to one's own differences and to reflect about them. However, for this we need plurality. Plurality is the "sine qua non" of acting which always needs other human beings. Plurality means equality and difference in the sense that we are all human beings who are natal and mortal, and that no human being is equal to any other human being who has lived, lives, or will live. Each human being is specific and differentiates herself or himself from other human beings in acting, speaking and many other ways. They may show who they are in action and speech. They do not show it in just being-for-the-other (selflessness) of the christian purity and goodness or in the against-the-other (selfishness) in crimes or wars, but only in being-with-each-other. We should not overlook, however, that capitalist societies based on competition and on the darwinistic concept of selection, *i.e.*, on the elimination of the others, are using the attitude of being-against-the-other as well.

One might argue that the notion of an autonomous authorized subject[18] is a prerequisite for the capacity to act. This would amount to an instrumental understanding of a capable subject who would be the condition for any political and societal change. However, Butler[19] observes that the person understood as instrumental agent confronts a social field in which power and politics already exist. The capacity to act is always and exclusively a political privilege. That is, if women are excluded from the political sphere they will not have the capacity to act. However, the pre-existing political sphere is not the only arena to act; also the private sphere can become political through action. Thus, we have to ask for the conditions of possibility of the capacity to act. And if the subject in her capacity to act is constituted by the present political and economic system of domination

---

[18] The notion of an "authorized subject" refers to the thought, mentioned above, that politically speaking the question who can act or speak depends upon the power structure of the political, cultural, and social system. Within the context of patriarchical thinking the notion of power means having power over someone or something. Within "androcracy" the notion of an unauthorized or weak subject would be a contradiction in terms.

[19] See Judith Butler, "Contingent Foundations: Feminism and the Question of 'Postmodernism'" in Praxis International, Vol. 11, No. 2, July 1991. Reprinted in German in: Seyla Benhabib, Judith Butler a.o., *Der Streit um Differenz, Feminismus und Postmoderne in der Gegenwart* (Frankfurt: Fischer, 1993).

and regulations, then there would be no possibility to go against and to transform these configurations of domination. Furthermore, women are traditionally treated as nobodies, they were not part of plurality but rather considered as a conformist group of equal objects which have no authorization to become subjects; or if there were differences then they would be defined by the male authority who certainly would not allow endangering voices and whose force differs from culture to culture, from society to society.

The role and characteristics of human beings are never completely constituted; s/he is neither an origin nor a product, but always a possibility of beginning,[20] a possibility of a particular resignifying process[21] which can be guided by mechanisms of power or violence. She represents in her struggle these mechanisms themselves. It is not the case that the subject is always already engaged in the political sphere, this is simply an insidious artifice of Western jurisdiction. The feminist subject is constituted in the *friction* of exclusion from the political sphere, one could say as pre-subjects who potentially step forward as "somebody". Before my birth I was nobody, now I am somebody; the woman excluded from the political sphere is treated as nobody, she is not an authorized subject. This is a lived contradiction! As the nobody she is not recognized, not even in the category of the discriminated, yet she is a "constituted silence", and silence is not the opposite of speaking. In this context, I speak of silence in the sense of having someone silenced. The precondition for her silence was/is an act of violence, or an exclusion. A silence that had been forced upon someone still has the potentiality to expression and the irritability imposed by the silencing, and hence silence has the power to break silence and this can be heard if one would be attentive. Silence for one might not mean silence for someone else. Any listening takes place by way of selection (consciously or unconsciously). Perhaps, somebody you believed to be silent, actually says something when you listen. What comes first, speaking or listening? Will

---

[20] "Because they are initium, newcomers and beginners by virtue of birth, men take initiative, are prompted into action". Hannah Arendt, *Human Condition* (Chicago: University of Chicago Press, 1958), p. 177.

[21] Butler, "Contingent Foundations: Feminism and the Question of 'Postmodernism'".

you speak if nobody listens? Even if someone is silent, her silence might mean something; for instance, the act of being silenced.

Acting always means beginning; something begins, and others must help in order to push the beginning forward. Thus, a beginning is also always a linking up with others. It takes place in reference to others and it is, according to Hannah Arendt, essential to the political space. Thus, the political space is endangered when plurality is subordinated to the will of one person, one group, or one particular political system; human beings are discriminated against and oppressed when they have in principle no access to the political and economic spheres of influence. An agent remains always in relation to other agents, s/he is never sovereign. Politically being free is synonymous with acting: as long as we act, we are free, not earlier, not later. Acting and being free are one and the same movement; to be free is not a condition for independence, but a doing, moving, acting, living, existing. Thus, to address the above: liberty is only achieved in relation to others, in linking up with others whereby the others live with their sexual, racial, ethnic differences without having to be ashamed of them.

The term "linking up" should not be understood as "relation to" in the sense of "I understand her and I am in communion with her. . . ." Linking up is beyond questions of understanding, agreement, or controlling. The principle of linking must be founded on a different logic, not on one which works with oppositions and ends up in devaluations. If it is true that neither women nor men, neither human relations nor history are fixed or formalizable, then we have to accept and respect an approach of a "non-positing consciousness, that is, of consciousness not in possession of fully determinate objects, that of a logic lived through which can account for itself, and that of an immanent meaning which is not clear to itself. . . ."[22] A thinking which is oriented by a principle of linking with other embodied and embedded subjects must live with and keep its composure in regard to the constant difference and transcendence of the others. Living by the principle of linking between men and women[23] can form a basis

---

[22] Maurice Merleau-Ponty, *Phenomenology of Perception*, trans. Colin Smith (London: Routledge, 1962), p. 49. Quoted in Elisabeth List, *Die Präsenz des Anderen* (Frankfurt: Suhrkamp, 1993), p. 116. She refers in the relevant passage to the experience, which is not graspable discursively and reflectively. It is strictly prereflective.

[23] This relation is primary in the growth or development of each person. The female/male socialization begins when the scrotum (or the lack of it) is detected.

for further possibilities of intra-cultural or trans-cultural relations and forms of communication.

The feminist subject cannot be one, she is not a subject striving for universality and self-identity; the feminist subjects are many, they are subjects in living their differences by a principle of linking and not by equating differences with either inferiority or superiority. Consequently, their relations must be less dominating. The subjects are constituted neither in the politics of identity nor in mere differences. The emergence of the subjects cuts across the politics of identity or of difference, *i.e.*, cuts across traditional bipolar oppositions.

In androcracy the principle of ranking, of ranking, for instance, of men over women, or of one class over the other, is emphasized. Within such hierarchy, which is based on force or violence, or the threat of force or violence, and hence, reinforced ultimately by destruction, human relations must fit into some kind of superior-inferior "pecking order". Hierarchies which are, as I have described, based on domination lead in the end to regressions such as destruction, wars, increasing pollution of land, sea, and air, industrial over-expansion, the computerization and genetic coding of individuals into numbers.[24]

The way out of this regression and the powerlessness of the individuals which many women as well as men actually feel is not the retreat to old religious views, *e.g.* becoming a born again Christian, or to nihilism, excesses of drugs, entertainment, *etc.* but to openness for a cultural transformation.

TRANSFORMATION

I have already mentioned the notion of "transformation" in relation to those of "liberation" and "having a vision". To envision a "feminist subject" is to presuppose a certain transformation of our thinking about the notions of subject and rationality. The need for transformation has also been pointed out in connection with the situation in the world and with regard to discriminations, such as sexism, racism, or classism. Cultural transformation cannot be a fiction. By transformation

---

Even, multiple identities are to be understood with reference to the affirmation or differentiation of the norms of female and male.

[24] Riane Eisler, *The Chalice and the Blade, Our History, Our Future*, p. 105/106.

I mean a change that is radical enough to so restructure culture—political, legal, economic, or social systems—that the "identity" of the system, and the principles by which the culture functions, are changed.[25]

By "transformation" I do not mean "evolution": evolution describes the biological, and, by extension, cultural history of living species. The term is often used normatively, especially by sociobiologists, as synonymous with progress from lower to higher levels of organization. Evolution involves a model of adaptation[26] within the system, hence, the system's identity will remain intact and be further affirmed.

When I speak of "transformation", I acknowledge a difference in the sense of a distance between the self and society; even though society "makes" the self, the self has still the capacity to act out of the difference between itself and society, and between itself and other selves. The subjects (or the pre-subjects) can never be totally identical with society or with any system of norms and regulations. "What we might call 'agency' or 'freedom' or 'possibility', is produced by gaps opened by the regulatory norms in the process of their self-repetition".[27]

Each iteration of action and meaning supports certain values and affirms the status quo, but also allows for transmissions of meaning-shifts out of the "gaps", *i.e.*, the differences, that emerge in the process of self-repetition. Each repetition of an act or a meaning takes place within a different context and at a different time, therefore, their attached values, and what people believe about them, differ each time. Also, the modality or style in which an act is performed or a meaning is expressed can open up differences. For example, the repetition of an action done very slowly and with a face filled with boredom will affirm a value slightly differently than an action done in enthusiasm. In both ways, there are possibilities already to open a "gap" in between the value that should be affirmed and the values that actually had been affirmed.

> Since every negatum and affirmatum is itself an Object posited as existent, it can, like everything else intended to as having a mode of being, become affirmed or denied. In consequence of the constitution

---

[25] See Drucilla Cornell, *Transformations* (New York: Routledge, 1993).

[26] Actually I believe that in the long run the androcracy is maladaptive because in the end it destructures itself.

[27] Judith Butler, "The Burning of Gender" (unpublished manuscript) cited in Drucilla Cornell, *Transformations*, p. 4.

of something as existent effected anew at every step, an ideally infinite chain of reiterated modifications therefore results.[28]

In other words, if the identity of a system or of a person is not a fixed essence, then it is ritualized and performed in each repetition and possibly reiterated anew. If the attributes of aggressive hierarchy and domination, "however, are not expressive but performative, then these attributes effectively constitute the identity they are said to express or reveal. The distinction between expression and performativeness is crucial".[29] If the attributes and acts of the androcratic system, the ways in which the system produces its cultural significations and identities, are performative, then there is no preexisting identity by which an act or a meaning, a law or a right, a norm or a value could be right or wrong, true or false; and the positing of "true gender identity" or "natural human aggression", "economic necessities" or "international competition", are mere fictions for us as women, which however regulate our lives when enforced and implemented. Certainly, the "reality" is there; "reality" is created through sustained social performances and as part of an androcratic strategy that conceals its own performative character, restrictions, and exclusions under the constitution of masculine domination and heterosexual conformities. Social constructions take place with regard to different institutional and social norms, which reinforce their routinized significations without more ado yet forcibly. While wondering about the nonexistence of preexisting identities for the evaluation of acts and values, I do not intend to suggest a form of relativism; rather, I want to say that for me as woman, the androcratic capitalist system puts forward certain "values", "norms", and "truths" which I see as mere fictions (which yet *became* our "reality").

Neither domination nor conformity is total; each member of society lives in some distance to the system, and in difference to the others. Out of these differences s/he can reflect or act. In other words, we are neither so radically free that we can create ourselves, nor are we always an instrument or product of a power which is totally external to our control.[30] In a way we are forced to repeat the conditions of

---

[28] Edmund Husserl, *Ideas pertaining to a pure phenomenology and to a phenomenological philosophy*, first book, trans. F. Kersten (Dordecht: Kluwer, 1982), p. 107.

[29] Judith Butler, *Gender Trouble, Feminism and the Subversion of Identity* (New York: Routledge, 1990), p. 141.

[30] Forms of totalitarian systems with their terror and violence can come (and do come) close to a total control of the individuals.

our genders, our social and cultural system; however, it is open to us how we repeat these norms. Do we affirm or negate them—criticize or doubt them—overexaggerate or parodize them? Do we speak with other women about them or are we actually aware of the implications of the different norms we repeat regularly?

By the procedure of reiteration and its slight shiftings I do not intend to suggest that on the basis of these conditions, therefore, individuals will begin to act. Acting is a striving towards making a difference. Simply repeating the traditions affirms the status quo; however, repetition of traditional values done reflectively and in a different style and by creating a different context may question the status quo and initiate transformations and their interpretation. With regard to their structure they differ: repetition in respect to the "how it is done" can be done in isolation and in anonymity. Actions are done with others, *i.e.*, they must be noticed by others, and they make a difference insofar as they begin something anew. Actions break free from the predictions of the system, from the repetitive reiteration of norms, from the status quo, from the thinking of means and ends. Actions, however, can only be done when differences, plurality, are realized, when the gaps are large enough, and when the urge to link among individuals and societies is privileged over principles of domination. Can she make herself heard? Can she hear the other's voices? Ultimately only actions, revealing the emergence of subjects, and the linking with others, the linking with other women, promise a liberation, empowerment for those who are oppressed now, and a transformation of the system's "identity".

The ultimate motivation for transformation comes from the experience of oppression, discrimination, and exploitation. This experience must not be just my own; the knowledge of oppression, discrimination, and exploitation of parts of humanity, *i.e.*, the systematic existence of injustice and powerlessness, initiates the search for the gaps, the niches, the political sphere (if one has access to it) in which we act and which we turn into a political sphere where we make a difference. However, if I am just behaving according to my own experience as an isolated individual, *i.e.*, according to an egocentric principle, then I cannot act; in case of injustice I would only be enraged and feel powerless. Transformation (out of the urge for liberation) can only be realized by an attitude of linking.

POWER

The demand for empowerment of women was put forward within strategies of emancipation. Rightfully women fought for their share of positions which were traditionally held by men. Strategies, as for instance affirmative action, were, and still are, initiated in order to realize equality for women. Women shall participate in the power structure on equal terms with men. However, the increasing militarism and environmental pollution, economic overexpansion and exploitation of large parts of society and in particular of people in the so-called third world countries let women question whether they really want to be accomplices of these androcratic strategies.[31] Presently some women still speak of empowerment in terms of distribution of power and justice (which I will also address in a moment), but I believe that if the androcratic strategy of aggressive hierarchies and domination are not transformed then we always will be faced with discrimination, on sexist, racial or whatever other grounds. Thus, I distinguish domination, which is ultimately reinforced by violence and power from the notion of "power" which goes back to Hannah Arendt's use of it.

I argue for a notion of "power" which inheres in the condition of linking with other human beings and their participation. Power is grounded in the acting-together of individuals and groups. Plurality is the condition of power; each group can be linked to other groups. It is important to notice that the sharing of power does not mean decrease of power but rather strengthening of it as long as it is done within a lively relation.[32]

Hence, the feminist subjects who live in a plurality with their differences may have power without creating powerlessness (*Ohnmacht*) of the others. The feeling of powerlessness is due to a system of regulations which is based on dominance. If society is ruled by strategies of conformity, which simply demand behaving but not acting, if political participation and acting is replaced by bureaucracy, economic strategies of colonization and exploitation, and androcratic norms, then power is understood only as domination. If women's behaviour is reinforced by violence (or the threat of it) then this is

---

[31] Christina Thürmer-Rohr, *Vagabundinnen* (Berlin: Orlanda, 1987). See esp. "Aus der Täuschung in die Ent-Täuschung, Zur Mittäterschaft von Frauen".

[32] See Hannah Arendt, *Human Condition*, p. 205.

not power but force. It is simply the muscle force of one (or more) man/men over a woman. And speaking of transformation, Hannah Arendt says: "The practice of violence, like all action, changes the world, but the most probable change is to a more violent world".[33]

In ancient and modern times the domination strategy has rather brutally handled cases of powerful, yet more "passive" approaches of non-violent challenges to the existing structure: Socrates and Jesus, then Gandhi and Martin Luther King, and an endless list of women. I name only one of them who had been killed by the government 4 years after the French Revolution: Olympe de Gouges.[34] Gandhi once said, "the aim is to transform conflict rather than to suppress it or explode it into violence". Accordingly, I think the aim is not just to transform conflict but the whole androcratic system; even the feeling of conflict is often silenced under the regulation of andro-cratic norms and occidental rationality.

To clarify the notion of "power" which I take to be valuable, I shall distinguish two senses of power: power for oneself and with others, *i.e.*, power as affiliation,[35] and power over others, *i.e.*, con-trol. The latter notion of power is generally seen as dangerous be-cause within the relation you have to control the others or they control you. The better the others develop and educate themselves the more they have to be controlled, hence the principle of androcratic sys-tem. Thus, control functions contrary to human development.[36] Along the same line, we can see the functioning of economic power: under present capitalist androcratic strategies, the increase of economic wealth for a few means an increase of poverty for many. Competition in the androcratic capitalist system stems from the attitude of being-against-the-other.

On the other hand, the idea of power as affiliation is the view that advancement must not mean, at the same time, imposition of a limit on the development of others. It is a non-destructive view of power which tries to privilege links with others rather than increas-

---

[33] Hannah Arendt, *On Violence* (Florida: Harcourt Brace, 1969), p. 80.

[34] "The woman is born free and is equivalent to the man", claimed the French suffragette Olympe de Gouges (7.5.1748–3.11.1793) in "A declaration for the rights of the woman and citizen", 1789. "Is it not time, that also among us women begin a revolution? Shall we always be singular? Will we never actively participate in the organization of society?" She ended on the scaffold.

[35] Riane Eisler, *The Chalice and the Blade, Our History, Our Future*, p. 193.

[36] See Jean Baker Miller, *Toward a New Psychology of Women* (Boston: Beacon, 1976), p. 116.

ing power over the other. It tries to affirm the others rather than to fear, control, or destroy the others. It values and respects the links among human beings, animals, and plants. Thus, power for oneself and with others means also the power to have responsibility. Miller suggests that this is the way women define power, as the responsibility of mothers to help their children to develop their talents and skills, or what Gilligan calls the feminine morality of caring. However, even though I believe it is a good idea to speak of power as affiliation and responsibility and I think it is a good "link" to the next section on justice, I would not want it to be restricted to the concrete face-to-face human relations.

Justice

Before I address the issue of justice more closely I have to readdress the way of "linking with" the others. On the one hand, "linking" could be understood in terms of relation, that is in the sense of a mutual and reciprocal understanding of concrete persons to whom I relate internally on the basis of mutual sympathy.[37] Accordingly, a community, of which justice would be the ideal basis, would be understood as a unification of individual persons through the sharing of subjectivities. Persons would understand one another as they understand themselves. But we all know that other persons never "really" see my world from my perspective; at best, they can imagine as if they were there. On the other hand, "linking" could be understood in the sense of an external relation according to an ideal of impartiality which is based on a logic of identity that denies and represses differences. Impartiality is guided by the will to unity expressed by an impartial and universal reason which generates an oppressive opposition between reason and desire or affectivity.[38] The logic of identity used by deontological reasoning eliminates otherness in at least two ways: it eliminates the irreducible specificity of situations

---

[37] See for critical remarks Iris Marion Young, "The Ideal of Community and the Politics of Difference" in Linda Nicholson (ed.), *Feminism/Postmodernism* (New York, Routledge, 1990), p. 309.

[38] See Iris Marion Young, "Impartiality and the Civic Public" in Seyla Benhabib, Drucilla Cornell (eds.), *Feminism as Critique* (Minneapolis: University of Minnesota Press, 1987), p. 59. And by the same author: Young, *Justice and the Politics of Difference* (New Jersey: Princeton University Press, 1990), esp. Ch. 4.

and the overall context of an action or an event, and the manifold differences among moral subjects.

Thus, in the end, both ways, the desire to have a mutual understanding with others and the desire to use impartial reason excluding affective and bodily aspects of a person and her particular situation, lead to a form of conformity that defines itself according to common attributes which can be either mutually understood or subsumed under the reasoning of identity. Thus, forms of "just communities" which follow either form of desire are partially the ground for discrimination in the form of sexism, racism, ethnic chauvinism, *etc.* According to the first way, "just communities" based on "mutual understanding", tend to subsume the others and other ways of living and thinking under a common paradigm of understanding. Differences are neither affirmed nor openly negated, but simply "non-existent" (until facts of injustices, made apparent by actual outbursts, cannot be denied anymore). In distinction to that impartial reason is used to illuminate and discriminate against deviations from the norms.

I think neither mutual understanding nor impartiality can be taken as the basis for justice; we are all different but not in the sense of being just differences and we are in some sense equivalent, *i.e.*, of equal value, but not in the sense of having a fixed self-identity or conforming identity. We are equivalent insofar as we are human beings. This is perhaps trivial, but it is not trivial in the sense of the thought that since we are human beings, we are generally beings in confirmation of humanity. And individually speaking in treating you with "the norms of friendship, love and care I confirm not only your humanity but your human individuality".[39] Our humanity is based upon the linking with other human beings understood as responsiveness[40] which is a listening to human beings and their relations. Thus, the linking can be understood as responsiveness among human beings not only on the one to one level but also as the general attempt to care for life as a whole with regard to the present and the future. If linking is understood as an attitude of responsiveness then the power of the subjects, let them be individuals or groups, must be under-

---

[39] Seyla Benhabib, "The Generalized and the Concrete Other" in Benhabib, Cornell (eds.), *Feminism as Critique*, p. 87.

[40] I choose here the term "responsiveness" because it contains the sense that it lives in the human links and relations themselves. Thus, it is neither an abstract concept nor an attitude which could be had by only one person. Responsiveness exists only within the link between at least two persons.

stood as responsibility towards themselves and others in the largest sense. As much as the parent's power is the responsibility towards the child in supporting her in her struggles to grow up, it is the economic subject's responsibility towards employees and dependents to regard them in their contexts and as being linked to other human beings as well. Thus, justice is based on the responsibility for the others, on partnership, the linking with the other, and on the respect for differences.

I like to take an example concerning work regulations: under the paradigm of formal equality[41] a woman on maternity leave is simply regarded as disabled and as a loss for the company, just as if a man would be sick. Formally speaking and it terms of androcratic rationality this is certainly the case, she is unable to work for a while. However, under the paradigm of partnership justice is not the question of equality according to some male standard but must be looked upon from both the general and the individual points of view. This particular woman is pregnant or just gave birth to a child and cannot work for a while. The company needs, say, replacement, somebody else who does her job; also from the individual point of view it is not just the woman who receives a child, there is also the father: what is he doing during this time? And from the more general point of view, the whole society receives a child. Human beings are linked: today's children are the instance of justice, or agents of justice, of tomorrow, we all have responsibility for them as much as they will have responsibility for us when we all are older.[42] Under the principle of ranking, women are just left along with the children who often grow up in a world in which the men are not there with them but only there to compete and to consume.[43] This is just a daily example of the reach of justice and a hint that justice must be, as it looks on the surface, gender sensitive. But in a deeper sense by

---

[41] Compare also the line of arguments against abstract equality by Mary E. Becker, "Prince Charming: Abstract Equality" in Leslie Friedmann Goldstein (ed.), *Feminist Jurisprudence, The Difference Debate* (Maryland: Rowman & Littlefield Publishers, 1992).

[42] Rhetorical question: Why shouldn't the grown up children get rid of their elderly parents in some institution, just as much as they had been organized in their day care centers in order for the parents to be equal in the economic world of competition and consumption? Nothing wrong, rather to the contrary, with kindergartens or homes for the elderly, the point is that women who are left along with the care of the family are forced to "organize family members away".

[43] See Maria Mies, *Die Befreiung vom Konsum, Wege zu einer ökolgischen und feministischen Gesellschaft* (Groß Chüden: Okodorf-Verlag, 1990).

respecting the principle of responsiveness, justice must not go by gender identities. If subjects are responsible for and with each other and if linking means a responsiveness among human beings, then men are also affected by women's "disabilities". Perhaps, specific persons are differently affected but if we are guided by responsibility then one must affiliate with the others and support or compensate equivalently.

Fundamental to justice is not only responsibility but also equal rights. Ranking takes place in terms of inferiority and superiority, linking takes place in terms of the rights of equality and differences. Empowering subjects with regard to their capacity to act means not, in my opinion, to set them free to choose between different ways of life just like choosing from different cereals in the supermarket. Amartya Sen suggests that capability mirrors the liberty of a person to choose between different ways of living. Cornell adds to it that the evaluation of difference which is grounded in equal rights, must reflect the possibility of choosing the way of life.[44] However, I believe that this sort of "freedom" is based upon the supposition that each individual lives in isolation (see above the arguments about identity and difference) "free from" other human beings ready to adopt a range of life styles. This conception is not only unrealistic, it also advances a notion of freedom which is threatened by the dependency of the other and the others themselves (as if a mother who cares for her children could never be free) and it is based upon the present capitalist system which is understood as if it would be a big supermarket in which one may pick one's ideal neighbor like one's favorite cereal. Thus, equal rights cannot just address problems of distribution within capitalist system and the freedom to choose a particular way of life. Empowering subjects with regard to their capacity to act rather means giving them the rights to link up with others, and hence, to interfere in the social, economic, cultural, and political sphere, and to speak up for their right to justice.

Derrida points out that the most fundamental aporia of justice is that it always addresses itself to singularity, to the singularity of the Other, despite or even because it pretends to universality.

> How are we to reconcile the act of justice that must always concern singularity, individuals, irreplaceable groups and lives, the Other or myself as Other, in a unique situation, with rule, norm, value or the impera-

---

[44] See Drucilla Cornell, "Gender, Sex and Equivalent Rights" in Judith Butler, Joan W. Scott (eds.), *Feminists theorize the political* (New York, 1992), pp. 280–297.

tive of justice which necessarily have a general form, even if this generality prescribes a singular application in each case? If I were content to apply a just rule, without a spirit of justice and without in some way inventing the rule and the example for each case, I might be protected by law (droit), my action corresponding to objective law, but I would not be just. I would act, Kant would say, in conformity with duty, but not through duty or out of respect for the law.[45]

The aporia of justice cannot be overcome, it must be lived, and for Derrida lived as a response to the call for justice. Law and justice need to be distinguished; laws can be just or unjust, they can be deconstructed, changed, rewritten, but justice must be just. However, contrary to the law justice does not have a (regulative or messianic) horizon of anticipation because of its urgency.

> Justice remains, is yet, to come, a venir, it has an [a-venier], it is a-venir, the very dimension of events irreducibly to come. It will always have it, this a-venir, and always has. Perhaps it is for this reason that justice, insofar as it is not only a juridical or political concept, opens up for l'avenir the transformation, the recasting or refounding of law and politics. "Perhaps", one must always say perhaps for justice. There is an avenir for justice and there is not justice except to the degree that some event is possible which, as event, exceeds calculations, rules, programs, anticipations and so forth. Justice as the experience of absolute alterity is unpresentable, but it is the chance of the event and the condition of history.[46]

And justice is the chance to set the (feminine) subject free to act, to make a difference, and, hence, make history. "It is precisely the reduction of justice to calculated proportion that has made it impossible to think of justice for women other than through our achieving equal measure to men".[47] The attempt to achieve "equal measure", "just distribution", "equal chances" has itself been condemned as unjust. Why is it "just" to take the men as standard? The rhetorical answer is: because it always had been that way (was it?), and because we (who? and to whom?) think justice in formal ways and thereby compound it with law. One (man) says that one cannot find a basis for evaluation in reference to women's comparable worth in

---

[45] Jacques Derrida, "Force of Law: The 'Mystical Foundation of Authority'" in *Cardozo Law Review*, Vol. 11, Nos. 5–6, 1990, pp. 969f.

[46] Derrida, "Force of Law: The 'Mystical Foundation of Authority'", p. 969.

[47] Drucilla Cornell, *Feminist Alliance with Deconstruction, Ethical Feminism, Deconstruction, and the Law* (New York: Routledge, 1991), p. 113/4. Here I like to enlarge the notion of "women" to the "feminine", that is, to the "other than men".

the economic realm. The reevaluation of comparable worth within
the capitalist system is condemned to injustice because each new
attempt will have to use again the leading paradigm of androcratic
standards. Thus, we know there is some injustice, even though we
cannot determine justice once and for all. Presently, any translation
of the injustice to her can only be stated in his system. Why is pregnancy considered to be a disease and correlated with some men's
medical disfunctioning and recoverable in insurance policies as dis-
ability? Natural necessity is hardly the foundation for reinforced gender hierarchy.

The acknowledgement for everybody to have a right to have rights
and, hence, to have responsibility, links not only human beings but
also the present with the future, and the present with the past. I am
responsive to my past as much as I am towards my future. Responsibility calls upon everybody in affiliation with others to engage and
to act beyond calculation, rules and programmes according to the
idea that justice is not simply a juridical or political concept. We
are called up by those who have suffered injustice to represent them
and to serve justice, that is, to serve justice for an opening up of
the horizon of the yet-to-come for a (cultural) transformation of the
political and legal structure and for a transformation of the basic
principles which are leading (in) our cultures.

UNDERSTANDING HUMAN ACTION: WOMEN'S FREE ACTS AS A CASE STUDY*

Chhanda Gupta

I

From very early times, different cultures, traditions and forms of life have produced deep fissures on the surface of human society. The image of the world given by one form of life seems so different from those given by others that the contrasting images are taken by many philosophers to be images of different social realities. Cultural diversity segments society into several closed worlds, as it were, each with an irreducibly native set of norms, beliefs, concepts and customs that seem alien to the other. There are "different worlds", these philosophers would say, the "worlds" of the culture of the East and West, for example, or of different countries, races, religions, tribes, communities—of any organized social aggregate in short, and also of particular periods of time.

Even within such a "closed world" diverse culture-forms in a plurality of contexts may create intra-cultural divisions, say between the woman's form of life and that of the man, which splits that world into two—into "Her Land" and "His Land". Indeed in "Her Land" too there may be conflicting perceptions of women's identity, subjection, struggle and freedom, which may lead to similar gaps in her understanding of her own world.

Are we to conclude then, in view of these gaps, that we cannot understand let alone judge the actions, aspirations and strivings of men and women simply because they are raised in other cultures and do not see from their standpoints what we see from ours?

There has been a confluence of streams of thought in the recent state of art of History and Philosophy of Science, Philosophy of Language and Mind, and also of the anthropological investigations of alien cultures, which impels one to give an affirmative answer

---

* A shorter version of this paper was published in Hiranmoy Banerjee and Tirthanath Bandyopadhyaya (eds.), *Action: Explanation and Interpretation* (Calcutta: K.P. Bagchi & Company in collaboration with Jadavpur University, 1990).

to the question. It is contended that notwithstanding the species-characteristics we have as humans, neither understanding nor *transvaluation* between different cultures can provide a basis of communication between them. My concern here is to oppose this radical relativistic answer.

A full answer to the relativist challenge, of course is not visible to me. Perhaps we have to live with an uneasiness that stems from the tension between "their" and "our"—an uneasiness that pervades the whole of our intellectual and moral life. Yet there seems to be something basically wrong about the extreme approach which infers irreconcilable gaps from the fact that we are culturally divided. Though we belong to separate social spaces and times, we do in fact communicate, compare and even learn from each other's experiences, and through this process of cultural symbiosis enrich the "space" and "time" we happen to belong to. The streams of thought in the fields mentioned above, which do not resonate to this claim and preach communication-gaps instead, spring from:

1. The thesis of "Incommensurability" authored by Kuhn and Feyerabend;

2. Wittgenstein's strictures against private languages that stand in the way of accepting "*verstehen*" as a means of access to the private mental states of an agent belonging to a different culture;

3. Wittgenstein's own thesis about understanding, though arguably, through participation in and following the rules of a particular society different from our own;

4. Quine's reflections on the problem of translation; and

5. The anthropological findings about the difference in connotation of terms used in different cultures, albeit the reference they have is common.

I wish to urge, on the contrary, concentrating mainly on 1, that:

a) the relativists draw wrong and anti-relativistic lessons from right relativistic insights;

b) it is possible to understand and evaluate others' actions in spite of cultural relativity.

II

Cultural Relativism claims that "all reality as known is cultural reality, and all human experience is culturally mediated . . . (All) . . . judgments, perceptions and evaluations are a function of, and are relative to, a given cultural system".[1]

This view is not likely to go unchallenged, especially in view of the passion many philosophers have for a detached investigation of hard facts of the matter of things and processes in nature as they are by themselves, and not as experienced by human beings from different perspectives due to different cultures. In fact, such investigation, characterized typically by an academic spirit of aloofness from the tumult of human existence, had long been the true haven of scientific research. So, many philosophers of science have refused to recognize cultural conditioning, if such conditioning stands in the way of an objective spectator's account. They extend this notion of objectivity even to the domain of human subjects, where their actions must be described without the intrusion of points of view and perspective of the social inquirer, who being a human and placed in a situation, is bound to have such perspectives.

However, inquiry by a social investigator is itself a human action, and as such, has an inalienable "subjective meaning" which among other things include a point of view, a perspective, a pro-attitude. Indeed, the "spectator" view of science may itself be a value towards which the inquirer as agent feels drawn. So the spectator image of science, though seemingly self-evident to its sponsors, is really a particular human orientation—and that too socio-culturally conditioned by a long-upheld image of science. Culture, therefore, seems to be one essential condition of all human experience, including cultural investigation itself.

Thus, breaking the "silence" into which she is socially driven, an immigrant feminist writer in Canada stresses the need of "gaining or giving a voice, a direct assumption of (her) subjectivity, creating a version of the world from (her) own standpoint, . . . speaking from (her) own 'self' or 'centre' of experience".[2] Her own act of investigation

---

[1] D. Bidney, "Culture: Cultural Relativism" in *International Encyclopaedia of the Social Sciences*, Vol. 3 (New York/London: Collier and Macmillan Inc., 1968), p. 544.

[2] Himani Banerjee, "Introducing Racism: Notes Towards an Anti-Racist Feminism" in *Documentation sur la Recherche Feministe*, Vol. 16, No. 1, (March 1987), p. 10.

as a social inquirer is not a detached spectator's account. Indeed, had it been so—culturally non-relative, objective and neutral, then paradoxically, her own understanding of her oppression and that of others like her, would perhaps be as distorted as that of a white racist feminist, who cannot "see" her or her culture. White feminists therefore should "re-examine the very ground of their historical-social identity, their own subjectivity, their ways of being and seeing . . ." in order to be able to see the immigrant woman's strivings for free actions. To understand her freedom then, even within the women's world or "Her Land", one ought to locate the "women of colour" in their historical and social context, and not substitute freedom *per se* or *the woman* as an universal entity for "freedoms" of concretely placed women in the plural.[3] One must not project the white woman's problems as "everywoman's problems"—her freedom as "every-woman's freedom"; to do so is to universalize something which is particular and relative.

This insistence on the methodological need of understanding and assessing subjects from the standpoint of their own culture is legitimate no doubt, as claimed by the immigrant feminist writer. But the relativity or "internality" is no less true of the white woman's understanding and evaluation than that of her subjects. So, her understanding too, being internal, may be said to be unable to reach out beyond the frontier of her own culture to assess and understand the actions of her subjects belonging to a different culture. Should that happen, one seems to be caught between the horns of a dilemma; either admit straightaway that the white feminist cannot really see from her centre of experience and point of view what the immigrant feminist sees from her's; and both being shut up within the prisons of their respective points of view, can hardly ever communicate with each other let along judge. Or, steeped in her own culture, she may impose, wittingly or unwittingly, her own norms, concepts etc. on her subject's mode of being, thinking that her view of freedom is "everywoman's" view of the same. I think both of these alleged consequences of a relativist approach are actually out of tune with the right relativistic insight. The former breeds ethnocentricity, a totalitarian control of everything under one authority, the authority of one particular group. The latter implies some kind of cultural imperialism that is blind to socio-cultural difference and autonomy.

---

[3] Banerjee, "Introducing Racism", pp. 11, 12.

The contentions listed at the outset under 1 to 5 are generally believed to lead ineluctably to this dilemma.

III

Kuhn's thesis of incommensurability (listed under 1) in its later modified form, tries to avoid the total collapse of communication between different cultures or "paradigms" embraced by different communities. In that modified version of the thesis, "local incommensurability" is intended to replace "total or global incommensurability". Global incommensurability is incoherent, as Kuhn, under pressure of severe criticism, admits. He concedes that "talk about differences and comparisons presupposes that some ground is shared...".[4] But in spite of recognizing overlaps in meaning of some expressions used in different paradigms, his thesis of "local incommensurability" enjoins that a few inter-defined expressions in one paradigm resist translation and do not have equivalents in the other. These expressions remind one of an example which W.V. Quine has used to bring up a problem that has exercised many philosophers, the problem of indeterminacy of translation. The problem and the example used are so well-known that I will be very brief in stating it here. The problem is: even if in the same perceptual situation in which we are, a native speaking a jungle language says *gavagai* prompted by the sight of a rabbit, and denies *gavagai* when there is no rabbit around, we cannot conclude that *gavagai* means "rabbit". For the native may view the world from within a conceptual scheme, which Quine and other anthropologists and linguists (Whorf and Sapir) think, is very different from the scheme which we use, positing full-blown objects. Consistent with the native's speech behaviour, these thinkers urge, *gavagai* may be taken to mean "rabbithood exemplified" or "undetached rabbit parts" *etc.* So "*gavagai*" may mean something very different from what we mean by "rabbit". Like Quine's *gavagai* Kuhn's locally incommensurable expressions belonging to one conceptual scheme are irreducibly native, and therefore a block to successful translation into the language of another scheme. Moreover these irreducible terms

---

[4] T.S. Kuhn, "Commensurability, Comparability, Communicability" in PSA, Vol. 2 (1982), Copyright c. 1983, by the Philosophy of Science Association, (privately circulated).

are said to be inextricably bound with certain other terms within one paradigm, which have meanings entirely different from the ones they have elsewhere in some other paradigm. So, when the local set of incommensurable expressions of one paradigm change meaning when transferred to another, it is likely to change the meanings of such other expressions too, which being bound and transferred with them, cannot but be infected by such change of meaning. This implies that the whole set of transferred expressions with changed meanings in a new paradigm would structure the world in a way that is very different from the way the set structured it before the transfer. It seems that "local incommensurability", too, cannot avert the threat of an irreconcilable gap in trans-cultural communication. For, the upshot of comparison which Kuhn ventured through his modified thesis of incommensurability was that the two world-views of the two paradigms are ultimately incomparable.

I have focussed on Kuhn's treatment of the problem posed by translation failure not only for want of space, but also because in spite of the moderation his later works show, his thesis does not hold the key to the question which is crucial here, that is, the question about understanding human action—especially the actions of agents in a different culture. Needless to say, Feyerabend, who has been more radical, can hardly be credited with having offered a better solution.

The consequence for the social researcher investigating actions in the human society segmented by deep divisions of culture, is grave. If what Quine, Kuhn, and Feyerabend, and also some anthropologists say about the hazard of translation is true, then we have to confront the dilemma stated earlier.

Was the action of the Hindu widow or "sati" who sacrificed herself on the funeral pyre of her husband a free and noble act which the alien rulers did not understand because it is impossible to translate "sati" into English without loss of meaning? The British simply did not and could not "see" from within their conceptual scheme the significance of the action; they did not see the connections which the term "sati" had with other expressions like "sadhvi" or "pativrata" (an ideal incorruptibly good wife devoted to her husband, though this does not convey the full sense of these expressions) and "charitrabati" (chaste and pure). These expressions are ineliminable in the sense that the meaning of the term "sati" cannot be acquired in isolation apart from them. In fact the term "sati" does not refer to the Hindu widow only who burns herself on her husband's pyre. It refers to any woman who is absolutely dedicated and devoted to her husband, chaste, pure, faithful. Her fidelity is part of her piety. If this term "sati" is "locally incommensurable" as Kuhn would say, and therefore has its meaning changed when transferred to an alien language, it is only natural that the other expressions too, with which it is inextricably bound, would also have their meaning changed, when transferred with it. The incommensurability of a set of terms including "sati" then, would not remain "local", but infect the whole network of terms in a language to which it is transferred. In the face of such an "incommensurability" which eventually turns out to be global, one may have to conclude despairingly that the British should have desisted from all efforts to understand the alien action. For the whole way in which the Hindus structured their social reality was very different from the way in which the British did it. This gap leads to the dilemma. Confronting it, a British may say: "to us it is a suicide which is barely voluntary because forced by social pressure, but to them it is a noble and admirable sacrifice".[5] But this amounts to the blatant contradiction that the same act can be both free and forced. To avoid the contradiction, one may have to succumb to the first horn, giving up all effort to understand and judge an alien practice, however bewildering and morally pernicious this may be, involving basic questions about the worth of human life. Or, if this is to be escaped, the alien investigators may continue their efforts, but in the face of failure of translation, may ultimately have to import their own concepts and standards and extend them to an alien and inappropriate context, thereby giving in to the second horn of the dilemma.

The moral cost in either case is too great. We cannot simply say that translation fails to bridge the gap and therefore there is no way left for cross-cultural understanding, and leave the matter at that. If this be the lesson drawn from the adoption of a relativist method, then, the British should never have tried to stop what was despicable in our society—burning of widows, child marriage, the brutal practice of killing female babies, to mention but a few. Alternatively, if they did try to translate the "incommensurable" expressions, forging their meanings upon ours, the moral cost involved would not be of any lesser consequence. For any such effort may impair the moral

---

[5] Roger Trigg, *Understanding Social Science* (Oxford: Basil Blackwell, 1985), p. 74.

image of a free and noble act of sacrifice beyond recognition, describing a free agent as a victim of social pressure. Can "sacrifice" be termed "forced suicide"? Is not the alien blind to the distinctive moral image of this volitional self-sacrifice based on norms which apparently are local? A free act of complete self-effacement of an agent who is prepared to renounce even her own life for an honour bound up with her conjugal and familial identity may seem strange to an alien raised in a culture that finds the last locus of freedom in the *individual* or *self*. Freedom, construed from the liberal perspective of that culture is expressed in *self-assertiveness* and *self-fulfilment*. The talk about *free self-effacement* consequently sounds mystifying and absurd. Yet self-denial, endurance, sacrifice are virtues constituting the feminine mystique that has engulfed Indian women down the centuries. Women who have been portrayed as paragons of these virtues in myths, epics, stories and history represent the icon of ideal womanhood.

Impressed by this reversal of moral perspective the relativist may urge that the virtues referred to are mere reflections of local traditions and values. Tied to a concrete form of life and a concrete history, these are likely to elude the alien's understanding. And what cannot be understood, cannot be judged either. Should we then endorse the "relativist denial that ethics, correctly understood, offers any trans-cultural norms, justifiable by reference to reasons of universal validity, by reference to which we may appropriately criticize different local conceptions . . ."? Or should we say that we can resort to "reasons that do not derive merely from local traditions and practices, but rather from features of humanness that is beneath all local traditions and are there to be seen whether or not they are in fact recognized in local traditions"?[6] To take an example, Padmini, a Rajput queen of a western state (Mewar) in medieval India, famed for her beauty that is said to have caused a blood-bath, performed the rite of self-immolation or "*jawahar brat*" with other ladies of the royal court when the Rajput men died fighting in the battlefield against a Muslim monarch who had come to capture her. They, and many other women in similar situations would rather die, being consumed by fire lit in a huge well (*kunda*) than succumb to ignominy, dishonour or indignity which inevitably awaited them, they felt, if captured by

---

[6] Martha Nussbaum, "Non-Relative Virtues: An Aristotelian Approach" in Martha Nussbaum and Amartya Sen (ed.), *The Quality of Life* (Oxford: Clarendon Press, 1993), p. 243.

the enemy. A life without their own men, father/husband or son, and the horror of molestation, rape and the prison walls of the Muslim victor's "*harem*" probably seemed insufferable, an existence worse than death. Are we to conclude that this collective act of self-annihilation, the peculiar sense of anguish, indignity and despair caused by severance from their men which culminated in the act, and finally the local conceptions, traditions and practices that motivated, sustained and sanctioned it, are all immune to appropriate criticism on the basis of trans-cultural norms justified by reasons of universal validity? To draw this conclusion would be a mistake.

First, the conclusion draws on the untenable presumption that any attempt to criticize and rationally defeat traditional ideas and societies in which these ideas are nurtured is wrong. Some radical relativists, Stephen Marglin and Frederique Marglin, (an economist and an anthropologist), to whose works Hilary Putnam refers in his book *Renewing Philosophy*, have actually advocated this view. Putnam sees this as what he calls "the revival of the myth of the noble savage". Traditional societies, he points out, are viewed by these relativists "as so superior . . . that we have no right to disturb them in any way".[7] The result is appalling. Borrowing Karl Popper's expression he calls this an "immunizing strategy" by which even institutionalized oppression can be protected from criticism. So even if it would be good for the victims of oppression to free themselves of the injustice of their situation, to conceive alternative ways of life, and to find out which among these would be better, the "Nobel Savagers" would choose not to criticize. They would refrain from playing the role of an "agitator" who stirs up the hitherto satisfied oppressed, living in blissful ignorance, on the pretext that agitation would disrupt stability.

Secondly, the so-called free and noble act of performing "*jawahar brat*" in a culture presumably inaccessible to the alien might have been an act into which powerless subjects were driven both by destiny and by local tradition and moral regulations which were imposed on them in a Procrustean manner. *Prima facie* the act was free, for the choice it involved was still a choice, one between death and dishonour. But in reality the option could have been the consequence of ideological manipulation which instilled a false sense of honour and dishonour, which though false, swayed the subjects *making* them

---

[7] Hilary Putnam, *Renewing Philosophy* (Cambridge, Mass.: Harvard University Press, 1992), p. 183, see also pp. 184–186.

feel that whatever they did was for the sake of a high ideal. This
high ideal again was a construct perhaps, built out of male dignity,
where women's dignity and honour totally fused with men's. So even
if the women who performed the "*brat*" did defy death through death
by being immortalized for moral excellence in the memory of their
race, in history and story, they owed this, it seems, to the roles they
played as mothers, wives or daughters of their men who died hero-
ically in the battlefield. In fact a similar interpretation in other
comparable situations is widely accepted by feminists in this country today. The author I referred to at the outset, Himani Banerji, observes
in an article in a paper brought out by a women's organization
"*Sachetana*", that the "construct of ideal womanhood" is a "creature
of pure ideology". The type of social subjectivity and agency that
women can gain through this construct is derivative from patriarchy.
It "is only as the mother, wife, daughter and sister of a hero that she
can become a heroine". So if the subjects we have been considering
turn out to be victims not only of male lust, incidentally of the Muslim
monarch captivated by tales of Padmini's beauty in the story nar-
rated above, but also of local tradition and moral regulations, then
this surely is a context in which one should invoke trans-cultural
norms to prevent anyone like them from being victimized. I agree
that there is a big element of truth in this interpretation. Indeed this
should make any researcher in women's studies conscious of the
enormity of social conditioning, especially of the Power that determines women's lives in the guise of ideology. However, I wish to
add a third point here which highlights the limitations of this interpretation though the point is not a deterrent to the acceptability of
the main argument being discussed, the argument against the "Noble
Savagers" and their "immunizing strategy".

The third point is that notwithstanding the enormity of social
conditioning women are to be regarded as *subjects* or *selves*, and not
as inert passive *objects* to whom no agency, no responsibility and no
personality can be ascribed. Those who speak of the ideology of "ideal
womanhood" as a construct, designed and utilized by male cunning,
seem to suggest (though this might not be their conscious intention)
that this construct is imposed on powerless patients who are doomed
to remain so. The idea that it is wholly *imposed* implies that the individual on whom it is imposed is a passive *patient* not an *agent*, and
so strictly speaking not an individual but an *object*. However, those
who want to combat the "Noble Savagers" and very rightly play the

role of "agitators" seeking to save those who have been duped by the cunning of male power in the guise of ideology, cannot treat women as "objects". Only humans can be saved, aroused, agitated, not objects. And only humans can be morally responsible for what they do whether or not the act is done due to external pressure. The invasive ideology contrived by male cunning and power may spread out invisible tentacles which women fail to perceive. These may coil round their whole social being, deceive, humiliate and afflict, but it does not follow that those who are sought to be subjugated are "objects". They are persons who have the potentiality of exercising the option either of submitting to or even imbibing an ideology, or rising against it.

So, the Padmini case seems to merit a fresh scrutiny. It is possible that the option she and the other ladies exercised by performing the "*brat*" was not imposed merely by peer pressure, by local tradition and moral regulations. It is possible that the indignity and dishonour she and others dreaded was not simply because local tradition stigmatized rape and molestation as disgraceful but because these were some of the cruelest forms of physical and psychological torture which these women as women could not endure. It could be that Padmini herself considered the imminent ignominy as an outrage on her honour, an assault on her person, for which she did what she did of her own volition. This act can even be interpreted as an act of tremendous courage, a deadly retaliation to the monstrous male ambition to possess her against her wish. The high ideal of not compromising with dishonour underpinning the act in this case seems to be trans-cultural, for anguish, indignity, suffering, and the feeling of resentment and protest are shared human sentiments, "features of humanness" in Martha Nussbaum's words. Despite cultural differences these features are there to be seen, though in addition to them there might have been other local norms which figured in the complex and intricate choice situation being considered. And seeing these features we could, like Nussbaum, recall what Aristotle said: "One may . . . observe in one's travels to distant countries the feelings of recognition and affiliation that link every human being to every other human being".[8]

I am aware that this can arouse vehement protests, for it ushers in

---

[8] This quotation from Aristotle's *Nicomachean Ethics*, 1155a 21–2, comes from Martha Nussbaum's paper referred to in note 6 above.

exactly that misconception which the second point discussed above seeks to eradicate. In the name of extolling what is supposedly a self-effacive free act, it glorifies bondage. This is the myth, not the reality about Indian women, deliberately intended to mask their true identity. Ironically the face that wears the mask does not see or know perhaps that something shrouds it. Engulfed in the "feminine mystique" that is compounded out of virtues of exemplars like the epic women Sita and Draupadi, and other mythological characters, the average women even today are overwhelmed by the ethos of sacrifice, self-denial, tolerance, fidelity and a strong sense of conjugal and familial identity that overshadows personal identity and fulfilment. Not only men, but these women themselves seem to believe that transgression of moral principles enjoined by society do not fall within the notion of femininity. Silence and infinite forbearance constitute feminine virtue.

I appreciate the spirit and substance of such possible criticism, which in fact is a reiteration of the second point I put across. But I think it misses the purport of the caution expressed in the third point I added. However forceful social conditioning might be, the right of an individual—of a woman who has suffered subjection to power in numerous forms—is still not a liberal illusion. To say that it is, is to turn her into an "object". The kind of things she accepts, compulsory monogamy, for instance, might have been enforced not only by an institution set up by men but also by herself, by a person who is torn inside between a "me" which is the personal, the subjective, and the "me" which has somehow meshed with the non-personal, the "other" or the institutional. This is why her actions are perceived as unfree, determined. And this is why we seem to confront the dilemma to which I repeatedly refer: is the act of self-annihilation of the "sati" who dies on the funeral pyre of her husband, or of the Rajput women who perform "*jawahar brat*", or of the epic queen Sita (wife of Rama, an incarnation of God) who enters the womb of her Mother Earth, as the story goes, on being told to prove her chastity by her husband for the second time even though she had proved it before by passing a test, a *free* act or one which is *forced*, forced that is to say by the traditional or institutional "other"? It seems to me that at this juncture the self/other relationship should perhaps be reconstrued and the reconstrual may weaken the force of the dilemma which has been exercising us. The "self" need not be viewed as a binary opposite of the "other" standing apart from it in its pureness with an identity that cannot tolerate the inclusion of any element from outside. Rather, as Richard Shusterman in this volume argues, it continually "reshapes and enriches itself by assimilating or appropriating aspects of the other . . ." and through "this process of . . . self-development by self-transformational absorption of the other . . . 'becomes what one is'". This relation of assimilation, absorption in contradistinction to that of determination reveals a fresh aspect of the self/other encounter. It shows how a self in its interface with the "other" may be influenced but not coerced into accepting something. The "other" therefore does not necessarily destroy the self or turn it into an "object", which precisely is the idea mooted by the third point. This is not to deny that the "other" in the form of local tradition, institution, practice, has its other hideous face too, which condemns the woman as evil/bad/fallen if she dared to transgress practice and principles deemed moral by a manipulative ideology. But to perceive both the faces of the "other", constitutive and coercive, formative, enriching, and also oppressive, is to exercise caution about the proper construal of the self/other relationship. It is a half-truth to focus only on one face to the exclusion of the other, a half-truth that tends to lead to the error of treating tradition, practice, principles *simply* as tools of oppression, and the oppressed as a *complete object* of male ruling power reflected in these. So, even if Ram did degrade Sita and banish her because she was forced to stay in the palace of her abductor Ravana till she was rescued by him, and even if in "this ideology of total male power Sita has no more say with her husband Rama than her abductor Ravana", it would be wrong to say: "She is a complete object of male ruling power" as Himani Banerjee writes in her article I referred to a few pages back.

Sita was not a *complete object* of male ruling power, even if she symbolised submissiveness. She too retaliated when asked to perform the second fire-test or "agni pariksha" for proving chastity. She *chose* to bid farewell to a life of indignity and return to where she came from, the womb of Mother Earth. Death, as in the Padmini case, is the tragic yet forceful retaliation to humiliation and dishonour. This is one way of giving expression to freedom, maybe mutely but still powerfully. Draupadi, the heroine of the other epic *Mahabharata*, was fiercely vocal, who by her powerful articulations could silence the wise and the aged in the royal court where she was pawned in a game of power by her husband. That was another image of expression of freedom.

Maybe feeling oppressed, subordinated, crippled and crushed under the dead weight of traditional injunctions a woman may not wish to emulate Sita. Draupadi, the more powerful personality may instead be the favoured icon. Thus it has been aptly observed that in "India we have been exhorted for several centuries to accept Sita as the model of womanhood. Indeed, she is admirable in many ways, but no *one* pattern of virtue will do for all times, and it may become appropriate for us to cultivate the virtues of Draupadi as well".[9] Indeed we must not project *one* pattern alone, that of Sita or Draupadi or of any other noble woman, so that this one pattern does not eventually overshadow many others, in which case we will tend to *impose* a single preferred model on someone who is presumably the passive recipient of that model. The individual may be besieged by many invasive ideologies from without or from within the bounds of her own culture. This may create gaps between different perceptions of patterns of virtue. But to bridge the gaps not one pattern should be *imposed* as remarked before, for that tends to treat the individual as "object", a point we should never lose sight of.

There are many patterns, many ways of being free, and hence many versions of "Her Story" of freedom. But plurality need not entail incomprehension. Mutual understanding across the boundary of different points of view of different cultures, and also within the same culture, is no less a fact of life than plurality and cultural relativity. To deny this is to deny history. Perhaps the most authentic witness of cross-cultural and intra-cultural understanding, transvaluing and synthesis is *history*, which would have been very different from what it has been, had there merely been sharp breaks and irreconcilable gaps. History gives strong evidence showing that gaps can be bridged. The question is how?

IV

We in modern India, who have lived through two hundred years of colonial history, have been an integral part of a process which has created fissures on the surface of our society, but has evolved means at the same time to cement the cracks. The process is the impact of

---

[9] Ketaki Kushari Dyson, "Towards a Multi-Dimensional Women's Movement" in Karabi Sen (ed.), *Her Story* (Calcutta: Prajna Publications, 1985), p. 45.

Western culture on that of our own. The old traditional walls were breached, but new modern liberal ideas disseminated to reform, re-build and reinforce the same, especially by providing a contrast image against which we could review our own heritage and reascertain where its real strength lay. In view of this lived experience of cultural syn-thesis, one cannot any more repeat the much worn cliche "the East is East and the West is West, the twaine shall never meet". How-ever, how can this fact of history—of cultural synthesis be satisfac-torily explained?

Kuhn no doubt was wrong in preaching incommensurability, the thesis of incommunicability between different cultures. He projected a wrong view of history. Indeed, as an eminent historian rightly points out that in describing some historians pejoratively as "antiquarians" who do not see any connecting thread between individuals and com-munities across time and space, one is creating a man of straw.[10] No one seriously maintains that there are sharp irreconcilable gaps, or else we would all be plunging into a collective amnesia. But even if we hold Kuhn guilty of propagating a position which cannot escape "antiquarian" implications, the problem he draws our attention to needs to be resolved.

If we do not have a translation manual which can translate with-out loss of meaning, and also without imposing alien ideas on a con-text which is resistant, then is there a third way to communicate, understand and finally absorb each other's viewpoints? Can empathic intuition or "*verstehen*" provide a third way through which the alien can have a direct access to the patterns of virtue we were consider-ing, the virtues enshrined in the two character-types for instance, the subdued Sita and the spirited Draupadi? Can this access extend, to take another example, to the solemnity, indissolubility and sanc-tity of the Hindu marriage form? Can the investigator resonate in an imaginative oneness to the spirit of sacrifice reflected in this marriage form or in the practice termed "*kanya dan*" which means giving away the daughter to the bride-groom's family, where she herself was to give through love, companionship, home-making, child-bear-ing and self-less motherhood without expecting anything in return?

---

[10] Ravinder Kumar, "Chance and Determinism in History: A Critique of the Historical Process" in Jayant V. Narlikar, Indu Banga, Chhanda Gupta (eds.), *Phi-losophy of Science: Perspectives from Natural and Social Sciences* (Shimla: Indian Institute of Advanced Study, Delhi: Munshiram Manoharlal Publishers Pvt. Ltd., 1992), p. 202.

Can *verstehen* discern the bond which this form of life has to the ideology of self-denial?

Wittgenstein's stricture against "private language" would immediately prompt a negative answer. But even if we concede pace Wittgenstein that empathic intuition can have an access similar to the first person access of introspection, that cannot lay a justified claim to being a *knowledge* of whatever comprises the complex "subjective meaning" of the numerous acts a Hindu wife performs, or is expected to perform.

The British did intervene in our form of life through legislation and other liberal measures, and thought they could see beyond the ideological veil and understand women's subjection, suffering and seclusion. Much in the same way as today's radical feminist critics of the ideology of the Hindu form of life, they too seem to have realised that this ideology created a myth for the Hindu wife, who *thought* she was free in her acts of self-denial for that was what her first person experience (supposedly) disclosed to her. But then the whole project of trying to understand and evaluate her actions would seem problematic for the perceptions of the investigator and the critic on the one hand and of the agent on the other fall apart. To resolve the problem an appeal to empathic intuition or "*verstehen*" that is believed to produce an awareness similar to the agent's own experience will hardly help. If the agent's own first person access to her feelings cannot validate the claim that what she *takes* as her freedom is *really* her freedom, then how can the investigator's surrogate for it, namely "*verstehen*" give a reliable knowledge of the same? Both the introspective and the empathic accounts seem to disclose a delusion, not the hard fact of the matter about real freedom. Of course one may give up the search for a non-doxastic, that is, non-epistemic account of real freedom, or freedom as it is in itself, not as known by this person or that. One may limit oneself instead to exploring social realities including freedom as known or experienced. But then this leaves us with the problem we are confronting from the very beginning. The social reality as perceived by the agent albeit mistakenly is freedom, while that which the investigator seeks to explore and expose is bondage. Shall we say that Kuhn was right after all in maintaining that different viewpoints produce "different worlds", different social realities in this specific context?

However, the facts of history suggest, contrary to the historiographical thesis about "closed" and "different worlds", that what the agent perceived as her freedom (may be mistakenly) was *not* a social reality *different* from what the alien was investigating. The accounts varied no doubt. But the subject of inquiry, the social reality being investigated was the same. Because the accounts varied, it seemed that what was being referred to from different cultural viewpoints were also different. This seems to be the case perhaps because *"verstehen"*, which the investigator could have availed of to bridge the gap in understanding, did not turn out to be a reliable guide for a trans-cultural journey to the alien heartland of any culture other than one's own. Still, there must have been some other way or ways of explaining the interactions which actually did take place. Or else we cannot answer why eventually there had been a new awakening in the Indian woman's life—a new freedom achieved both at home and in the public world outside, which, partially at least, owed its sustaining force to ideas underpinning the process of Westernization. Probably she too realized that what she was hitherto perceiving wrongly as freedom was in fact bondage, and that realization saw the birth of a new vision of freedom, a freedom which she strove to and did achieve.

Whether this new awareness and achievement of freedom was a mere projection forced from outside, and therefore different from the actions being investigated which were really unfree, is a wrong way of posing the question. It is wrong because the self/other relationship is not merely one of determination and coercion, as noted before, but also of absorption, assimilation and enrichment through incorporation of elements borrowed from the cultural "other". And this is precisely what history has testified to in the case of the emergence of the new woman in this country during the latter half of the last century. There were contrasting images of women's status, but an interactive process as well which led to the resolution of the conflict stemming from these contrasting images. The process of social change that began with the enactment of laws prohibiting burning of widows, child marriage and other cruel practices, gradually evolved a new consciousness through a new educational system and social reforms in which both men and women of the country played a leading part. The synthesis of cultures in which the process culminated cannot be said to be a sudden surge from nowhere—or a rootless shift of paradigm. The historiographical thesis of "closed" or "different worlds" was mistakenly supposed by its sponsors to be a consequence of reflections upon history. Social change in India is a multidimensional continuous process: its history is a story of synthesis in which the new culture of the West and also a reawakened consciousness of our own heritage mingled to form a rich mosaic. The aliens not only contributed directly to the nation's cultural history; they also helped indirectly in evolving a new ethos by bringing back to the Indian mind its own contrasting identity. This unification was made possible through continued, interactive and interpretive dialogue—through a rethinking of concepts and values—through a shared form of life.

V

This may be construed as a gross misreading of history by radical relativists. There cannot be a cross-paradigm debate, understanding and synthesis of standpoints, not to speak of transvaluation, according to them. They would even refuse to perceive, it seems, the most pernicious moral consequences of the segregation of standpoints. Thus it has been observed: "The British administration waged a long campaign against (the Hindu practice of female infanticide) based on the Christian premise that they were no less than murder without really understanding the Hindu preference for sons, let alone the overpopulation problem".[11] But even if an action cannot be torn out of its cultural context and treated as if it is in fact very different from the way the agent conceived it, would anyone consider that infanticide is defensible, or unjudgable because the person killing the infant did not see it as murder? The relativists would not admit the need of sensitizing social inquiry to such moral issues, if the moral judgments are believed to have a global significance. If there are standards of evaluation, these are purely internal—internal to a community or society. But the question sought to be ruled out is bound to arise if the social reality referred to and judged is the same, notwithstanding the differences of the ways in which it is looked at from different perspectives. For a debate erupts usually when contradictory claims are made about the same matter. Since the relativists refuse to believe in this sameness, they see no point in raising questions about trans-cultural evaluation.

However, there is no good ground for saying that the descriptions

---

[11] This quotation from V. Reynolds and R. Tanner's *The Biology of Religion* is borrowed from Roger Trigg's book *Understanding Social Sciences*.

which are different or even incompatible, must necessarily be descriptions of different realities. One may recall at this juncture a parallel problem in the context of natural sciences which Putnam discusses. He explains how incompatible descriptions can still be said to be "equivalent" referring to the *same* events. To understand how this is possible one may consider the Special Relativistic description of two events: an explosion on the moon, and an explosion on Mars, abbreviated as X and Y respectively, which he cites to explicate his notion of "equivalence". If X and Y are described in neutral observational terms then, in two different frames, say, the earth and a rocket-ship moving almost at the speed of light compared to the earth, there would be two incompatible descriptions. For example, if the word "simultaneous" used for describing the events is construed observationally in neutral terms, say, in terms of light signals received in each frame, then, the description given by observers on earth would say "X and Y happened simultaneously", while the one given by those in the rocket-ship would say "X happened before Y". But "how can two such flatly contradictory accounts both be true"?[12] Both can be true, according to Putnam, despite the incompatibility of the two descriptions: "X and Y happened simultaneously" (A) and "X and Y did not happen simultaneously" (B). For even if the incompatible descriptions A and B given by observers on the earth and the rocket-ship respectively, do not agree on the *temporal* distance between the events which produces this incompatibility, they may agree on an "invariant quantity" namely, the *space-time distance* between any two events like X and Y. This implies of course, a relativity underpinning ascriptions of simultaneity, and brings out the theory-laden character of observational terms. But if terms like "simultaneous", "distance" *etc.* are incompatible given a neutral observational definition, then such terms may be avoided, or be interpreted theoretically. And if they are avoided, the events in question can be described in the language of "invariants". Moreover, since each of the frame-bound descriptions can be recovered from this invariant description, namely, "the space-time distance" when we are given the co-ordinate systems associated with the frames, the two framebound descriptions A and B can be said to be *equivalent* notwithstanding their incompatibility. The invariant description is the basis on which the terms figuring in

[12] Hilary Putnam, "Equivalence" in *Realism and Reason: Philosophical Papers*, Vol. 3 (Cambridge: Cambridge University Press, 1983), p. 34.

description A can be translated into the language of description B. For given the space-time distance between the events, and given that the earth moves with a velocity v much less than the speed of light c, the observers on earth can determine the co-ordinates of an event in the rocket-ship from the co-ordinates in the frame which they presently occupy (the earth). They may therefore be able to make predictions about what they will observe in case they are transported to the rocket-ship. And if they can do so, then, the observation sentences they use in describing X and Y by A on earth, can be mapped on to corresponding observation sentences used by observers in the rocket-ship. This is another way of saying that the observers on earth will be able to identify the events they describe by A, as referents of B, though B alters the description A. They can legitimately claim that the events they describe, namely, X and Y, are the *same* as the events countenanced by observers in the rocket-ship.

I am not suggesting that this can be regarded as an exact parallel of the situation we encounter on numerous occasions in the action context, the situation, that is to say, in which incompatible descriptions are given of what presumably are the *same* acts. Even if events and actions are not treated as ontologically disparate by some thinkers, they are *semantically* different, and few would be ready to erase this difference, which is why we cannot speak of an exact parallel. To describe an *action qua action* we cannot fall back on notions similar to that which is mathematically expressed in terms of a space-time invariant and for describing *physical events*. Using this invariant description as basis, one can translate terms figuring in one physicalistic description of events into the language of another physicalistic description of the same. One can make predictions about what others using this other description will observe from their position. We cannot make such exact predictions in the action context. Still we can look for and perhaps find a rough analogy, though not an exact parallel. And the lesson to be drawn from a rough analogy to the notion of "equivalence" of incompatible descriptions is that incompatibility may be attributed to circumstantial difference. The incompatible descriptions may still be said to refer to the same social reality, as in the case of natural realities, if of course these descriptions can be recovered from an invariant description. This description may not be one which is mathematically formulable. Nevertheless it could be such that one could use it as a basis for recovering incompatible descriptions. The question is: what, if any, is the invariant basis in the context of action?

There are many ways in which one can be free and many accounts of such freedom too, some of them being incompatible. For
instance, one can freely be self-effacive and perform acts which are
not self-fulfilling. One can on the contrary be free in the sense of
being self-assertive performing acts which do lead to self-fulfilment.
As in the case of the two incompatible descriptions: "simultaneous"
and "not simultaneous" (interpreted observationally), can we say that
the two incompatible accounts: "self-fulfilling" and "not self-fulfilling"
are "equivalent"? "Simultaneous" and "not simultaneous" are expressions which referred to the same events, namely, explosions on the
moon and Mars, despite incompatibility. Observers on the earth
adhered to the description "simultaneous" and would not call the
events "not simultaneous" like the observers in the rocket-ship. The
disagreement was in respect of the temporal distance between the
two events as stated before. Those who adhere to the description
"self-fulfilling" to refer to free acts likewise would not characterize
them as "not self-fulfilling". The disagreement here too is in respect
of one specific aspect of being free. However, despite disagreement
and the incompatible descriptions it leads to in both cases, the
descriptions can count as "equivalent", if Putnam is right, being about
same events and/or acts, and can be shown to be so by being recovered from some invariant basis. This invariant basis in the context of
action perhaps is the *choice* of the individual, the choice which each
of us can make as an agent who is "autonomous" not "heterono-
mous" in the sense given to these expressions by Kant. It is perhaps
the minimal core of what we understand by freedom. This does not
mean that the autonomous chooser must stand aside from the mainstream of social existence, in complete isolation, in order to be able
to think and choose for himself/herself. He or she may authentically
and autonomously choose even that which their "form of life" or
society enjoins, provided it is not thrust upon them. Much is absorbed by the choosing agents from the institutional "other", as I
said, which does not merely coerce.

However, saying that choice is the invariant base of freedoms may
sound implausible, for it is too abstract—too thin in content from
which different descriptions can be recovered, and in terms of which
the shared features of those descriptions can be understood.

To repeat, autonomy of choice by itself seems to have too thin
a content to have any explanatory worth for showing sharedness
between different images of freedom. To what extent it can serve as
an invariant basis consequently is unclear and problematic. To add

content we should be able to figure out *what* we ought to choose. Probably, if we did posses a capacity to know some "inclusive human end" by the "natural light" of reason, we could have secured sharedness in the sense that our free choices, however different, are in fact made in the light of such an inclusive end. But reason by itself can hardly *reveal* such an end. Moreover, if the inclusive human end was thus "revealed" one could hardly say that in choosing it, an agent was thinking for herself. A revealed end that is believed to *determine* choice takes away its autonomy. A person exercises free and autonomous choice to the extent she is able to think for herself as subject, even when she is, or might be subject to numerous influences. She exercises free choice when she is not coerced into accepting any "revealed" end.[13] How then can we find an invariant base that has a richer content than the ability of exercising an autonomous choice?

A full answer to the question is not visible to me, as stated at the outset. Broad pervasive features of the human form of life and its natural history are often recognized as the basis of trans-cultural understanding. Peter Winch, for instance, following Vico refers to three human customs that are common to all nations. All have some religion, all contract solemn marriages, all bury their dead. He himself takes some concepts as "limiting notions" which are of utmost importance for understanding alien action. Can these notions be treated as "ideal types" which help to locate what is really universal about human nature, and thereby provide the needed points of contact between societies? Can these notions, to be more specific, help one in figuring out *what* one ought to choose in the light of features they show to be really universal about human nature? It seems they cannot. For the "ideal type" is construed as a heuristic device which does not correspond to anything in the real world.[14]

Even the "individualistic" version of the "ideal type" which is said to be abstracted by inspecting actual cases, is so removed in its ideality and abstractness that it can hardly be given the status of a universal that is true of all individual instances.

---

[13] This is a point persuasively argued by Hilary Putnam in Lecture III: "Equality and our Moral Image of the World" in his book *Many Faces of Realism* (La Salle, Ill.: Open Court Publishing Co., 1989).

[14] See. J.W.N. Watkins, "Ideal Types and Historical Explanation" in H. Feigl and M. Brodbeck (eds.), *Readings in the Philosophy of Science* (New York: Appleton Century Crofts, Inc., 1953), pp. 724–726.

It seems to me that this whole effort of looking for linkages be-tween conflicting images of women's freedom, or of any other social reality for that matter, does not get off the ground because we look for these linkages in the wrong place. There simply is no hard fact of the matter, no *fixed essential* trait of the subject of investigation that can provide the base for the linkage. Even if self-assertiveness, self-fulfilment are powerful expressions of women's freedom, these are not to be projected as the hard fact of the matter about *everywoman's* freedom. Nor can free self-effaciveness be the chosen model for *everywoman*—the intrinsic hard fact of the matter revealing something that is really universal about feminine nature.

If we do want to have a fuller account of the basis from which we may derive the various images of freedom, then we do not need to look for a "revealed end", or an abstract "ideal type" or a fixed essence. We may begin with some experiences—our own or of other members of our community. On the basis of these experiences a word may be used to refer to whatever is the content of those experiences, say, the sense of feeling free in choosing something. At this point nobody has a more concrete account or idea about this. "But the experience fixes a subject for further inquiry" as Martha Nussbaum writes though in a different but comparable context. She explains, following Aristotle, how a sphere of human experience that figures in more or less any human life can be isolated, and in which more or less any human being will have to act in some way rather than some other. For instance, in the sphere of fear especially of death, one will have to act with courage. Little is known about this virtue word "courage" but its reference is fixed by this sphere of experience, which Nussbaum calls a "grounding experience". The "grounding experience" gives a thin account but provides a basis for, further investigation leading to a fuller specification of the word "courage". We begin with a "thin" or "nominal" account. As experience grows, we come up with fresh ideas, with competing explanatory theories which make rival claims about giving a fuller and "thick" account.[15] Which among these will be gradually entrenched depends on our experiences. When we understand what problems humans beings encounter in their lives with one another, what circumstances they confront in which choice of some sort is required, we will have a

---

[15] See pages 245, 247–248 of Martha Nussbaum's article referred to in note 6 above.

way of assessing competing responses to those problems as Nussbaum points out. Maybe one such response, one image of freedom that portrays it as self-assertiveness and self-fulfilment will get entrenched and assume the status of a socially and culturally evolved universal, which all concerned, the agents, investigators and critics alike agree to accept as the basis from which other images are to be derived. This image, assumes the status of a "social universal" not because it expresses an intrinsic hard fact of the matter about what freedom is, if at all, by itself or in itself. It assumes this status because the agents and investigators interpret it as such, or agree to accept it as such. If we do have a base for understanding and transvaluing different cultures, it is something which grows as a commonly accepted converging viewpoint. And the convergence depends largely on experiences of common human concern—of "features of humanness" that lie beneath all local traditions, features which constitute the "feelings of recognition and affiliation that link every human being to every other human being" as Aristotle said.

EPILOGUE: CULTURE THEORY AND PRACTICE: A FRAMEWORK FOR INTER-CULTURAL DISCOURSE

J.N. Mohanty

When we speak of the culture of a country, we obviously speak of the dominant culture, and more likely of certain high-level elements of that culture—elements such as philosophy, the arts, music and dance. However, it should be granted that there are, as contrasted with this high-level culture, also low-level cultures which we look for in the everyday lives and practices of ordinary members of the community. In the case of India the high-level elements derive from the Sanskrit texts, or rather for each such element theoretical texts were composed, and the low-level elements have to be found by discerning observers in the lives of simple men and women living in the villages. The cultural beliefs and practices of the latter sort are not sanctioned by texts; if they are, the texts are not the Sanskrit texts of the elites but local language books and literature which are read, remembered and recited by people who are far from being scholars. If we consider that part of Indian culture which we can call "religious", the high-level beliefs and practices derive from the Upanisads and the Rg-Vedic sources, the low-level beliefs and practices, consisting of numerous *pujas*, *vratas* and practices are of "local", non-textual origin. If this distinction is valid, then one should add that at no level, the high or the low, there is a monolithic culture. On the contrary there are pluralities, differences and oppositions at each level. One could perhaps say that the pluralities and differences belonging to the lower level are considerably "overcome" at the higher level, but even there the texts, which are the common sources of ideas and practices are themselves capable of being variously interpreted which makes room for fresh difference. The "local" differences to be found in low-level culture are now replaced by large, and trans-local, conceptual differences. At the same time, one must also recognize that there are, between these two extremes, many intermediate, and mediating links which bear testimony to a sort of intermingling of the two levels, where the lower is interpreted in the light of the higher and the higher is brought down to the level of the masses.

It may be supposed that the "lower level" culture embodied in the so-called "lifeworld" of the community is *practical*, and the higher level culture, articulated by the elites (for the elites) is *theoretical*. One of the contentions of this essay is that that way of drawing the distinction is false, that at every level of culture theory and practice are intertwined. No culture is merely practical, none is merely theoretical.

In earlier papers and on earlier occasions, I have taken Husserl to task for holding the view that Indian thinking was practically oriented ("How to get rid of suffering, and to attain *moksa* or *nirvana?*"), whereas western thought, beginning with the Greeks, developed a purely theoretical thinking *i.e.* purely interest-free contemplation of the nature of things. We know that neither was early Greek thinking purely theoretical nor was the logical totally separated from the mythical. Likewise, Indian thinking was far from being simply practical. From the very beginning it asked theoretical questions which, in course of time, blossomed into theoretical systems. In neither case, theory and practice were as sharply sundered as philosophers make them out to be.

There are definitions of "culture" which make it out to be a theoretical structure. There are also definitions which emphasize its practical character. Both these aspects are to be found in Talcott Parsons's writings. Parsons on the one hand looked upon culture as having its objective reality in the subjective representations of actors and in their ability to systematically deal with the rules that help the actors to construct and use their action-orientations in an intersubjectively coordinated manner. But Parsons also realized that culture can play this action-guiding role only if it is itself a *system*, which for him is a subsystem of the general action system (other subsystems being "personal system", "social system" and "behavioral system"). This system is an exclusively symbolically organized system of abstract *Sinnzusammenhänge* or meaning structures, a set of *Idealfaktoren*.

Parsons's attempts to understand "culture" bring to light that there are two levels of systems: one a system of *actions*, *Handlungsordnung* (which one may want to keep apart as the *social* system) and another, *a system of meanings* (which one would then want to regard as the *cultural* system). But one may want to regard both the systems as constituting "culture", as I would do in this essay. What mediates between these two layers, and holds them together is the concept of intentionality. Intentionality is then *either* actional *or* theoretical: in each case it creates *meanings*.

PRACTICAL INTENTIONALITY

There is a widely shared assumption that any theory of intentionality, and also any theory which makes intentionality fundamental, must be suffering from an intellectualist prejudice. In the present context, it would follow from this assumption that a theory of culture which uses the concept of intentionality as fundamental must be incapable of taking into account irreducibly practical, or rather actional, side of every culture. That assumption, and therefore this conclusion, are, in my view mistaken. Intentionality is not merely a matter of theoretical consciousness. Another prejudice dies hard, namely, that consciousness is *eo ipso* theoretical, intellectual or thinking consciousness. Both these prejudices are countered by a fundamental theorem: there is "consciousness in action",[1] intentionality in action that is not reducible to the intentionality of thought. So that may be called practical intentionality. If every intentionality intends an object as having a certain significance or meaning, then we can speak of "practical meaning". The so-called *Handlungsordnung* is the system of such practical meaning. A system of actions is a system of practical meanings. When Heidegger defines "Sinn" as "das Woraufhin des primären Entwurfs, aus dem her etwas als das, was es ist, in seiner Möglichkeit begriffen werden kann" (*S u Z*, sec. 65), he has this practical meaning in view.

Every action is cultural to the extent it is directed towards, aims at, lays bare the world as having a certain meaning. This meaning has not only the temporal component "to be done" (pointing to a future possibility) but also a valuational component: "by being done, a state of affairs will come into being which will satisfy some purpose, and so is a good". There is also a reference to the past, for every matter of possible action falls into a type, with an intersubjectively recognized meaning, which *has been* established in one's culture. In this sense, one's life-world is present with its past and also with its predelineated future.

A community lives in an originally living tradition which belongs to the people, inherited from earlier generations through communication and narration by the ancestors. All that has "meaning", is understood—primarily for social praxis, ritual, religion and relation-

---

[1] David W. Smith, "Consciousness in Action", *Synthese* 90, 1992, 119–143. Also see Castaneda, Hector-Neri, *Thinking and Doing* (Dordrecht: Reidel, 1975).

ships—even if in vague indeterminacy. At a primary level, cultural meanings must be non-conventional and rooted in the organic: in the basic needs, drives and experiences of humans, in hunger, thirst, sexual drive and experiences of birth and death. To recognize this is not to say that any of these is merely natural, but to say that even in the most unfamiliar culture we can expect to find that men do whatever they need to do, in whatever manner their cultural rites require, to eat, drink, satisfy sexual urge, and to celebrate/ mourn birth and death. The social, in all its dimensions, need not be conventional.

I think, the urge to court conventionalism with regard to meanings is due to a refusal to recognize the subjective and bodily aspects of the birth of meanings. The conventionalist recognizes only one other alternative, namely, essentialism which he rejects. But there is a third alternative: the subjective creation of meanings.[2] When I say this, I include the bodily within the subjective, largely following Merleau-Ponty.

Acting need not be thought about acting. Nor is acting reducible to events, both bodily movements and bodily movements bringing about change in things around. Acting has always an intentional content, not a propositional content, but what Castaneda calls a *practition*. This content belongs to a system of such contents, and also draws upon as well as determine the theoretical meanings embedded in the culture. Heidegger describes this when he describes the world of a carpenter as a system of references. He goes wrong in one-sidedly insisting that these practical meanings are a self-contained system. I wish to emphasize that practical meanings draw upon sedimented theoretical meanings as well. In other words, there is a continuing "communication" between theoretical and practical meaning-systems.

Tradition as Sedimented Meanings

When meanings, both theoretical and practical, become detached from intentions of individuals or groups, and lead a life of their own, conditioning the way individuals act and think without self-consciously

---

[2] Eugene Halton, "The Cultic Roots of Culture" in Richard Munch and Neil J. Smelser (ed.), *Theory of Culture* (Berkeley: University of California Press, 1992), pp. 79–102.

invoking them to their aid, the meanings have already constituted a
culture. Some degree of anonymity of meanings, *i.e.*, functioning
unrecognized, is needed for the constitution of a culture. A culture
that is more reflective and self-conscious seeks to rescue such meanings from their anonymous functioning, and to bring them to explicit consciousness, and in that process to modify them, for such
reflective efforts generate new meanings—theoretical and practical—
which may then, as determinants of the culture,—for succeeding
generations—sink into relative anonymity.

Two things should be noted in the above account. For one thing,
as already emphasized, I do not wish to place either practical or
theoretical meanings at the origin. One reason why one is inclined
to place *pure* practical meanings at the beginning, is that one fails to
distinguish between pre-reflective meanings and practical meanings,
and consequently between reflective and theoretical meanings. In other
words, in my view, there are pre-reflective but theoretical meanings,
just as there is reflective practice. As a result of not making the above-
mentioned distinctions, one tends to posit a phase of mankind's (or
a society's) life which is *purely* practical, uncontaminated by any theoretical thinking, where there is only knowing-how but no knowing-
that, so that the emergence of theoretical thinking is seen as a threat
to the integrity of that seamless practical life. This, I think, is a mistake.
That romantic positing of a life of practice undisturbed by any thinking
is exactly so: *i.e.*, a romantic positing.

Body, Intentionality and Habitus

One finds this naively in the otherwise interesting notion of *habitus* of
Piere Beaurdieu. Regarding the so-called *habitus* as the practical meaning of social actions, Beaurdieu wants to cut it off first from subjective intentions, and then from all theoretical thinking. Locating the
habitus in the body amounts, for him, to detach it from all intentionality— thereby committing the initial mistake of taking all intentionality
as intentionality of thinking. If *Sinn* is not merely *Sinn* of thinking but
of action as well, there is also a practical intentionality besides the
theoretical. This practical intentionality need not be construed as a
thought of action, it can be located in the acting itself. Beaurdieu, it
would seem, does not make use of Merleau-Ponty's discovery of bodily
subjectivity and bodily intentionality.

Beaurdieu rightly locates his understanding of *practice*, including the concept of *habitus, within* "real activity as such", *i.e.*, in the practical relation to the world, where "the world imposes its presence, with its urgencies, its things to be done",[3] and by doing so he claims to be able to avoid both positivistic materialism and intellectualist idealism. So far so good. The *habitus* is accordingly construed as "the system of structured, structuring dispositions . . . which is constituted in practice and is always oriented towards practical functions".[4] The objects of knowledge are, he holds, as against "objectivisim", constructed. However, subjectivism needs equally to be avoided, for it is quite "incapable of giving an account of the necessity of the social world".[5] We do not need a rootless, pure, unattached subject for the constitution of the practical world. The *habitus* is rather a product of history and produces individual and collective practices (*i.e.*, more history); it makes possible that the past is actively present in the form of schemes of perception, thought and action. Thus the *habitus* is embodied history, embodied in the body of the agent, the members of a community, and is "a spontaneity without consciousness or will".[6] It is also objectified in institutions including language, exhibited in "the intentionless invention of regulated improvisation".[7] In so far as practical sense and objective meaning are in harmony, a commonsense world is constituted. The question of intention is superfluous. Practice is significant without a signifying intention. Actions determined by *habitus* are strategic, without being the result of genuine strategic intentions.

It is this *habitus* which has become "nature" in the motor schemata and automatic bodily reactions that are socially necessary. What the body has learnt is not possessed as a fund of knowledge, but rather is the person himself.

I believe that this entire concept of *habitus* finds its natural home in a theory of bodily intentionality and subjectivity. Without the latter, *habitus* would be nothing other than a mechanically self-perpetuating habit, and would lack the historicality which must belong to it if it is to be the foundation of a theory of culture.

---

[3] Piere Beaurdieu, *Critique of Theoretical Reason*, p. 52.
[4] *Ibid.*, p. 52.
[5] *Ibid.*, p. 52.
[6] *Ibid.*, p. 56.
[7] *Ibid.*, p. 57.

BELIEFS

But is a culture fundamentally a system of practical meanings embodied in individual and social action, possibly weaving such actions into a system, or does a culture necessarily involve a set of beliefs? As a reaction against the over-intellectualist view of structuralism that a culture is a theoretical system of scientific beliefs, a conceptual structure, inherently rational, one tends today to fall into the opposite trap: an overemphasis on the practical, a refusal to ascribe to all cultures, especially the primitive cultures anything like beliefs, any theory in any sense. One then conceives of the primitive man (and possibly men in all cultures) as tool-using, ritual-practicing, etiquette-observing, food-gathering creatures, whose surrounding world has only practical meaning, all understanding tied to practical projects, all things are like tools. Both the theoretical man, contemplating the order of things and the practical man, planning, projecting and doing, are abstractions. The practical man must believe that by adopting a certain means, a certain goal can be reached, he must believe that the goal is worth achieving, that it is a good, and the various goods between which he may have to choose must be ordered for him, in his culture. There must be practical beliefs ("*This* should be done, in order to achieve that goal") and theoretical beliefs ("Achieving that goal will be conducive to a good") inseparably interwoven. Likewise situational beliefs and some generalizations over like/unlike situations must be around. For this to be accepted one need not look for belief-like verbs in the language, there can be beliefs without self-ascription of belief ("I believe . . ."), nor need one require that the language must have semantic predicates such as "is true" or "is false". But there must be some equivalent of them, which does their job. My submission is, that a certain unity of theory and practice, of belief-systems and action-systems, is a cultural universal. Out of this universal matrix, cultures develop different theories and different practices.

CRITICAL PRACTICE AND CRITICAL THEORY

The risk of a Beaurdieu-like theory is that it reduces all practice to the mechanism of *habitus* historically engendered by a culture. While a large segment of social action can be explained by such a theory, an equally large and important segment cannot be. Under the latter fall all actions which require deliberation, thinking, theoretical legiti- mation, application of rational criteria and choice. Even if we set aside the higher level reflective judgment as undertaken by philoso- phy, there is a limited reflective judgment aiming at legitimizing one's life's decisions in terms of large goals and meanings that a culture already has prescribed for individuals belonging to that culture. In the latter case, legitimation and deliberation are not as radical as philosophy claims to yield or at least undertakes to deliver, but none- theless within the presuppositions of that culture one does attempt to confer a meaning on one's life's major decisions. So one may distinguish between three levels: first, action guided by *habitus*, con- forming to the expectations and prescriptions of a culture (rituals, etiquettes, ethical action, *etc.*); a limited deliberative legitimization in case of conflicts, choice—in terms of goals and meanings already available within the culture; and a more theoretical, reflective, at- tempt at "grounding" the latter goals in strictly philosophical terms. The second of these three is what I call critical practice, the third a theory of the practice.

Likewise, with regard to theory. If there are beliefs, interwoven with practice, both practical beliefs and low-level theories—wher- ever there are predicative judgments claiming either truth or some equivalent of "truth", Husserl finds the presence of the "logical"— these are, for lack of a better expression, I shall call pre-critical or dogmatic theory. At some point, such theories—an individual or a culture may entertain many such—come to explicit conflict, and a rational individual may want to resolve such conflicts to make his practical (and religious and ethical) beliefs more livable. You have then the beginnings of critical theorizing, which is radicalized by philosophy.

At this point, one should distinguish between two levels of philoso- phizing. There is a kind of philosophizing which is intra-cultural. At this level, philosophy thinks within the parameters and presupposi- tions of the culture within which it comes into being. In the Indian tradition, such thinking does not question the validity of the Vedas, but proceeds to introduce new interpretation-principles to be able to achieve its goal of legitimation (theoretical justification). The *darśanas* first develop as intra-cultural. Amongst themselves, they do not raise the issue of the authority of the Vedic texts. But no culture, in its totality, is a seamless whole. The seeds of radical questioning are within its own life. The *lokāyatas*, Buddhism, and many other heretical thinkers raise strong sceptical challenge, making it necessary that the philosopher goes beyond intra-cultural thinking, and undertakes to justify the fundamental presuppositions of the culture. Thus arises the second, the highly theoretical and idealized mode of thinking which claims universality and independence of the cultural matrix from which it was born. But thereby it adds a new dimension to that very culture.

INTER-CULTURALITY AND UNIVERSALITY

Not all cultures exhibit this idealized theoretical discourse which we call philosophy. Many cultures stop at the intra-cultural, critical theorization; perhaps some cultures stop at the first level *i.e.*, pre-critical theory. It is when theoretical thinking becomes philosophical in the sense of an idealized thinking claiming universality that one steps outside the bounds of one's tradition, and claims to be capable of *inter-cultural* discourse.

In the face of cultural relativisms, one may point to two meeting grounds of cultures: one at the beginning, the other at the end. At the beginning, there is the bodily, rooted in nature, the biological and the organic; at the other end, there is the universality-claiming discourse of philosophy. Keeping those two "kindred points of heaven and earth" in mind helps us to develop a framework for inter-cultural discourse. In this paper, I wanted to make such a framework visible in its outlines.

INTERCULTURALITY AND TRANSCULTURALITY

The next step in our thinking about culture would go beyond the perspective of interculturality and beyond the need for reaching the universality of idealized philosophy. The pursuit of interculturality presupposes that there are well-defined cultures *between* which one positions oneself in order to establish mutual understanding and to open means of communication. I myself in several earlier papers represented a culture as a sphere and have made use of the picture

of intersecting circles to make communication amongst cultures intelligible. But is the representation of a culture as a circle correct?
Here we are coming face to face with a deeply rooted prejudice—a
myth about "culture"—which needs to be questioned, and eventually overcome.[8]

Let me begin by asking, what is *a* culture? Is individuation of
cultures unproblematic? A very common means of individuation is
the political state. If India and Bangladesh are different political states
now, or India and Pakistan, or Bosnia and Serbia, they must have
their respective cultures. But only fifty years ago, India and Bangladesh
and Pakistan formed one political entity. Hardly a few years ago,
Bosnia and Serbia were not different states. If political boundaries
do not define *a* culture as distinct from all other, then what else
does? There are two other claimants: language and religion. The
same language may be spoken in many different regions of the world,
and one may not want to say that the British and American cultures
are the same. To say that the languages—American and British—
are quite different (as Oscar Wilde realized on his first visit to America)
would not do, for then the New Englander and the Texan, the
Londoner and the Oxford Don do not speak the same language.
Similar considerations apply to religion as the principle of individuation. It is not also true that the neighboring language is closer to
the home language. How could after all Lithuanian be close to Sanskrit and Hungarian to the Finnish?

Another answer to my question is suggested by Husserl in his late
manuscripts. The identity of a culture is definable in terms of the
continuity of a historical tradition, and the history has to be a generative history. But who can guarantee that a people's cultural-generative
history does not contain tributaries that we know nothing of. A unique
generative history is not guaranteed by all the known facts about it,
it can only be stipulated based on the assumption that the home
culture is a unique one.[9]

---

[8] Wolfgang Welsch has pointed out that the representation of a culture as a sphere
goes back to Herder. Welsch finds in Herder three features of a culture: first, a
culture moulds the whole life of a people and so is unificatory; secondly, it is always
the culture of a folk; it is, next, separatory, *i.e.*, delimits other cultures. Each of these
features needs to be drastically revised if the present argument holds good. (Welsch,
"Transculturality—The Changing Form of Culture Today" in *La Shuttle: Tunnel-
realitäten Paris-London-Berlin*, ed. Kunstlerhaus Bethanien, [Berlin, 1996], pp. 15–30.)

[9] I can not resist the temptation of quoting the following text from Carl Zuckmeyer,
cited by Welsch in *loc. cit.* ". . . just imagine your line of ancestry, from the birth of

What all this leads up to is that any identity of culture, on the one hand, dissipates into endless internal differences ("Indian Culture" into Bengali, Oriya, Gujrati, and so on, each of these latter likewise into further differences) and on the other, may be exemplified, at least in some of its features, in other supposedly foreign identities. Thus every claim to uniqueness of a culture is provisional, every identity can maintain itself by suppressing internal differences (as well as external repetitions). Cultural uniqueness is a claim—not sustainable by empirical research. It is an ideology, sometimes amounting to nationalism, chauvinism and religious enthusiasm. As Wolfgang Welsch has been pressing, the more appropriate concept should be trans-culturality instead of inter-culturality.

With this revision of our concept of cultural identity, we also overcome a familiar form of cultural relativism. The representation of a culture as a self-contained sphere implies that the fundamental concepts and criteria (of truth, rationality, moral goodness, *etc.*) within each sphere is valid only within it and no such concept and criteria from another sphere could retain their validity outside of that domain. The only way this relativism could be overcome, consistent with this conception of culture, is by postulating one large sphere to which all the others belong as sub-spheres, and with regard to that global sphere posit universally valid concepts and criteria. Note that you do not, by taking this step, give up the representation of a culture as a sphere, only you accept one all-comprehensive sphere, one Universal Culture. Since this kind of universalism seems too abstract and arbitrary, I would prefer overcoming relativism by abandoning that root metaphor for a culture, and postulate infinite interpenetration of cultures and so infinite differentiations within every identity

---

Christ on. There was a Roman commander, a dark type, brown like ripe olive, he had taught a blond girl Latin. And then a Jewish spice dealer came into the family, he was a serious person, who became a Christian before his marriage and founded the house's Catholic tradition. And then came a Greek doctor, or a Celtic legionary, a Grisonian landsknecht, a Swedish horseman, a Napoleonic soldier, a deserted Cossack, a Black Forest miner, a wandering miller's boy from the Alsace, a fat mariner from Holland, a Magyar, a pandour, a Viennese officer, a French actor, a Bohemian musician—all lived on the Rhine, brawled, boozed and sang and begot children there—and—Goethe, he was from the same pot, and Beethoven, and Gutenberg, Mathias Grunewald. . . . They were the best, my dear! The world's best! And why? Because that's where the peoples intermixed. Intermixed—like the waters from sources, streams and rivers, so, that they run together to a great, living torrent." (Carl Zuckmeyer, *The Devils's General*, in *Masters of Modern Drama*, [New York, Random House, 1963], pp. 911–958.)

and the failure of any geographical-political boundaries to contain, delimit and define the identity of a culture. By doing so, relativism becomes pointless, for we loose our grips on any way of answering the query, "relative to what?"

"Indian Culture"

No one better expressed the nature of Indian culture from the perspective just developed, than the poet Rabindra Nath Tagore in his lines "*hethāy ārya, hethā anārya, ... ek dehe halo līn.*" The Aryans, the non-Aryans, and later in history, the Sakas, the Hunas, the Pathans and the Moghuls (and let me add, during the pre-historic period, the Aryans, the Mongoloids, the Australasians, the Negroids) all merged into one and constituted the stream called "Indian culture", of which no simple essentialistic definition is possible.

The same needs to be said of "Hindu Culture". Here I will refer to an excellent paper by Julius Lipner. Lipner speaks of the "decentering conceptual tendency" on the one hand and "its concurrent counterpart, a perspectival (and potentially plural) recentering on the other", the consequent "dynamic polycentrism" as one of the distinctive marks of Hinduness.[10] To speak of Indian culture (as of German Culture) is to indulge in a high level construction whose use is legitimate in contexts and not *per se* as long as we bear in mind the "differences" it is built upon and as long as we do not marginalise those differences in the political and power interest of the constructed identity.

Summary

Two theses are advanced in this essay. The first part argues for an inter-involvement of theory and practice within a culture, and for the claim that the primary, organic and the higher, *i.e.*, the reflective level harbour seeds of universality. The second part criticizes the much touted thesis of cultural relativism by questioning if we have a satisfying criterion of what is a culture, by rejecting as misleading

---

[10] Julius J. Lipner, "Ancient Banyan: An Inquiry into the Meaning of 'Hinduness'", *Religious Studies*, 32, 1996, pp. 109–126, esp. p. 117.

the representation of cultures as self-contained spheres and by arguing for the positive thesis that cultural identity is a higher order construction whose tendency is to marginalise and eventually destroy internal differences. I think both parts together constitute a viable picture of a cultural life-world.

CONTRIBUTORS

D.P. Chattopadhyaya	Director, Project of History of Indian Science, Philosophy and Culture, Delhi.
Fred Dallmayr	Dee Professor Government, University of Notre Dame, Notre Dame, Indiana.
Chhanda Gupta	Department of Philosophy, Jadavpur University, Calcutta.
Frank J. Hoffman	Department of Philosophy, Westchester University, Westchester, Pennsylvania.
Krishna Mallick	Department of Philosophy, Salem State College, Salem, Massachusetts.
Joseph Margolis	Professor of Philosophy, Temple University, Philadelphia, Pennsylvania.
J.N. Mohanty	Professor of Philosophy, Temple University, Philadelphia, Pennsylvania.
Christina Schües	Department of Philosophy, University Hamburg, Hamburg.
Pranab Kumar Sen	Professor of Philosophy, Jadavpur University, Calcutta.
Kalyan Sen Gupta	Professor of Philosophy, Jadavpur University, Calcutta.

INDEX OF NAMES

INDEX OF SUBJECTS

Philosophy of History and Culture

1. HERTZBERG, L. and J. PIETARINEN (eds.). *Perspectives on Human Conduct*. 1988. ISBN 90 04 08937 3
2. DRAY, W.H. *On History and Philosophers of History*. 1989. ISBN 90 04 09000 2
3. ROTENSTREICH, N. *Alienation*. The Concept and its Reception. 1989. ISBN 90 04 09001 0
4. ORUKA, H.O. *Sage Philosophy*. Indigenous Thinkers and Modern Debate on African Philosophy. 1990. ISBN 90 04 09283 8
5. MERCER, R. *Deep Words*. Miura Baien's System of Natural Philosophy. 1991. ISBN 90 04 09351 6
6. VAN DER DUSSEN, W.J. and L. RUBINOFF (eds.). *Objectivity, Method and Point of View*. 1991. ISBN 90 04 09411 3
7. DASCAL, M. (ed.). *Cultural Relativism and Philosophy*. North and Latin American Perspectives. 1991. ISBN 90 04 09433 4
8. WHITE, F.C. *On Schopenhauer's* Fourfold Root of the Principle of Sufficient Reason. 1992. ISBN 90 04 09543 8
9. ZEMACH, E.M. *Types*. Essays in Metaphysics. 1992. ISBN 90 04 09500 4
10. FLEISCHACKER, S. *Integrity and Moral Relativism*. 1992. ISBN 90 04 09526 8
11. VON WRIGHT, G.H. *The Tree of Knowledge and Other Essays*. 1993. ISBN 90 04 09764 3
12. WU, Kuang-ming. *On Chinese Body Thinking*. A Cultural Hermeneutic. 1997. ISBN 90 04 10150 0
13. ANDERSSON, G. *Criticism and the History of Science*. Kuhn's, Lakatos's and Feyerabend's Criticisms of Critical Rationalism. 1994. ISBN 90 04 10050 4
14. VADEN HOUSE, D. *Without God or His Doubles*. Realism, Relativism and Rorty. 1994. ISBN 90 04 10062 8
15. GOLDSTEIN, L.J. *The What and the Why of History*. Philosophical Essays. 1996. ISBN 90 04 10308 2
16. BARRY, D.K. *Forms of Life and Following Rules*. A Wittgensteinian Defence of Relativism. 1996. ISBN 90 04 10540 9

17. VAN DAMME, W. *Beauty in Context.* Towards an Anthropological Approach to Aesthetics. 1996. ISBN 90 04 10608 1
18. CHATTOPADHYAYA, D.P. *Sociology, Ideology and Utopia.* Socio-Political Philosophy of East and West. 1997. ISBN 90 04 10807 6
19. GUPTA, C. and D.P. CHATTOPADHYAYA (eds.). *Cultural Otherness and Beyond.* 1998. ISBN 90 04 10026 1

Brill — P.O. Box 9000 — 2300 PA Leiden — The Netherlands